THE HAUNTED INKWELL

Mark Patrick Hederman

The Haunted Inkwell
ART AND OUR FUTURE

the columba press

First published in 2001 by
the columba press
55A Spruce Avenue, Stillorgan Industrial Park, Blackrock, Co Dublin

Cover by Slick Fish Design
Origination by The Columba Press
Printed in Ireland by Colour Books Ltd, Dublin

ISBN 1 85607 347 5

Acknowledgements
The author and publisher gratefully acknowledge the permission of the
following to use material in their copyright: Doubleday for *The Heart
Aroused* by David Whyte; Harvard University Press for *Soul Says: On
Recent Poetry* by Helen Vendler. Copyright © 1995 by the President and
Fellows of Harvard College; Harvard University Press for *The Breaking
of Style* by Helen Vendler. Copyright © 1995 by the President and
Fellows of Harvard College; Cambridge University Press for *Myth,
Literature and the African World* by Wole Soyinka; Lilliput Press for
Reading the Future: Irish Writers in Conversation with Mike Murphy;
Excerpts from James Joyce's writings reproduced with the permission
of the Estate of James Joyce; in this instance special permission has been
given to reproduce a few excerpts from James Joyce's letters which deal
explicitly with his oeuvre. Copyright © Estate of James Joyce; *The Irish
Times* and Seamus Heaney for two articles by Seamus Heaney. Faber
and Faber for quotations from Seamus Heaney, Ted Hughes and T. S.
Eliot.
Every effort has been made to trace copyright holders. If we have inad-
vertently used copyright material without permission we apologise
and will put it right in future editions.

The author wishes to thank Aideen Quigley for her careful and considered editing of the manuscript.

Contents

Introduction

This book is written at the beginning of the twenty-first century. This century can either continue to roll inexorably forward as evolutionary history, following the ebb and tide of random forces that will buffet it towards its chronological conclusion, as wind and waves shunt driftwood towards some shore; or it can be fused into compelling intentionality by those with a capacity to understand in a certain way, and to express what they perceive in a prophetic and irresistible rhythm, shape and form.

The future is not something out there that we step into as an already designed space. The future is ourselves as we choose to become, melded with the world as we inherit it and as we choose to arrange it. The future is alive with possibility to the extent that we are open to change. Change occurs most profitably in the wake of fundamental shifts in our way of being. These occur mostly because someone has imagined and described them.

How do we even begin to envisage such possibilities? This vision of humanity and of the world we inhabit is the artist's task. Writing the icon of our future face, preparing the skins that can carry the new wine, digging the trenches into which the waters can flow, such is the pioneering work of the artist. Others do not have the sensitivity, the authenticity, the flair for capturing such evanescent originality.

But others do have to build the future. We are those others. So, in whatever way and to whatever extent is possible, we must become aware of the direction in which the trailblazers are pointing and the contours of whatever expansiveness they are proposing. As a civilisation we are required to read their poetry and understand their art until it becomes part of the instinctual gesture with which we mark out our future.

This does not mean that we have to write poetry. It does not even mean that we have to read poetry ourselves. It does mean that someone has to produce the appropriate work of art and that our socio-cultural ambience has to become infused with the understanding that such art inspires, so that the movement forward which we instigate is initiated, energised, directed and informed by the spirit of that art, shaped by the space cleared for us by such work.

The point of view that I am presenting here, which is the point of view offered by a monk, is not necessarily the same as that of an artist or an academic. It will certainly not be as polished or as perfect. However, it is a point of view that might shed some complementary light. There is a kind of reading exercised by monks which is called *Lectio Divina* or 'spiritual reading'. It is reading as rumination, in the way a cow might chew the cud – slow, attentive but dispassionate assimilation of a text. Such reading is usually exercised on the Bible or on theological or spiritual texts. It can also be exercised on works of art and literature in a reading of 'the signs of the times'.

Philosophy collects and articulates ideas which are haunting the ether at specific times, and which are sensed by artists, who, like animals, foretell by their behaviour the earthquake that is on the way. So, art and philosophy, in their different ways, are in touch with 'Being', which is the way things are in their ultimate reality, rather than the way they appear to our myopic, self-obsessed, contemporary vision.

Art is a privileged space, which allows room to dimensions and structures that otherwise remain buried in the everyday. Artists are prophets, in the literal sense of speaking out before their time. As they become the unwitting mouthpiece of the psychic secrets of their age, they are often as unconscious as sleepwalkers. So the philosopher is required to record, unravel and present their dreamtime.

There are at least three kinds of art: there is an art of propaganda, which tries to persuade you of a particular point of view; there is an art of entertainment, which can be high-brow or low-brow, depending upon whether your taste is for street ballads or metaphysical sonnets; and there is an art of excavation and exploration, seeking meaning where scientific words or normal human discourse can no longer be trusted to register the subtlety of what is being experienced. In this book my concern is this third kind of art.

As such it is the same as 'poetry' in the most original and the deepest sense of this word. Here language is not a tool, expression not a technique, both are the way in which Being, what really is, can appear. When we are trying to convey the Being of a situation, we don't so much devise a language to do justice to it, we try to find the language that the situation demands. How do things appear as they are? They do not appear by devices of human making; nor can they appear without such human co-operation. Poetry is a kind of making that responds and recalls rather than represents or explains. It provides representation of beings with regard to their Being. Wallace Stevens, in *Of Modern Poetry*, makes a stab at describing it:

It has to be living, to learn the speech of the place.
It has to face the men of the time and to meet
The women of the time. It has to think about war
And it has to find what will suffice. It has
To construct a new stage. It has to be on that stage
And, like an insatiable actor, slowly and
With meditation, speak words that in the ear,
In the delicatest ear of the mind, repeat,
Exactly, that which it wants to hear, at the sound
Of which, an invisible audience listens,
Not to the play, but to itself, expressed
In an emotion as of two people, as of two
Emotions becoming one. The actor is
A metaphysician in the dark, twanging
An instrument, twanging a wiry string that gives
Sounds passing through sudden rightnesses, wholly

Containing the mind, below which it cannot descend,
Beyond which it has no will to rise.[1]

Matisse has said famously: 'If you want to dedicate yourself to painting you must start by cutting out your tongue.' Artists rarely speak of their work. Bridget Riley explains why: 'There is an area, and a very sensitive primary area for an artist, which cannot be referred to directly without damage. It is as though the impulse which is about to be expressed should remain unavailable to the logic of the intellect in order to find its true form in whatever field or metier the artist has chosen.'[2]

Another reason why it is wiser for an artist not to talk about his or her work is expressed by Thomas Mann at the end of his novella *Death in Venice*:

Verily it is well for the world that it sees only the beauty of the completed work and not its origins or the conditions whence it sprang; since knowledge of the artist's inspiration might often but confuse and alarm and so prevent the full effect of its excellence.[3]

However, there is a kind of thinking that can be undertaken, which is the long task of listening to and hearing the almost archaic and ancient language that emerges in the art work. Such thinking and explanation are necessary if the art work is not to remain an unavailable enigma.

The purpose and the meaning of this book can be summed up in a quotation from the philosopher Martin Heidegger, who has painstakingly elaborated this point of view about certain kinds of art and this way of listening and presenting it in a coherent fashion:

But there would be, and there is, the sole necessity, by thinking our way soberly into what this poetry says, to come to learn what is unspoken. That is the course of the history of Being. If we reach and enter that course, it will lead thinking into a dialogue with poetry, a dialogue which is of the history of Being. Scholars of literary history inevitably consider that dialogue to be an unscientific violation of what such scholarship takes to be the facts. Philosophers consider the dialogue to be a helpless aberration into fantasy. But destiny pursues its course untroubled by all that.[4]

This book concerns a possible meeting-place between philosophy, literary criticism, art and truth. Poetry, if understood in a certain way, is where the truth of Being manifests itself at the beginning of the twenty-first century. If this is the case, then poetry is far too important a matter to be left to the so-called 'experts'. It concerns each one of us, as each one of us is required to understand why we are alive at this moment on this planet. No one can usurp this role, nor can we delegate the task to anyone else. The truth of Being is something we must engage for ourselves.

On 1 January 1901, *The Times* of London welcomed a new century with a series of questions: 'Will the last generation of the twentieth century differ very much from the first? Will they be healthier and longer-lived, wiser, better, and more intelligent, or will they remain substantially the same as the people we have known and the people whom history has portrayed to us?' The *New York Times* hailed the 'Twentieth Century's Triumphant Entry' with banner headlines, and declared that 'the advance of the human race during the past hundred years has not been equalled by the progress of man within any of the preceding ages'. Randolph Guggenheimer, president of the city council, is quoted as hoping that in the new century: 'the rights of the individual man shall continue to be regarded as sacred, and that the crowning glory of the coming century shall be the lifting up of the poor, the annihilation of all misery and wrong, and that the peace and goodwill which the angels proclaimed shall rest on contending nations as the snowflakes upon the land'.[5]

Our experience of that same twentieth century has taught us differently. These are destitute times. There may have been other times, other eras, when the truth of Being became available in other ways, through other sources – through politics, religion or philosophy for instance – but in these times in which we live, the traces are few and the scent is poor. We have to rely for their detection on highly trained watchdogs with a keen sense of smell. Artists are in one specific order, prophets are in another. People need both orders. It is not necessary, nor is it advisable, for the poet to move into the second order of prophecy, although some do with varying degrees of success. 'In our time,' says W. B. Yeats, 'we are agreed that we "make our souls" out of some one of the great poets of ancient times, or out of Shelley or Wordsworth, or Goethe or Balzac, or Flaubert, or Count Tolstoy, in the books he wrote before he became a prophet and fell into a lesser order.'[6]

I agree with Yeats about three things here: that 'poets', in the sense he means here, are artists of whatever kind, whether novelists, painters, sculptors; that the work of the poet is different from that of the prophet or the preacher, although they have been, and can be, combined; that the prophet or preacher is in a lesser order than the poet, whose task is paramount because essentially original. The artists and poets are like water diviners and prospectors, whose task is to find the water and the ore. It is usually the task of others to mine and refine, collect and distribute.

There might seem to be a contradiction here: on the one hand the work of certain poets is 'prophetic', and, on the other, the role of the prophet is of a lesser order to that of the poet. Two things should be distinguished. Poetry as 'prophecy' is something that happens to a poet. It concerns the whole being of the poet, the total personality. It passes through poetic sensitivity and emerges as poetry almost as if the words of the poem were drops of sweat. The poet may not even be aware of all that is happening. In a certain sense he or she is being used as a mouthpiece.

This does not mean, therefore, that such a poet then assumes the role of a prophet, preaching, teaching and calling to order. That is a very different stance. It may be that the poet is called to assume both roles, but whether or not this is the case, the second role is a lesser one. Whereas, on the contrary, in the order of poetry, the prophetic kind is of the highest order. Other kinds of poetry, whether propaganda, protest, or popular song, are less important. What I am calling 'prophetic' poetry is where, and how, something more than the poet could have accomplished on his or her own infiltrates and emerges with the poem. This 'something more' is what is being referred to here as the truth of Being. Such truth demands total commitment of the artist to the poetic act. It is a matter of *being* rather than *doing*, and it requires the complete life and person of the poet to accomplish it.

This is why it usually requires another person and another kind of criticism to assess and to interpret what the poetry is saying. Another kind of thinking and commitment is required to articulate such realities into a discourse available to those who can read and follow logical thought. Sometimes such assessment and interpretation take centuries to unfold. However, the better outcome would be to make this truth available more immediately, so that the poet's contemporaries might also profit from the truth he or she has allowed to enter our world. The second work of explanation or interpretation is the task of thinkers, monks, prophets – those who stand on the edges in the watchtowers of the night, waiting for signs of the dawn that is approaching.

What is approaching, in this sense, is something to do with Being, something ontological. It is not political or social, although it can have an effect on these and can be influential in many and beneficent ways.

My own watchtower happens to be in Ireland on the edge of Europe. Some of the poets who have helped me to catch glimpses of this possible future are Irish. They have accompanied me on this journey for over thirty years. It is my privilege to share with any reader who happens to open this book, and is interested in the kind of truth that it hopes to promote, the strange way they have led me to such understanding.

The quotation from Heidegger with which I open this search is forthright and daring to the point of being arrogant. It says that there is a way of reading poetry that gives access to Being. This is neither the way philosophy has worked in the past – even though philosophy is supposed to understand and explain Being as its most specific purpose – nor is it the way literary

criticism proposes, which is meant to be the ultimate interpreter
of poetry. A third path has to be forged, which is a specific kind
of dialogue between poetry and thinking.

If this is not done, our generation will have no access to Being
or truth of the most fundamental kind. If it is done, it will probably
be discounted by philosophy and disdained by literary critics.
Too bad about that, says Heidegger, Being will whisper to those
who have ears to hear with, and will become manifest, will enter
history through the humility of those who are ready to undertake such a dialogue. It may not have the kind of influence it
should have, but at least it will be there as a presence. Without
the fosterage of at least some members of the human race, it can
gain no access to our world. In fact, Heidegger is suggesting that
there was perhaps only one person in the nineteenth century
who can be identified through his work as having been ungain-
sayably privvy to this presence. This was Friedrich Hoelderlin
(1770 -1843), a contemporary of the philosopher Hegel. He had
suffered from schizophrenia from his early thirties and was
virtually ignored during his lifetime and for the rest of that century. It was only when his collected poems were published in
1913 that his work became available to those who were able to
detect the truth of Being that it contained.

This kind of poetry is in what T. S. Eliot calls 'the first voice' –
that of the poet talking to him or herself or to nobody at all:

What you start from is nothing so definite as an emotion, in
any ordinary sense; it is still more certainly not an idea; it is –
to adapt two lines of Beddoes to a different meaning – a

Bodiless childful of life in the gloom
Crying with frog voice, 'what shall I be?'

[The poet] is oppressed by a burden which he must bring to
birth in order to obtain relief. Or, to change the figure of
speech, he is haunted by a demon, a demon against which he
feels powerless, because in its first manifestation it has no
face, no name, nothing; and the words, the poem he makes,
are a kind of form of exorcism of this demon.[7]

My aim in writing this book is to articulate in the simplest form possible the findings I have gleaned from many years of such dialogue. If there have been such artists in Ireland, and, of course, there is no reason why there should have to be, it would make it easier for Irish people to access. Obviously, there is no premium attached to being Irish, no ontological aristocracy; it just makes it easier for me, as another Irish person, to achieve that kind of discernment in their work which can separate the wheat from the chaff, the absolute and definitive from the local and idiosyncratic. I choose James Joyce and Seamus Heaney as test cases whose lives and works span the twentieth century.

Before undertaking such exegesis, which will be the essential burden of Chapters Six and Seven of this book, a number of other tasks are essential to clear the way. The first of these is to describe the kind of literary criticism that is involved, because, after all, these are works of literature. This can be achieved by first of all showing what such criticism does not mean. Secondly, something must be said about philosophy and how it must end up in dialogue with poetry or art if it is to achieve its fundamental purpose.

One of the reasons why philosophy, like Moses, is prevented from entering the promised land, is because it has been from its beginnings a European and all-male preserve. Its advantages and its strengths in terms of clarity, precision and muscularity of thought are the very reasons why it becomes powerless in the realms of Being. This is not just because the heart has reasons which reason cannot know, as Pascal has said, but because our understanding is wider than the narrow compass of our reasoning. Art and literature, as W. B. Yeats knew, is made 'by what is still blind and dumb within ourselves'. The enlargement of experience that makes us capable of the truth of Being 'does not come from those oratorical thinkers, or from those decisive rhythms that move large numbers of men, but from writers that seem by contrast as feminine as the soul when it explores in Blake's picture the recesses of the grave, carrying its faint lamp trembling and astonished'.[8]

The reasons why philosophy must decrease and art increase in face of this mystery can best be elaborated through the works of one of the great philosophers of the twentieth century, Iris Murdoch, who chose to accomplish her work through the medium of art rather than through her profession, which was philosophy. Chapter Four will study her work in this regard.

Western European philosophy as a comprehensive net of universal understanding is pretentious and provincial when portrayed against the tapestry of other and older systems and cultures. Its endemic purblindness can best be conveyed by an artist from outside this tradition, and I have chosen the African playwright Wole Soyinka. Chapter Five will be a presentation of his work both in drama and in philosophy, which provides a salutary corrective of and instructive alternative to the Western European tradition.

When I say that I am trying to keep it simple, I mean that I am trying to make something important as widely available as possible. The work of artists is original; my work is derived. In this book I attempt to explain as clearly and as simply as I can, without thereby losing the subtlety of what has to be elucidated, the truth that I have gleaned from following behind artists, harvesting possible shapes for the future.

Because the important possibility is this: there is no future as some kind of panorama laid out beforehand. There is no God, no soothsayer, no fortune-teller who can describe its contours and its shape by some magic or psychic insight. The future does not exist until it happens. And we are the ones who make it happen. The future is neither a blank page nor is it an already designed house into which we are required to move. The future is what we build together, what we create together. It can be an ugly, vulgar extension of what we already are, or it can be an invitation to Being to infiltrate and expand the reality of what we might become. Being has to await our participation before its form as history is allowed to take place. This happens through the aegis of those who are gifted with metaphysical insight, who in our times are mostly artists and poets. So, I repeat, there is no such thing as the future. There is only the next move that we make. And that move can be originating truth, if it is poetic, and it can be repetitive impersonation if merely political.

The twentieth century was a blundering between ideologies. Ideologies are false futures drawn in big pictures by those who take it upon themselves to shape our destiny. History as we have known it is mostly a concatenation of disasters followed by clean-ups afterwards. The truth of Being is otherwise. It requires that we inch our way forward with constant reference to the subtler music of who and what we really are.

The twentieth century moved into the future with the speed and panache of a joy-riding technology. We have moved so far and so fast that it will be a long time before our souls catch up, or any clean-up can take place.

Our approach to the future at that time was as brash and in-sensitive as our approach to the past. In 1922, Howard Carter made one of the sensational archaeological discoveries of all time. In the valley of the tombs of the Kings of Egypt he found the burial place of Tutankhamun. For over three thousand years this funeral vault had been sealed off and forgotten. Every other royal Egyptian burial place had been ransacked from a remote date and there were no known tombs intact since the fall of the Egyptian empire in about 1085 BCE. Experts thought Carter was crazy to insist on excavation. He had exhausted the patience of his fellow-workers and the resources of his sponsors when he uncovered the steps leading down to the entrance gallery. The actual task of unsealing the burial chamber and penetrating the tomb was given to Carter himself. His eye was the first in over three thousand years to look into this vault. He describes in his memoirs how they bored a small hole through to the chamber and then stood back to let him be the first to see inside. He looked through the tiny aperture. Light and air also entered the vault for the first time. Carter saw lying on the sarcophagus a large multicoloured feather. As he watched and as the air en-tered the chamber for the first time, he saw the ostrich feather curl up and disintegrate within seconds before his eyes. He understood that this penetration and invasion of the past destroyed the very mystery it was attempting to retrieve. Millions of tourists who have since then viewed the relics salvaged from that excavation, displayed in the National Museum of Cairo, are witnesses to the resurrection of an empty tomb. The event is symbolic of another kind of excavation of the past, namely our own psychological past, and the story is a way of describing how intractable the past is to the predatory fingers of the present.

We cannot remember yesterday any more than we can remember tomorrow. Obviously, we can use memory as a clothesline with images of our past hung out to dry like linen. The more determined our interest in each piece displayed, the more available each will be for whatever purpose we want to put them to now. It is the past presented as booty for the carpet-bagger of the present.

The past, according to Proust, is stored in 'that inaccessible dungeon of our being to which habit does not possess the key'. Every moment of our past life is 'imprisoned in a vase filled with a certain perfume and a certain colour and raised to a certain temperature. These vases are suspended along the height of our years, and, not being accessible to our intelligent memory, are in a sense immune, the purity of their climatic content is guaranteed by forgetfulness, each one is kept at its distance, at its date. So that when the imprisoned microcosm is besieged in the manner described, we are flooded by a new air and a new perfume.'[9] The reality of our past remains a hermetically sealed surface, which we can use and interpret for whatever purpose our present opportunism, greed or suffering choose to impose upon it.

But more importantly for the present investigation, so is our future. In the same way that the truth can be lost through clumsy excavation of the past, so too the future, which is an even more delicate and sensitive opening, can be desecrated. Mission statements, ten-year plans, vision documents, can be a way of levelling the future and imposing upon it our own myopic architecture, unless we harness the sensitivity and clairvoyance of

certain artists who are gifted with insight about our own particular singularity of contour and the approaching plasticity with
which this should be fused. As for the past, so into the future. As
Heaney said, 'All I know is a door into the dark.' We need to harness eyes that can see. The way forward is evolution.

'If revolution is the kicking down of a rotten door, evolution
is more like pushing the stone from the mouth of the tomb.
There is an Easter energy about it, a sense of arrival rather than
wreckage, and what is nonpareil about the new conditions is the
promise they offer of a new covenant between people living in
this country. For once, and at long last, the language of the Bible
can be appropriated by those with a vision of the future rather
than those who sing the battle hymns of the past.'[10] This is
Seamus Heaney writing on a Saturday after a significant Friday
in the peace process in Northern Ireland. In the context of this
book, his words apply to the future in general and to every door
and every step we take towards that future.

Ireland as an outpost on the edge of Europe can be a poet's
perch, sensing the rhythm and the shape of the next move forward. In destitute times it is the fool, not the king, who takes us
by the hand. But what does it mean to 'feel' our way forward,
and what is the precise role of the artist in this regard? I am not
saying that the fool should replace the king or that the artist
should take up the reins of government. I am suggesting that the
body politic is in fact a body, that it has different constituent
parts. Unless each of these is working in its particular way at its
appropriate function, the movement of the total organism is im-
paired.

The artist has a very precise and indispensable role to play. It
is certainly not everything, but it is something akin to yeast in
dough. Its accurate and pervasive participation allows every
part of the whole loaf to take a certain contour. Without this specific ingredient, the whole batch remains flat and cannot achieve
its purpose or assume the shape it was intended to take. How
this happens is a matter of organisation, but the end result must
be correct valorisation of the artist's place and role, sufficient

security and support to allow the artist to attend to the specific work of art, and effective, even ruthless, clearance of all channels to allow the truth of that work to penetrate every fibre and particle of the total organism. Whether this means the establishment of a parliament of artists, or the incorporation of such a constituency within existing structures of representative government, is optional. What is not optional, and what must be accomplished in whatever way allows it to happen, is that the voice of the artist be heard.

Such a voice may not make itself heard in any of the media which currently constitute our preferred channels. These consider art only as entertainment or as propaganda. Art as prophecy is unrecognised. It may make itself heard in the most obscure and even sometimes perversely obscurantist sound bytes. In face of our accustomed channels of garrulous and facile communication, art can appear dumb. Art can be despised 'when arrayed against the moral zeal, the confident logic, the ordered proof of journalism'. It can appear as 'a trifling, impertinent, vexatious thing, a tumbler who has unrolled his carpet in the way of a marching army'.[11] But we must make it our task to detect such tremulous sounds and translate them sufficiently to make them available to our corporate future as a marching army.

As Yeats has said so disdainfully: 'It is not the business of artists to make themselves understood, it is the business of the people to understand them.' Sometimes translation can destroy what it purports to convey. In such circumstances it is necessary to wait and remain attentive to the truth which is present in the work of art, until it reveals to us the appropriate way to transform it into architectural energy. The burden of this book is neither politics nor sociology, although it has important implications for both. It is concerned as much with religion or spirituality and the way in which those responsible for our growth and evolution envisage the future and identify their task.

CHAPTER ONE

Art and Spirituality

Spirituality describes the way we relate to the world of the spirit, the way we connect with whatever we describe as our God. Each culture has to find its own way through to the dimension of the 'Other'. Each people, embedded in varieties and layers of culture, must burrow their way to transcendence, to freedom, to appreciation of what is other than, or different from, their particularity. Otherwise they remain immured within, never reaching any dimension beyond themselves.

How to accomplish this, how to reach such dimensions, is the problem. There can be no all-purpose technique, no abstract and universally applicable solution. Each of us is irretrievably enveloped in our own particular cocoon, from which it is impossible to escape completely. However, we can prevent ourselves from being obtusely atavistic by making some effort to identify our more unyielding cultural reflexes. What the French call *la hantise d'être insupportable* is difficult to translate, but it suggests being haunted by the probability that we are unbearable; this last word in a double sense: that others cannot abide us and that we are incapable of gaining access to a world other than the one we were born into. Those most capable of making us aware of these probabilities and of pointing out the hidden and subtle ways in which each of us may be so, are artists. Specifically, the people of the last century who explored the spiritual dimension of life, in ways that make it accessible to others, are artists. Artists are the best guides we have.

Sometimes such people are not very admirable in themselves. Sometimes we are freed from our chains, as Nietzsche says, by those who were unable to free themselves. The path to freedom is not always very glamorous; the things we have to do to get there are not always edifying; the people who help us are not always paragons of virtue.

Part of my argument requires the repudiation of a certain kind of criticism of artists. There is a high-minded superiority and nitpicking disdain that characterises some contemporary assessment of the work of people, past or present, whom the critics judge guilty of actions or attitudes now proclaimed to be 'politically incorrect'. Some artists or thinkers are excommunicated completely for attitudes or activities that later generations find inexcusable.

It is salutary to remember how many of us had ingrained attitudes twenty or forty years ago, which at that time we accepted as perfectly normal, but which we now find unthinkable: such aberrations of cultural complacency would include attitudes to women, to children, to peoples from other races, etc.

Thomas Jefferson remains, for me, one of the most striking examples of such cultural blinkeredness. Cultivated, imaginative, intelligent, philanthropic, his drafting of the American Declaration of Independence and his sensitive commentary on the social situation in France leading up to the French Revolution, on the eve of which he was in Paris, might have led to the hope that his cultural awareness would have been beyond the ordinary. And yet, he arrived in Paris with two slaves, one of whom was still a mere child, his concubine, pregnant with one of his children. The culture that welcomed him in Paris made it *de rigueur* for such a man to have a lover among the great ladies of the court. The only question was: upon whom should he bestow his favours. The husband of his chosen was expected to be a good sport, if not indeed flattered by his choice. But even such moral and social laxity and broadmindedness did not extend to concubinage with a teenage African-American slave-girl. The clash of two very limited but different cultures, even though it did awaken his slaves themselves to the anomaly of their situation, causing them to insist upon eventual freedom, did not seem to ruffle in any way the cultural complacency of Jefferson himself.

However, does this allow us to conclude that if he were alive today Jefferson would have been a child-abuser, that the politician he would have most admired would be Pol Pot, or that he would have condoned the 1995 bombing of the Federal building in Oklahoma? Such seem to be the suggestions of Conor Cruise O'Brien in his study of Jefferson and the French Revolution.[1] Furthermore, Cruise O'Brien's intention is not only to destroy Jefferson's credibility but to vilify him, to make it shameful to admire such a person. He knows that many Americans, and others, have been taught to love and admire Jefferson. He knows that these people will be outraged. The very purpose of his study, in his own words, is to 'go on outraging them … out of existence'. The fact that Jefferson was an uncritical supporter of the French Revolution, 'hot with enthusiasm of the great French struggle', makes him, for Cruise O'Brien, the equivalent of a contemporary terrorist. The September Massacres of 1792 were atrocities that Jefferson condoned. These were numerically on a larger scale than their 1995 equivalent in Oklahoma City. Therefore Jefferson is 'worse' than one of the Oklahoma bombers. It seems to me that such comparisons fail to take into account the painful awareness imposed upon us by the logic of historical confrontation with cultural blindness. Before the Second World War most Christians were saturated with attitudes towards the Jewish people which, when followed through to their logical and inexorable conclusions, led to the hideous reality of the Holocaust. This reality in turn made it less possible for subsequent generations to be blinkered by such prejudice.

This does not necessarily mean that we are making cultural 'progress'. It would seem more likely, using a phrase of Herbert Butterfield, that each generation is equidistant from barbarity. However, visible evidence of the scale and scope of our atrocities makes it less possible to be unaware of these propensities in ourselves and less capable of turning a blind eye. Perpetrators and condoners of such atrocities in the first years of the twenty-first century must be more 'responsible' for what they do than were their peers at the beginning of the nineteenth century.

So, I shall continue to admire Thomas Jefferson as a person who did try to make sense of life as it stepped up to him, and who used his time on earth constructively, even if he was prisoner to the culture of his times and even if he had – as who has not? – weaknesses and deficiencies. And I shall continue to disregard the efforts of those who set themselves up as the ultimate tribunal establishing the validity of other people's lives. History is one thing; the last judgement is presumably another.

We would do better to examine our own consciences and try to imagine what our children will think of our present prejudices. The most dangerous decoy is to presume that we are, or ever can be, without them: insensitive attitudes to races other than our own, to those of a different sex, class, age, state of health. Secret sins shouted from the rooftops, ugly war crimes perpetrated in dark rooms, writ large and suddenly on TV screens, must constitute a rude awakening, an irreversible jostling of public consciousness. The revelation of evil in day-to-day existence, its detection and identification in some of our most automatic responses and reactions, must surely show it up for what it is, for both the perpetrators and the public at large. It can no longer hide itself as habit and be condoned as our way of dealing with things, our 'rough justice', our little foibles, our home-made pesticide.

Sensitisation does not always have to come from lived experience, exposure, humiliation, revolution, necessity. It can also come through the work of certain artists. They bring us to the edge of our culture, to the hall door, even if we are not going to be able to get further than that. However, the hall door is a major step in the right direction. It allows us to open it and to dialogue with others of the same or of different cultures. More than that, artists help us to detect what the future holds in store. This 'prophetic' quality of the artist need mean no more than a heightened sensitivity, which makes them capable of sensing what is coming in the future, as animals 'sense' a thunderstorm or as Cezanne sketched future shapes in the plane trees of Provence. More than that, they can invent the future by sketching the possibilities that none of us ever thought of.

The point of view I am presenting here, which is the point of view offered by a monk, is not the same as that of an artist or an academic. However, it is a point of view that might shed some complementary light. Both Dostoevsky and Yeats were aware of the connection between the work of certain artists and the life of the monk, identifying the contribution that the latter should and could make to the future of civilisation. Yeats compared Synge to those who:

> sought for the race not through the eyes or in history, or even in the future, but where those monks found God, in the depths of the mind, and in all art like his, although it does not command – indeed because it does not – may lie the roots of far-branching events.[2]

Yeats and Synge believed the inhabitants of the Blaskets and Inishmaan to be living 'under the weight of their necessity' in such a dimension: 'in the orgiastic moment when life outleaps its limits'.[3] This is the moment of transcendence from which a literature can be created 'by what is still blind and dumb within ourselves'.[4] Artists who work also in this dimension 'speak to us that we may give them certainty, by seeing what they have seen'.[5] A certain type of 'criticism' can and should accompany such artistic effort. It constitutes a kind of thought and, therefore, a philosophy, which is a coherent and comprehensive articulation of that thought. The thinker who has, in my view, most successfully articulated it is Martin Heidegger:

> Such reflection cannot force art and its coming-to-be. But this reflective knowledge is the preliminary and therefore indispensable preparation for the becoming of art. Only such knowledge prepares its space for art, their way for the creators, their location for the preservers.[6]

However, before even examining such a text, we are forced to ask ourselves at least two important cultural questions: 'What does Heidegger actually mean?'; and then, even more importantly: 'Is this philosopher worthy of our attention, if he personally is guilty of behaviour and commitments that remove him from the arena of civilised discourse?'

Art, he is saying, can be as powerful a modifier of human being as genetic engineering. Its modifications would be more aligned with what we should be, more appropriate to what we are, because grounded in the truth of Being. A certain kind of thinking is necessary to prepare art for its essential task and to prepare us for awareness of its achievement.

As a general principle, it should surely be conceded that such a possibility concerning art must remain valid, no matter who is responsible for articulating it. Once the argument has been made, it cannot be obliterated simply by denouncing the person who formulated it. Would we, for instance, give up using penicillin if it were shown that Alexander Fleming was a monster?

What Heidegger has revealed to us about art is as important to our spiritual life as penicillin has been to our physical life. And this, very simply stated, is that art is a starting point. It is what makes history original. The movement of history is neither an inexorable flow, nor is it a human decision entirely; it is neither fate nor politics. It can be a more subtle conjunction, which lies between these two options. The growth and the shedding of cultural skin which determine the movement of human history are, according to this theory, a combination of philosophy and art, with art playing the original role. Philosophy lifts art to the opening at the top and catches it as it falls on the other side. But art establishes the actual escape route and does what is necessary to lead us through. Art has the imagination to sketch out the possible.

In the mythical story of the escape from the Labyrinth at Cnossus, philosophy plays the role of Ariadne and art the role of Theseus. But just as each culture weaves its own particular labyrinth, so each one has to find its own Theseus. Each Theseus will also be provided with the particular silken thread at the mouth of that labyrinth which will allow him or her to encounter the minotaur at the centre and then find the way back outside.

All of which is a mythological metaphor to describe a kind of knowing, which combines science on the one hand and mysticism on the other, with art as the nexus between the two. This specific phenomenon of art as a vehicle of transcendence is what Joyce describes as 'the Haunted Inkbottle'.[7] It is that use of language which allows some possibility for another dimension to eke its way into the text, if the art work is a written one. In a letter, Joyce tells his brother: 'I like the notion of the Holy Ghost being in the inkbottle.'[8] Which means that the way of access to this world of ours, for all that is beyond its reach, happens in the space between the paintbrush and the canvas, the nib of the pen and the paper, between the fingers and the computer screen.

The Holy Spirit, who cannot enter our world without camouflage, without disguise, hides in the inkwell so that inspiration can exceed the most extravagant efforts of the artist. Within the space created by these words or images, by this poetry, by this art, something as yet unheard of can infiltrate. We can call this other dimension the thirteenth cone, the fifth province, or the fourth stage, the image or the name are always inadequate to the task. However, it is through artistic ecstasy that such a transcendent dimension is allowed to penetrate the opacity of our cultural labyrinth.

The kind of thought that can help such an event to occur and can make it more available to others once it has occurred is 'criticism', which places itself between the artist and the inspirational event, holding open the space wherein the extra breath from elsewhere accrues. This, as I see it, is the real business of such criticism. It is thinking with the artist.

What kind of artist are we talking about here? There is a paradox that historical example and individual biography almost impose: the more overtly religious the artist, the less convincing the art. Conversion, for instance, is not a great career move for the artist as artist. One only has to think of Tolstoy. Art, of the kind I am talking about here, has to do with the unconscious in a way that is difficult to articulate but which means that such art happens through an artist in ways that remove any identifiable copyright or exclusivity of authorship. So many artists have given testimony to this reality, it is hardly possible to gainsay.

'Only that which does not teach, which does not cry out, which does not persuade, which does not condescend, which does not explain, is irresistible,' Yeats reminds us. That is why overtly 'religious' art, or art that is a form of preaching or teaching, fails to exist as art. Yeats was talking about J. M. Synge, 'who was a drifting silent man full of hidden passion, and loved wild islands, because there, set out in the light of day, he saw what lay hidden in himself'. 'All art is the disengaging of a soul from place and history, its suspension in a beautiful or terrible light to await the Judgement,' Yeats decides. The Greek word for judgement is *krisis*, which is the origin of our word 'crisis'. Schiller has said that 'the history of the world is the judgement of the world'. This sentence can be taken in at least three ways: that each step history makes depends upon the discernment that 'the world' makes about how to proceed; or that history is continual crisis management, the stages of which are what we call 'historical epochs'; or that history as it unfolds is an indictment of the world – meaning us – who should have changed its course.

Yeats sees the artist as having a prophetic role in the unfolding of history's direction. In Synge's art, for example, he saw 'the roots of far-branching events'. Where does such art come from? From that place, Yeats tells us, 'where the monks found God, in the depths of the mind'.[9] Art should provide the form of truth that the future might assume at the beginning of each epoch.

The twentieth century happened in Paris in the 1920s, says Gertrude Stein. She was referring, no doubt, to all the artists who were exiled from elsewhere and who ended up in the only place that would take them in. There are two kinds of time – chronological time and creative time. When we suggest that the twentieth century happened in Paris we are saying two things: the century we have just been through, probably the cruellest and most devastating the planet has survived, began its march. But we are also saying that there were artists who foretold what would emerge, forestalled, perhaps, or mitigated its full impact somewhat, and helped us to survive it. They sowed seeds for an alternative version, and the monuments they left have survived. These enduring works of art give us further opportunity to reestablish ourselves as their beneficiaries by becoming their contemporaries, even if somewhat belatedly a hundred years later.

Roger Casement (1864-1916) sent a report to the British government about the inhuman treatment, the barbaric exploitation of what was then the Belgian Congo, at the beginning of the twentieth century. He was British Consul in the Congo (1901-1904). James Conrad is supposed to have read this report, although it was only published in 1904, and, whether he read it or not, he wrote *Heart of Darkness*, published in 1902. In a letter of 1895, Conrad says: 'All my work is produced unconsciously (so to speak) and … it isn't in me to improve what has got itself written.' This kind of art is inspired. It comes from a depth where its authorship is no longer quite traceable. T. S. Eliot read Conrad's book. He wrote *The Waste Land*, from a corresponding place in his own beleaguered unconscious in 1922, between the two world wars:

> What are the roots that clutch, what branches grow
> Out of this stony rubbish? Son of man,
> You cannot say, or guess, for you know only
> A heap of broken images, where the sun beats,
> And the dead tree gives no shelter, the cricket no relief,
> And the dry stone no sound of water. Only
> There is shadow under this red rock,
> (Come in under the shadow of this red rock),
> And I will show you something different from either
> Your shadow at morning striding behind you
> Or your shadow at evening rising to meet you;
> I will show you fear in a handful of dust.

When I say that the Holy Spirit is in the inkwell, I am using an image for a kind of inspiration which artists have often been aware of themselves. But are not these words no more than pious platitudes? 'It is only through the psyche that we can establish that God acts upon us,' says Jung in his *Answer to Job*,[10] 'but we are unable to distinguish whether these actions emanate from God or from the unconscious. We cannot tell whether God and the unconscious are two different entities. Both are border-line concepts for transcendental contents.' Jung is not saying, as he has so often been accused of, that God does not exist, or that God is a creation of the unconscious. He is saying that it is empirically impossible to distinguish between the 'God-image' and 'the archetype of the self', even though we can 'arbitrarily postulate a difference between these two entities, but that does not help us at all'. For all practical purposes, he thinks, we must remain agnostic on this point, because our conscious minds are the only means by which we can formulate the possible connections that happen in the unconscious, but this is beneath any radar screen to which we have conscious access. The reason for this impossibility has nothing to do with God; it is entirely to do with the inaccessibility of the unconscious. We have no idea what happens, or who's who, down there.

However, it is from the unconscious that all great spiritual or religious art emanates. It does not come from a conscious embracing of religious creeds or principles; nor does it arise from implementation of a strategic religious plan, a propagation of a particular set of credal formulae, or the adoption of a specific code of religious conduct.

Art of this kind is truth entering history and emerging in a recognisable and durable work. Art of this kind is theology. It does not merely illustrate a theology. It is itself a theological act or deed. It is God actively involved in the work: divine energy. The word 'energy' comes from the Greek *en ergon*, meaning 'in the work'. It is God's Spirit at work. Such truth does not come to us; it comes through us. We do not open up the truth; we are the opening through which truth can announce itself. Truth does this through language; not language as a tool of ours, which we can manipulate, but language as a river in which we swim. Truth seeps into our pores, starting from the feet. It cleaves us in two and breathes through us in song. We are torn and turned upside-down before this can happen. And it can only happen through individual people. It doesn't come through a group or out of a seminar. As Rudolf Steiner has said famously of Goethe: 'Truth is always only individual truth of significant human beings.'

Such truth emerging in significant words is poetry of the deepest kind. It is what Rilke calls 'heart-work':

Work of sight is achieved,
now for some heart-work
on all those images, prisoned within you; for you
overcame them, but do not know them as yet.

This 'turning', or conversion, which is required to become an artist of the other order – Rilke calls it the angelic order – is a reversal of our normal stance. The artist has to hang upside-down like the hanged man in the tarot cards. A scooped-out turnip with a candle inside. The head is buried in the earth and the feet become explorers of the rhythm. Iambic pentameter: the Greek words refer to the rhythm of the lines as the language reverberates through the poet. *Iamb* is a foot and the metre is measured according to the number of times the footbeats hit the earth. Wordsworth and Coleridge walked all their poetry into the earth: pedestrians. Humility is the virtue or the fundamental attitude required (the word 'humility' also comes from the Latin word *humus*, meaning earth). Dancing is the original medium. It is the unconscious movement of the whole body from the ground upwards. Remember Synge on the Aran Islands:

Last night, after walking in a dream among buildings with a strangely intense light on them, I heard a faint rhythm of music beginning far away on some stringed instrument.

It came closer to me, gradually increasing in quickness and volume with an irresistibly definite progression. When it was quite near the sound began to move in my nerves and blood, and to urge me to dance with them.

In a moment I was swept away in a whirlwind of notes. My breath and my thoughts and every impulse of my body, became a form of the dance, till I could not distinguish between the instruments and the rhythm and my own person or consciousness.[11]

In his 1970 Nobel lecture, Alexander Solzhenitsyn (1918-) distinguished between two kinds of artist: 'One artist sees himself as the creator of an independent spiritual world: he hoists onto his shoulders the task of creating this world, of peopling it and of bearing the all-embracing responsibility for it ... Another artist, recognising a higher power above, gladly works as a humble apprentice beneath God's heaven.'

Inspiration of the second kind means thinking together. It means a kind of artistry that is both active and passive at the same time. The Greek language had a grammatical term for this, a middle voice. We have lost both the grammar and the practice. For us, everything is either active or passive. Either I kick you or I am kicked. Either I compose this piece or somebody else composes it. However, inspiration is more than 'I think', or 'I compose'. It is better expressed by 'it thinks' or 'thinking happens'. Even the word 'compose' comes from the Latin *cum*, meaning 'with', and *pono, ponere, posui, positum*, meaning to 'place' or to 'pitch'. So it implies acting with someone or something else. Two sources, two simultaneous currents, mingle and unite wherever you have authentic inspiration of the second kind.

No one can teach us the techniques required for this second kind of inspiration. There are no techniques. Techniques are in the domain of genius, of accomplishment, where one is given the gifts to be a great artist. Asked by the government in Paris what should be done to improve the standard of art in the French educational system, and especially in the various third-level art schools and colleges, Picasso replied: 'Give them rotten conditions, and let the teaching be bad, bad, bad.'

Great art cannot be taught; it must be submitted to and then it will do the teaching. Rumi, the thirteenth-century Persian mystic, puts it appropriately:

Then new events said to me,
'Don't move. A sublime generosity
is coming toward you.'

The chess master says nothing,
other than moving the silent chess piece.

That I am part of the ploys
of this game makes me
amazingly happy.

Great art of the second kind, which allows God's creative spirit
to take shape in the world, requires humility. We have to yield
to this spirit, we have to give up our copyright, our exclusive
right as author, our signature at the bottom of the painting or at
the end of the book. It means diminishing the self so that the
other source of inspiration may increase.

The claim I am making is that certain kinds of poetry and art
have been doing work of a similar nature to that accomplished
by the religious seers of previous centuries. Further, I am proposing a certain kind of criticism of such works of art as the most
appropriate way to uncover this dimension.

There is a reading of certain poetry, an understanding of certain art works, that is 'ontological', or metaphysical, because
such art is the way in which Being (or, in my perspective, the
Spirit) can register presence in our world.

Such a task can only be achieved by a dedicated and subtle
dialogue between poetry and thinking. Such a dialogue is neither
the creation of poetry by thinkers, nor is it the formulation of
ideologies by poets. It is the recognition by both parties that we
are living in destitute times, when all the structures we have
created, all the languages we have learnt, and all the 'truths' that
we have believed to be fundamental, have somehow proved
themselves inadequate to the task of catering for our common
future.

In such circumstances, the role of the artist becomes essential.
And the task of 'thinkers' is to listen and to learn. The sobering
lesson of these destitute times is that we have become almost
irretrievably estranged from our potential future by the ideological constructs of our various pasts. To extricate ourselves from
this war of worlds, it is not enough to invent yet one more illusory

utopia; it is essential to re-establish contact with the reality of what we are, with the truth of history, even if it has to find words that are beyond the vocabulary of all the languages we currently know how to speak. 'In the buginning is the woid,' Joyce suggests in *Finnegans Wake*. And in that punning conjunction of 'word' and 'void', he provokes the 'thought' (because the pun is 'two thinks at a time') that poetry makes 'nothing' happen and that art 'lets truth originate'.

This means that the origin of our historical existence as people rather than as pawns, and the hope for our existence as it might be in a more imaginative future, is art. Heidegger tells us that 'art is of its nature an origin, which means a very distinctive way in which truth can come into being and become historical'. We are not necessarily determined by some inexorable flow of history. We can stop the world and redirect it, if we have sufficient understanding and imagination both to point out the better way and make it compelling enough to accomplish. Art is an original truth of this kind: it can reveal the way towards a more sensitive future.

In the combination required to achieve such an event, the poets have one role and the thinkers another. This does not mean that thinkers are trying to abuse poetry and make it into fodder for philosophy. It means that 'there would be, and there is, the sole necessity, by thinking our way soberly into what the poetry says, to come to learn what is unspoken'.[12]

In accomplishing such an event, we reach the place of transcendence, which, although it can never dislocate itself entirely from the cultural place to which we belong, at least gives us access to the world or the reality beyond ourselves. Through the language of poetry, the work of art, a breath beyond the breathing space of the artist can impress itself upon our hearing.

CHAPTER TWO

Art and Criticism

Artists are of paramount importance to us at this time, and a certain kind of criticism is, perhaps, preventing them from accomplishing an essential task. Poetry, in the broadest sense, is probably our only way forward in destitute times. Perhaps it is unfortunate that we have to rely on such fragile antennae, but, at the moment, it is all we have. At other turning points in history, science, philosophy, ethics or theology may have been sufficient; in the complicated and unpredictable times in which we live, there is no other way. Art can provide the weak, yet indispensable instruments available to chart the way forward. It is almost as if the place we have reached in the tunnel we are burrowing is too narrow for grown adults to scramble through, and we have to persuade children to ease their way through the opening, take the fall on the other side and then help us to negotiate a passage for the rest.

The kind of criticism that can prevent this from happening is that which declares certain artists and thinkers unworthy of our attention because of personal actions or views that are deemed unacceptable. For example, Ezra Pound, T. S. Eliot and W. B. Yeats are accused of fascism or anti-semitism.

Denis Donoghue[1] calls his own point of view liberal and bourgeois. He feels embattled by 'Marxists and feminists to the left of us, Tories to the right of us.' He finds it 'tedious to be forced into the extremity of defending Yeats, T. S. Eliot, D. H. Lawrence, or Shakespeare on diverse charges of fascism, anti-semitism, male chauvinism, royalism, or whatever; when all we want to do is read "Among School Children" for the extraordinary achievement it is, a true act of imagination and composition'.

While I am sympathetic to this point of view, I do not share it entirely. The idea that one should be able to read the poetry of Idi Amin or the Yorkshire Ripper without any reference to the lifestyle of the author is the other end of a spectrum that needs more subtle and comprehensive negotiation.

However, the crucial and very circumscribed point here is whether or not the views I wish to endorse about art and poetry, because they derive in great part from those articulated by Martin Heidegger, should be dismissed because he, at a certain moment in his life, seemed to support Hitler's regime and a fascist philosophy. And, in this situation, I am inclined to use Denis Donoghue's argument. Let the point of view stand on its own. It is a truth about poetry and poets and, whatever its source, it should be judged on its own merits.

There is another point of view, however, most decisively articulated by Emmanuel Levinas, the Jewish philosopher: Heidegger's thoughts on poetry are in themselves fascist; they instigate a sacral religion that promotes invasion of the human by totalitarian energies with racist implications. The religious aspect of such thought leads us back to a primitive pagan spiritism demanding the sacrifice of the alien on the altar of the incumbent.[2]

I do accept the seriousness of these arguments. However, the point of view I am presenting in no way depends upon any individual thinker. One of the main reasons for selecting Heidegger's thought as an *apologia* for the primary status of the poet is that he, as one of the foremost philosophers in Europe in the last century, was able to articulate, with a rigour and a depth that is difficult to match, a point of view about art and poetry which only became apparent to him at the end of his life but which was understood and practised as a reality by several artists of the past, who neither had the capacity nor saw the point of elucidating it as a philosophy. It was certainly a change of direction for Heidegger to declare that poetry was the essential way forward.

Thinking, for the later Heidegger, is secondary to poetry. It can bring us to the point where poetry 'founds' and accomplishes existence and it can elucidate the implications of this original thrust in history. But it cannot usurp the fundamental role that poetry alone can play.

Even if we condemn Heidegger as a person, we are still obliged to assess the argument he puts forward for this primacy of poetry. Indeed, there is a similar tradition connecting poetry, prophecy and religion in the Celtic tradition, some experts tell us. The normal word for poet in old Irish is *fili*, which means a seer or a wise man. Poetry is *filidecht* (what the poet says). Another verb applied to poetry is *canid*, cognate with the Latin *canere*, meaning to sing, chant or recite. An older Irish word for poetry is *creth*, which implies the magic transformation of something into something else, in contrast with the Greek notion of production or craftsmanship, which is implied in the word *poiesis, poieo*. The Irish word for prophecy is *fath*, cognate with the Latin *vates* (poet/seer). Poetic art in Irish is signified by *ai*, which is cognate with the word for wind. The image is of wind or of breath as in-spir-ation.[3] In many traditions poetry or 'song' is understood as something much more than production or craftsmanship. Poetry is more like an event, in which the poet is a filter that decreases continually in the creative accomplishment of the poem. One example of such a poet is Rainer Maria Rilke, and by describing what I understand of his *Duino Elegies* (see chapter three), I hope to enlarge upon the kind of poetry essential in destitute times.

Because in the sense I am trying to elucidate here, we are not talking about any kind of poetry. Ezra Pound puts it this way: 'I believe in everyone writing poetry who wants to; most do. I believe in every man knowing enough music to play "God Bless our Home" on the harmonium, but I do not believe in every man giving concerts and printing his sin … It is tremendously important that great poetry be written, it makes no jot of difference who writes it.' The term 'great' when applied to poetry can be misunderstood. What I am talking about here is a kind of poetry that explores. 'The poet,' to use T. S. Eliot's phrase, 'is occupied with frontiers of consciousness beyond which words fail, though meanings still exist.' This is consciousness before and after it enters the idiom of rational thought. Consciousness is not just in and from the mind. It pervades our total presence. The mind is certainly an important part of the poetic act, but it is only one element. The kind of poetry I am referring to is 'metaphysical' in the terminology of Hart Crane, because it records 'absolute experience':

> Such a poem is at least a stab at the truth, and to such an extent may be differentiated from other kinds of poetry and called 'absolute'. Its evocation will not be toward decoration or amusement, but rather toward a state of consciousness, an 'innocence' (Blake) or absolute beauty. In this condition there may be discoverable under new forms certain spiritual illuminations shining with a morality essentialised from experience directly, and not from previous precepts or pre-conceptions. It is as though a poem gave the reader as he left it a single new word, never before spoken and impossible to actually enunciate, but self-evident as an active principle in the reader's consciousness henceforward.[4]

Where does this poetic word come from? The finished form is filtered through consciousness, but this does not answer the question. Consciousness is the place where many forces and energies meet to emerge as self-expression. The act of poetic creation opens the poet to worlds beyond the conscious mind. The poem is a use of words in whatever way is necessary to convey the new kind of consciousness that the poet experiences. Hart Crane attached no intrinsic value to the means he employed 'beyond their practical service in giving form to the living stuff of the imagination'. Which means that there is no 'recognised technique'. Success in poetry is how you succeed in expressing what you have received. 'It is part of the poet's business to risk not only criticism – but folly – in the conquest of consciousness.' There are no limitations or restrictions involved in the choice or invention of form, but once the form crystalises, it becomes the only and the exact measurement of the work. There are no marks for effort or good will. The poem's worth will be judged on how it 'approximates a formally convincing statement of a conception or apprehension of life that gains our unquestioning assent, and under the conditions of which our imagination is unable to suggest a further detail consistent with the design of the aesthetic whole'. Poetry must be judged by formal standards. The movement from anarchical life experience to the actual concrete structure of the poem is governed by the innate sense of form and the coordinating power of the intellect. This technical skill, the capacity to encompass the energy that percolates without spilling a drop or crushing a leaf, will define the genius of poetry as form. Form is the fruit of the poetic effort, but it cannot aspire to be its root or source as well. Although technique is the *sine qua non* of any poetry worthy of the name, it cannot usurp or replace energy or source. Yeats warned his readers:

> Living in a time when technique and imagination are continually perfect and complete, because they no longer strive to bring fire from heaven, we forget how imperfect and incomplete they were in even the greatest masters ... for he who lives in eternity endures a rending of the structures of the mind, a crucifixion of the intellectual body.[5]

My argument in this book is that poetry, if understood in a certain way, can be, and should be, a guide towards the future, an essential voice in the drama of creating a more habitable planet.

I am aware of the dangers if poetry is invited to undertake such a role. It can become 'political', either in the sense that it produces politics or derives from politics. And I do not believe that it should be political. However, that does not mean that the discoveries it makes and the dimensions it reaches should not somehow be incorporated into the structures that are devised to achieve optimum quality of life for all inhabitants of the globe.

Otherwise the pendulum swings into the other danger area, where poetry is syphoned off into its own space and is cultivated for its own sake, without connection with, or influence on, the way we live. Such limitations relegate it to the level of entertainment.

Poetry is neither purposeful, rational creation by the conscious ego, nor is it impersonal, atavistic energy from the unconscious. It is the means whereby we can attain to another centre, a psychic space, which otherwise remains inaccessible. Jung puts it this way:

> The centre of the total personality no longer coincides with the ego, but with a point midway between the conscious and the unconscious. This would be the point of a new equilibrium, a new centering of the total personality, a virtual centre which, on account of its focal position between conscious and unconscious ensures for the personality a new and more solid foundation.[6]

This does not mean that it belongs to the domain of psychology, or that it can be reached by some science or method other than a certain kind of art. It is an ontological space giving access to the transcendent, which goes beyond the psychology of the individual. The artist, the poet, can provide access to this space by accomplishing a certain kind of poetic form. It is through the brokenness and vulnerability of such artists that history and culture can cooperate as both continuity and rupture.

Art is original. Whenever it happens a new era begins. The poet allows him or her self to be the filter of something beyond that self, something transcendent. This means that the poetry is not the work of their own hands entirely; but it does not mean that they are taken over by some impersonal or sacral force. The original source is open to what is beyond the autonomous powers of the poet's creative activity. Through the particular gifts of the poet, what is always entirely new – because never before encountered in history – becomes embedded in the familiar because it emerges in the form of a poem. The place of this punctured seamlessness and broken continuity is the virtual space available to the artist. An artistic metaphysics allows for creation and preservation to be accomplished through the filter of this space.

This explains the connection between art and history, which is not political but rather *sui generis*, original. It is not the subjection of history to one's imagination, nor the enslavement of imagination to fate. It is an essentially human movement of history, which is neither an inexorable flow of impersonal fate, nor the arbitrary construct of our free will. Between these two 'logical' possibilities, there is a space, which is both uncovered and kept open by the artist – a middle voice between active construction and passive surrender. This third way entails an inner journey through the labyrinth of the poet's own history and situation towards the universal dimension, the open space of transcendence.

However, poetry cannot achieve this on its own. It must be accompanied by a certain kind of critical understanding that will be guarantor of its authenticity and exegete of its accomplishment. In other words, a certain kind of critical thought can facilitate the journey to and from the protectorate of poetry, that centre of equilibrium for which poetry clears the space. This space is not a detached and self-contained realm of its own. It is always attached to a particular culture, and the poet has to travel through the psychic hinterland of that culture before reaching it. The journey to the top of the world must take you through your own back yard, which might be what Patrick Kavanagh called connecting 'the parish with the universe'.[7] It is through the very act of transcending their own culture that poets open out the protectorate of poetry itself. Apart from the act of exodus, the bursting through, of the poet, which makes the protectorate available, there is actually nothing there at all. The act of reaching this dimension has an effect upon the poet that allows him or her to become spokesperson for the new and unheard of. Critical thought should be the companion and helpmate, the exhortation and encouragement for such an arduous task. Mozart is supposed to have said 'I can only play for you if you love me.' The kind of 'criticism' that accompanies poetry in its specific and demanding task should be cherishing, self-effacing and open to every possibility imaginable. It should be scrupulously vigilant but at the same time humbly aware of its own limited powers of assimilation, its inevitable obtuseness.

To explain what kind of criticism this might be, it is useful to contrast it with the kind it should not be. The poet whose work will act as the major source for my overall thesis is Seamus Heaney. I will, therefore, use criticism of Seamus Heaney as my example here. He has attracted every kind. Not since Hemingway has so much ink been spilt assessing, advising, admonishing and analysing a 'natural' artist. The first writings of Hemingway were hailed as 'inspired babytalk'. By the time the critics had finished with him, and his foreshortened career had ended so tragically, his writing was just babytalk. Or, so the critics said. And Hemingway knew, with the critics, that his first efforts were very good. But he didn't know how to keep it up. He was unable to maintain the first fine careless rapture. And he was wounded to the depths by the critics, who told him relentlessly what he already knew – that his later efforts were uninspired.

In Ireland, the one pleasure more intense than seeing one of our own reach the top, is watching them tumble down again. We cherish the magnificent failure. Seamus Heaney, as far as the popular imagination is concerned, has reached the peak of poetic fame. We now wait patiently knitting at the foot of the scaffold.

Heaney was recognised from the beginning as a 'natural' re-shaper of the remembered world of childhood. Christopher Ricks and John Carey, for instance, were two of the first trainspotters, although James Fenton suggests that this was because they thought he was 'a successor to Ted Hughes'.[8] He was reviled by Al Alvarez for precisely the same reason:

> If Heaney really is the best we can do, then the whole troubled, exploratory thrust of modern poetry has been a diversion from the right true way. Eliot and his contemporaries, Lowell and his, Plath and hers had it all wrong: to try to make clearings of sense and discipline and style in the untamed, unfenced darkness was to mistake morbidity for inspiration.[9]

This is criticism both in terms of theme and tradition: Where is he coming from and what's he on about? The 'When, for fuck's sake, are you / going to write / Something for us?' school of criticism. On the one side you have those who claim that Heaney is not supporting the nationalist cause, not putting his art at the service of his 'people', and on the other side there are those who hold that his poetry is being used to bolster a sophisticated version of the nationalist ideology, that he is 'the laureate of violence'.[10] James Simmons sees him as 'retreating into the tribe, excluding Protestants, fostering resentment', when he had thought of him 'as an ally in the general struggle to liberalise and reform Ulster'.[11]

Most of these critics, naturally enough, come from these islands, where it would be advantageous to be able to canvas the support of a Nobel laureate for whatever political viewpoint one promotes. Some would claim that his poetry is not of this stature at all. One of the quotes of the year 2000 was made by the British author and journalist A. N. Wilson, to the effect that 'Heaney, whose talents wouldn't, in a sane world, have taken him beyond the parish magazine, is a Nobel-Prize winner because he's a Catholic from Northern Ireland'.[12]

In America, Heaney's most prolific and perceptive critic is Helen Vendler. She is a 'no-nonsense' critic who has taken the trouble to spell out for us what that means. In a review of *The Oxford Companion to 20th-Century Poetry in English*, she hopes and predicts that most of the poems therein will be forgotten, that 'In 2500 AD . . . the 1500 poets here included will have shrunk to about fifty.' She deplores the way this poetry is marketed by trying to show how interesting the poets are: 'Twenty-seven here had nervous breakdowns, nineteen served time in jail, fourteen died in battle, three were murdered, one executed, etc.' This, she says, 'points to the real vacuum in the publishing world of things to say about poetry itself'. She castigates many of the 'critics' who present the poems, because they concentrate only on the first act of criticism, when three acts are essential.[13]

The first act is discussion of the themes and the imagery of the poetry. But more important than that is 'the poetic form itself'. This form is external and internal: 'Are these poems short or long, in free verse or metrical verse ... tragic or ironic or comic, narrative or meditative ... and if original, in what measure and in what way? ... There is always something to be said about how a poet either follows a formal or technical trend or begins one.' As far as she is concerned, much of what passes for poetry nowadays is not 'real' poetry, but rather 'versified prose'. The third act is identifying how the poet's imagination works – in symbolic form. Unless the poet transforms the theme (family, love, memory, etc.) into symbols, it is not a poem: 'theme untransformed is theme unimagined'. There is, according to Vendler, a 'crucial absence of a serious and widely-shared cultural discourse applicable to poetry'. Which is why most critics are allowed to say anything that comes into their heads.

In her view, Heaney changes his style from poem to poem, and in her book *The Breaking of Style,* she shows in elaborate detail how this happens, using the different parts of speech (nouns, verbs, adverbs, etc.) to show the 'bareness and simplicity of some recent poems', which spring 'from a poem's concentration on a single grammatical element'.[14]

Vendler herself prefers the unassuming and the reticent. She finds that 'Heaney is not entirely at home in allegory', and her suspicion in this regard is 'borne out' by 'the nonallegorical pieces he has been publishing … many of them exquisitely reticent and unassuming poems, often recalling moments almost too evanescent to be described. They are "allurements, elvergleams," expressing phases of sensation neglected by the poetry of sturdy fact or political contention.'[15] In other words, Vendler finds Heaney's strength as a poet in what the other critics might describe as his weakness. She is more on the side of poetry for poetry's sake and certainly decries the vulgarity of propaganda. James Wood, too, sees in Heaney's collection *The Spirit Level* that 'this new verse has got beyond proving things, and is just a sweet engine for the propulsion of its lines'.[16]

Desmond Fennell, on the other hand, sets out to show that this cunning trickster, with a keen eye for poetry as a commercial enterprise, has had the brashness and bad taste to prostitute his small talent in the gaudy American marketplace where they wouldn't have the subtlety to tell first-rate poetry from its pretentious and posturing rivals. The real connoisseurs of poetry were never consulted, of course, when the coronation of Paddy the Prophet was being orchestrated on the East Coast of America. Helen Vendler, as self-appointed queen of omniscient academia, saw the immediate correspondence between New England prudishness and Heaney's taciturnity. Fennell muses, 'this world of theory, especially on the East Coast, accommodated his kind of poetry. If it wanted puritanism, the cool chastity, emotional restraint and guilty introspection of his work supplied it.'[17] Fennell's pamphlet, *Whatever You Say, Say Nothing — Why Seamus Heaney is No. 1*, begins with a quotation from Alan Bold in *Marxism Today*, which sets the tone and the agenda: 'Eliot is, in my opinion, a greater poet because his poems, finally, say more about the human condition than Owen's do.'

Moreover, Heaney should not be wasting Irish taxpayers' money seducing the academic elite. He should be back here with his people. His job as poet is to provide 'clear light thrown on the human condition, or a voice raised memorably to exhort, decry, console or celebrate'.[18] Presumably all this would be within the philosophical and political framework elaborated by Fennell himself.

'What good is poetry to people?' he asks:

This, naturally, raises questions which will not go away. What good to people is this goodness of poetry? Has poetry, has the puritan lyric, any intelligible social function, and if so what? How can the poet who 'says nothing', and leaves the world in darkness, do good socially? In a civilisation which prides itself on its social concern and its democratic culture, these are pointed questions. They concern Seamus Heaney, not least because he would like to believe that his work does good to people, and in particular to those Six-County Irish whom he keeps looking back at over his shoulder and feeling guilty about.[19]

Whatever the point of view, this kind of criticism, which sees poetry as either protest or as propaganda, indulges in its own rhetoric and usually appeals to the mob beneath the scaffold for judgement. The danger is that in a poet of Seamus Heaney's sen-

sitivity and, perhaps, exaggerated vulnerability, it induces a
sense of guilt. The kind of hectoring proselytism that such criticism involves gives no encouragement, no sympathy; its only
purpose seems to be dismissive and polemical entertainment for
the begrudgers.

Indeed, James Wood believes that 'from the very beginning,
Heaney's poetry has been badged with guilt'. He sees the
Oxford Lectures as an attempt to prove poetry's right to exist
and to justify Heaney's own choice of it as a vocation. Heaney
seems to be addressing himself to 'the scepticism of those in
Northern Ireland who might question poetry's rights'. The re-
lentless attacks of such critics as we have described, force
Heaney to engage in a false problem: 'Out of his own need to answer on behalf of poetry, he constructs a theory of poetry's need
to answer on behalf of poetry.' In other words, the scepticism of,
or about, poetry, which makes up the major theme of his prose
writings, doesn't really have its origin 'in poetry itself but in certain sections of his audience'.[20]

However, returning to Fennell's views about what he thinks
Heaney's poetry should be, I am inclined to agree with Neil
Corcoran that there is something here that needs to be answered.[21] Specifically, Fennell's cynical observations on what
Heaney himself thinks poetry is. And here Fennell comes very
close to what I am saying about poetry, except that he is, once
again, calling on the mob to laugh this nonsense out of court:

> Heaney seems to me to envisage the poet's beneficent social
> action on the analogy of the monk in an enclosed religious
> order, who, Catholics believe, helps to atone for the world's
> evil – to assist Christ in the world's redemption – by his de-
> tachment from the world, his chastity, and above all his life
> of meditation and prayer. Heaney's repeated injunction that
> the poet must reflect the affairs of the contemporary world in
> his poetry – but in his own way and without intervening –
> corresponds to the monk's promise, much-prized by the
> faithful when they receive it, that he will 'remember' or 'in-
> clude' their worldly concerns and 'intentions' in his prayer.

Given belief in God, in the efficacy of prayer, and in the sincerity of the monk's dedication, it is easy, and indeed logical, to believe that, through the processes of the spiritual economy, the monk's prayer effects good in the world, atones for evil, stays the punishing hand of God. It is not so easy to believe that, with no part in it for God or a spiritual economy managed by him, a man of no proven virtue, perhaps even a bad man, effects social redress – corrects the world's imbalances – by meditating and delivering verses which 'contain the coordinates of the surrounding reality'.[22]

Fennell is saying to Heaney: 'If you think you can get away with an irrelevant poetry of mutism that says nothing at all, by persuading your friends in Oxford and Harvard, where they are all atheists anyway, that you are really a monk performing meaningful rites in the sanctuary, then I'm going to blow your cover. This is exactly what the academic elite wants to hear.'

That is my synopsis of Fennell's 'criticism', here it is in his own words: 'In short, the poet par excellence becomes a sort of ruminating, groaning shaman, delivering oracles which his academic acolytes interpret to the students within the temple and the heedless multitude beyond the gates.'[23] This is the worst kind of charlatanism and hypocrisy, says Fennell, and don't quote Simone Weil at him as prototype or role model, because 'Simone Weil was a mystic whose mysticism was intellectually disciplined by Christian Doctrine'.[24]

This sounds to me as if Fennell is saying to Heaney: 'If you are trying to hide in there in the monastic sanctuary in the belief – or the pretence – that you are performing some legitimate function, then come out, you whore, or I'll tell them all a thing or two about your private life. Do you realise that you have to believe in God to be in there, you have to be a Catholic or at least intellectually disciplined by Christian Doctrine. And what about your prayer life, your daily meditation, not to mention your detachment from the world?'

Criticism of this kind is born of self-righteousness, which insists upon brain scans for ideological heresy, and tests in conventional moral rectitude, before spiritual exploration can be taken seriously. On the contrary, the qualifications necessary to undertake such poetry are quite other, and Heaney himself was attempting to delineate them in his Inaugural Lecture at Oxford in October 1989.[25] Such qualifications belong to a long and distinguished tradition of poets from every nationality, none of whom had anything but their vulnerable humanity, their accurate sensibility and their dedication to the task, as mandate.

Vendler takes up this point most interestingly in her assessment of Heaney's aesthetic integrity:

There have been singular and individuated selves who never wrote a word. But without a singular and individuated moral self, there has never been a singular and individuated literary style. The writing self does not have to be virtuous in the ordinary sense of the word; but it does have to be extraordinarily virtuous in its aesthetic moves. It must refuse – against the claims of fatigue, charm, popularity, money, and so on – the *idée reçue*, the imprecise word, the tired rhythm, the replication of past effects, the uninvestigated stanza. It is this heroic virtue in the realm of aesthetic endeavour that courses in great authors exist to teach (as courses in 'texts' do not). And Heaney stands by this aesthetic arduousness ... the strict morality of the imaginative effort toward aesthetic embodiment. That morality is almost unimaginably exhausting.[26]

In the end, what both Heaney and Vendler are saying about aesthetic judgement, criticism at this level, is that it 'can only say whether or not a writer has successfully deployed the moral, imaginative, and linguistic resources needed for the artwork in hand'.[27]

To achieve such a 'reading' is to keep your whole being alive to the being of the poem. Heaney praises Geoffrey Grigson's criticism of Auden, for example: 'The way it teases out the cultural implications and attachments which inhabit any poem's field of force is a critical activity not to be superseded, because it is so closely allied, as an act of reading, to what happens during the poet's act of writing.'

'Real' poetry has to 'find ways to create a work and a life that are as yet only imagined'.[28] Heaney often quotes Mandelstam's notion that poetry is addressed to 'the reader in posterity', and Vendler reports him as having said at a symposium that this means 'it is not directed exploitatively towards its immediate audience – although of course it does not set out to disdain the immediate audience either. It is directed towards the new perception which it is its function to create.'[29] Vendler analyses Poem xxiv from *Seeing Things*, especially the line: 'You knew the portent in each setting' and suggests that 'the command behind' the poem is 'an epistemological one: know':

> One knows first a phenomenology perceived through the senses, a 'setting'. But that does not complete knowledge: one must also know the portent. This portent is not known through a deduction which succeeds phenomenological perception. Nor is the portent known emblematically, through the setting, but sensuously, in the setting. The task Heaney has set himself is not one of allegory but one of what we might call clairvoyant perception. The settings are symbolic not of something beyond themselves but of something in themselves. A setting is something now re-seen, in the retrospect of middle age, as portending at the time it was experienced, even if one did not, in the past moment, recognise the portent in the setting.[30]

All of which makes me aware that in order to really understand what Heaney is doing, we have to invent a critical faculty worthy of the task, and this involves nothing less than a metaphysics: 'A new rhythm, after all', Heaney tells us, in connection with Grigson's criticism of W. H. Auden, 'is a new life given to the world, a resuscitation not just of the ear, but of the springs of being.'[31]

It must be a prerequisite for critics to have 'been there' where the poem actually happened. It means the difference between 'seeing things as one would have them and seeing them as they really are'. Clifford Geertz has interesting insights that serve us here, from his point of view as an anthropologist. The ability of anthropologists to get us to take what they say seriously 'has less to do with either a factual look or an air of conceptual elegance than it has with their capacity to convince us that what they say is a result of their having actually penetrated (or, if you prefer, been penetrated by) another form of life'. And he uses the example of artistic works: 'As the criticism of fiction and poetry grows best out of an imaginative engagement with fiction and poetry themselves, not out of imported notions about what they should be ...' so an anthropological study should be undertaken. The two dangers that threaten such engagement are: 'hearing the words but not the music' (which is the possibility with too textual a study) or: 'hearing music that doesn't exist' (which the examination of theme alone or of extra-textual phenomena can cause).[32] In another context he says that 'a good interpretation of anything – a poem, a person, a ritual, a history, an institution, a society – takes us into the heart of that of which it is the interpretation. When it does not do that, but leads us instead somewhere else – into an admiration of its own elegance, of its author's cleverness, or of the beauties of Euclidean order – it may have its intrinsic charms; but it is something else than what the task at hand – figuring out what all that is about – calls for.'[33]

Having examined the various kinds of criticism exercised on one particular poet, I will, in the next chapter, try to identify what constructive critical thinking about poetry can accomplish. This will be done by presenting Heidegger's views on poetry and his critical analysis of the poetry of Rilke.

I will return to the poetry of Seamus Heaney in Chapter Seven and try to apply these criteria in his regard.

CHAPTER THREE

Poetry as Truth

The danger and the difficulty about recent discussions on Heidegger as a man are the embargos they impose upon examination of his discoveries at the deepest level of human existence and his contribution to the history of philosophy. What could such a person have to teach any of us, and what could be the interest in a philosophy so tainted?

The burden of works such as *Heidegger et le Nazisme* (1987) by Victor Faria, and *Martin Heidegger* (1991) by Hugo Ott, is to show that Heidegger was a paid-up member of the Nazi regime in Germany during the Second World War and that his international standing and fulsome support gave credence to the doctrine of National Socialism, which might have been less plausible without such sponsorship.

I do not think it is possible to deny these ugly and disturbing facts. However, we still have to consider the possibility that even so vilified a philosopher could have made an important discovery and one that we would all be impoverished to ignore.[1] Are we to close off a whole dimension of ourselves and declare it a no-go area because the person who discovered it is denounced as a reprobate?

Heidegger's alliance with National Socialism in Germany, far from being a sycophantic attempt to attach his career to its rising star, was rather an attempt to direct this movement and ensure its destinal purity by attaching it to his. It was no petty political ambition that tempted him to flirt with this movement. His ambition was extravagantly more cosmic. He saw himself as one of those few people in world history whose name would survive as a household word when centuries had obliterated

every military or political figure on the contemporary horizon.
Heraclitus and Heidegger would make up two mountain peaks
still visible when every other name in the twentieth century had
been submerged in the valley of detail.

His weakness, it seems to me, was neither greed nor ambition, but a creative infatuation that allowed him to project his
own purposes onto the prevailing situation, imagining that his
worldview coincided with the destiny of Germany. If he became
the inspirational force behind all university education in Germany,
he would fashion a whole generation in the light of his understanding of truth.

This belief was not based upon political ambition or personal
lust for power. It was based upon his conviction that he, and
only he, was capable of guiding the universities along the path
of truth, and that he was destined to do so. His own experience
as a very gifted teacher, confirmed by anyone who knew him in
that capacity,[2] was that of being able to lead his students to a
completely new way of living the truth. He believed that by
multiplying this situation in as many universities as there were
in Germany, he could both revolutionise the way of teaching
and learning that characterised university education, and make
that vital connection between the youth of Germany and genuine contact with Being, which would realign the Western
world with its true destiny.

This infatuation was shortlived. Both sides quickly realised
that the other had a different agenda. And as soon as these fundamental differences became apparent, Heidegger became as
arrogantly dismissive and courageously forthright as was his
wont. Heidegger admitted that he had made a great blunder
('*grosse Dummheit*') in aggrandising Hitler, but he regarded this
as Hitler's fault and Hitler's business rather than any reflection
upon his own thought or behaviour. In the famous interview
given to *Der Spiegel*, he held that he had been betrayed by Hitler.[3]
Needless to say, Heidegger's understanding of what should
happen in Germany and in Europe, once genuine contact had
been re-established with Being, bore absolutely no resemblance

to what was perpetrated by the Nazis and what constituted their political agenda. His opportunistic partnership with them even for a short time shows him to be culpably blind and politically naïve, but it does not allow us to suppose that his philosophy was ever identifiable with theirs.

In fact, at the end of his life, Heidegger repudiated all forms of idealism, any political manifesto. Thought was only a pathway to another kind of truth. Philosophy should lead us to poetry. 'The end of philosophy' for Heidegger is a place – but not a local or geographical one – a 'clearing', which makes way for the 'Other'. Heidegger's commentary on Holderlin and Rilke suggests two things: that there is a presence of the divine in nature, an infiltration; and that it is beyond 'thought'. Poetry is a way of human consciousness that reaches beyond the modality of thinking, which is philosophical or scientific. But his work as commentator allows him to salvage for philosophy some of those realms 'beyond thinking' that stretch out before us when we reach that place where philosophy ends. The infiltration is not a power that invades and overwhelms our freedom, it is a sound that appeals to the sensitivity of those who have ears to hear with.

Heidegger believed that 'Art is truth setting itself to work.'[4] The poet is 'like a passageway that destroys itself in the creative process for the work to emerge'. (PLT, 40) 'By contrast, science is not an original happening of truth but always the cultivation of a domain of truth already opened'. (PLT, 62) Something happens 'through' the poet, which is contained in the work. This 'something' is the emergence of truth. All art is essentially poetry. (PLT, 72) The poet engages in a kind of saying that is 'projective'. Projective saying is saying which, in preparing what we are able to say or put into words, simultaneously brings the unsayable as such into the world. (PLT, 74)

The function of the philosopher 'at the end of philosophy' is to embark upon another kind of thinking. This thinking will be repudiated by both the disciplines of philosophy proper and by literary criticism. It leads 'thinking into a dialogue with poetry, a

dialogue that is of the history of Being' and that involves learning 'what is unspoken' by 'thinking our way soberly into what
the poetry says'. (PLT, 96) The objects of such attention are 'the
traces of the fugitive gods'. These traces are not visible. 'Traces
are often inconspicuous, and are always the legacy of a directive
that is barely divined.' (PLT, 94) But 'poets stay on the gods'
tracks and so trace for their kindred mortals the way towards
the turning'. (PLT, 94) 'Turning' is a kind of conversion, a new
way of being human.

Heidegger recognises in Rainer Maria Rilke someone who
has 'in his own way poetically experienced and endured' (PLT,
98) this new approach to both Being and truth. Rilke describes
the order to which his poetic vocation summoned him as 'angelic'. In *The Duino Elegies*, Rilke is describing the 'angelic' life to
which he has been called: 'This world seen no more with human
eyes but in the angel, is perhaps my real task.'[5] This so-called
'angelic' order is the place to which the poet is summoned. If we
can understand this place better, we will be nearer to understanding this very specific poetic vocation.

Rilke had been married. He and his wife had found the demands of art incompatible with their life together. Rilke felt
called to and by 'the angelic order', 'a much higher order whose
right I have got to acknowledge'. This call made him a different
sort of person to the ordinary dweller in the world. His presence
to the world demanded a sacrifice of the 'normal' presence. He
had to 'see' the world as 'angels' do, and speak out this reality.

It was suggested to him that if he underwent psychoanalysis
he could return to the normal order and take up married relations with his wife again. This he acknowledged as a possibility,
but he refused to do it. He believed that it was required of him to
'record the utterly wonderful line along which I've come
through this strange life of mine'. He knew that it might be possible for him to be 'normalised' back into the 'ordinary' way that
people live, but this would be to betray his conviction that he
had been born as the poet of another way of life, another way of
living in the world, and that if he failed in this task – if he did not

live and give expression to this kind of life – the earth would be disappointed and would have to wait, how long he could not tell, for another champion of her secret.

All his life Rilke knew that he carried this task with him. Suddenly he knew also that the time was ripe. He had to give birth to the expression of this reality. For this he had to go somewhere entirely alone. He loathed solitude. He found it physically repulsive and abhorrent to him. But it was necessary. His friend Princess Marie von Thurn und Taxis-Hohenlohe lent him Duino Castle near Trieste, which was then part of Austria, as the perfect setting for his solitary confinement, 'where the Elegies can howl out of me at the moon from all sides, just as they please'. Here he stayed for months, waiting until he became sharp enough to write.

> I get up day after day and try myself out in the quietest most regular things … expect nothing of myself … I have wanted for a long time to be here alone, strictly alone, to go into a chrysalis, to pull myself together; in a word, to live by the heart and nothing else … That will bring certain regions that have lain there for ages within reach of whatever is beginning to stir in me. I creep around all day in the thickets of my life, shouting like mad and clapping my hands – you would not believe what hair-raising creatures fly up.

'Then all at once,' Princess Marie tells in a letter, 'in the midst of his brooding, he suddenly stopped short, for it seemed to him that he heard a voice calling to him out of the roaring wind: *"Wer, wenn ich schriee, horte mich aus der Engel Ordnungen?"* ("Who, if I cried, would hear me from the angel order?" – this is the first line of the first Elegy) … He took out the notebook he always carried with him and wrote down these words together with several more verses that formed themselves without any effort on his part … By evening the entire Elegy had been written down.'

Rilke recognised each Elegy as it came and when it came. There were ten in all. They were not completed at Duino. In fact he carried them around inside himself for ten years, during which time Duino was destroyed and rebuilt again. When at last, after ten years, the 'work' was completed, he knew that it was done: 'At last, the blessed, how blessed day when I can announce to you the completion – so far as I can see – of the Elegies. Ten! From the last, large one (the opening lines begun, long ago at Duino …) from this last one which was intended even then to be the last – from this – my hand is still trembling! Just now, Saturday, the eleventh, at six o'clock in the evening, it is done! … That I was still permitted to experience this … experience being it … I would not have held out one day longer … All tissue and ligature in me cracked in the storm … I must be well made to have withstood it … The blood cycle, the legendary cycle of ten (ten!) strange years has come to an end … It is done, done!'[6]

Throughout those ten years Rilke had lived this vocation. No monk of the desert could have found himself a stricter master:

When I look into my conscience I see only one law; it stubbornly commands me to lock myself up in myself, and in one stretch to finish this task that was dictated to me at the centre of my heart. I am obeying – for you know it's true, in coming here I wanted only that, and I have no right to alter the course my will has taken, until I have completed this act of sacrifice and obedience.

The *Duino Elegies* celebrate a second way of being in the world. The first way is known to us all: it is celebrated everywhere. The second has been forgotten. Now and again certain people stumble upon it – as a person might find, through a hole in a tree, an unperceived wonderland and return transformed by this experience. But they are never allowed to register this way of being as an alternative to the norm of happy families, even though this second way is necessary also, because through it 'the earth' is 'redeemed'. Rilke's 'voices' were really the earth calling him to this way of life, asking him this favour:

Not that you could endure
the voice of God – far from it. But mark the breathing,
the unbroken word that builds itself out of silence.

It rustles towards you now from those youthful dead.
Always in Rome and Naples wherever you stepped
into a church, did not their fate calmly address you? (D1)

The world is a place complete in itself. It is possible to live there as the birds, animals and insects do. What is it, then, about human presence that makes it so different? 'Just as a crack goes through a china cup. The way the wing of a bat rips through the porcelain of evening' (D8). Animals live entirely within!

O blessedness of tiny creatures,
who *remain* forever in the womb that bore them;
O joy of the gnat, that can still leap *within*,
even on its wedding day: for the womb is everything.

We alone, of all the inhabitants of the earth, are haunted by the 'without'. This never disturbs the animal. The shadow of death never casts itself on its way. 'His being to him is infinite, incomprehensible and without sight into his situation, pure, like his outward gaze.' (D8)

We both dwell in the same valley, human and beast alike. But we are strangers while they are at home. At the end of this Elegy, Rilke gives a poignant description of our situation in the world:

Just as on
the final hill that shows him his whole valley
one last time, a man will turn, and stop, and linger –
so we live and forever take our leave. (D8)

'Like the moon', Rilke says elsewhere, 'so life has a side that is constantly turned away from us, and that is not its opposite but its completion to perfection, to plentitude, to the real whole and full sphere and globe of being ... Death is the side of life that is averted from us, unillumined by us.'

What do we mean by death in this sense? It is not death as an end: this we share with the animals. It is death as the shadow that follows and whose very following down-curves and oppresses the vertical stance of man and makes his flight like 'the fountain whose starting spray is already teased into falling.' (D7)

We are not like the animals:
We have never, not for a single day,
that pure space before us, into which the flowers
endlessly open. (D8)

This is not just because humankind is 'blessed' with an 'awareness' of death, to which the animal world is blind. No, at the root
of our soul there is a real presence of death, which makes us a
different kind of being from the animals, and makes of our
world a different kind of space. 'Here all is distance, and there it
was breath. After the first homeland this second is a drafty, hybrid place.' (D8) Death is a draft from the 'outside'. Others have
died. This is not just a pious thought; it is a place at the apex of
the soul, a sharp immortal diamond that pierces through the
patch-work of the world. It is 'without'; it is an absence. The
draft casts a chill on the cosiness within.

   All the dead die young. They were cut off. There was more
there – more sap, more growth, more youth. Where did this
'more' disappear to when the husk fell to the earth? It was
sucked out into the great void that swirls beyond the 'inside' of
our world. The silence after they fell was louder than any noise.
It is the absence that makes up the presence of death. Nothing
remains. This nothing, absence, silence, is the permanent space
of death in our midst. We can never shake it off. It is the reverse
side of our life.

   Death is the element that ripens the greenness of our natural
life. Fruitfulness is the advancing through us of decay. The one
who goes down to the ground of him/herself, to the apex, to the
place where life meets death, and who releases there the valve of
the great unknown outside, allows 'the other side' to illumine
the whole of reality, making it ripe. It is this ripeness that makes
everything 'cool like laid-out market fruit, held public from the
shoulders'. (D5)

   The task of humans in the world is to achieve the balance between the clustering pull of the earth and the suctioning vortex
of the abyss – as you might wave your arms to regain balance on
a tottering wall or a fence. This space is between the within and
the without. This space is the order of the angels.

We cannot shut out the 'Open'. Every shutter holds it in its curve. It is always there *in absentia*. Its mode of presence is absence, so that no amount of walling up can seal it off. In the fullest meaning of these words: 'nothing' haunts us. To live for the 'outside', to allow its breath to seep up through us 'like a song' into the world, to spread ourselves fully so as to become a sound-box for this 'organing impulse' – this, according to Rilke, is what the earth is asking of us.

> Yes, the springtime did need you. Many stars demanded
> that you sense them. A wave
> long since gone by lifted itself toward you
> or when you passed a window that was open, a violin
> gave itself up. All this was a charge.
> But did you complete it? (D1)

It is a kind of poetry and a mode of being that is certainly not useful in any recognisably commercial sense; and it claims to lead beyond the paralysis of everyday existence. It is almost an ecstasy that accomplishes what Rilke terms 'angelic life'. It calls us to be 'more', as Rilke puts it, 'by this trembling endurance'. A strange way, we might think, of being more. Rilke can only agree:

> True, it is strange to live no longer on earth,
> and to practise no longer customs scarcely acquired;
> roses and other expressly promising things,
> not to give them the meaning of human future;
> what in endlessly anxious hands one used to be,
> to be this no more, and even one's own name
> to lay aside, like a toy that is broken.
> Strange not to go on with one's wishes. Strange
> to see all relations go loosely
> fluttering in space. (D1)

Rilke had experienced the destitute times. He was a channel through which the 'song' emerged. Heidegger tells us that 'we are unprepared for the interpretation of the *Elegies* and the sonnets, since the realm from which they speak, in its metaphysical constitution and unity, has not yet been sufficiently thought out in terms of the nature of metaphysics … We barely know the nature of metaphysics and are not experienced travellers in the land of the saying of Being.'[7]

It is as if there are two ways of being in the world: one convex, the other concave. 'To put something before ourselves, propose it, in such a way that what has been proposed, having first been represented, determines all the modes of production in every respect, is a basic characteristic of the attitude which we know as willing.'[8]

Rilke is trying to change this kind of willing. This is what is meant by the 'turning', by conversion – another way of willing, another way of being. Rilke is calling for the establishment of a centre of gravity other than 'the physical gravitation of which we usually hear'. He calls it, therefore, 'the unheard-of centre'. This marks the contrast between the two ways of being in the world. The first kind of person searches for the perfect physical centre through which to realise destiny in the order of humanity. The second kind is drawn towards a secret centre, which constitutes what Rilke refers to as 'the order of angels'. The earth has need of both these centres and of both these 'orders' to realise its survival, and to survive this realisation.

Because it is not enough merely to subsist; we also need to accomplish existence. This happens if we are prepared to relinquish the 'covetous vision' of things, which we find natural, and adopt the 'double vision', which – when we juxtapose ourselves concentrically above the secret centre – allows us to see as 'a work of the heart' as much as of the eyes.

But where is the 'space' and when is the 'time' of the convex world, the 'outside' world-space that Rilke calls 'the Open'? By a movement of interiority we turn ourselves inside-out and surface in the element of the order of the angels. From this situation we become a different kind of being to the ordinary mortals – we become 'more venturesome', and, through us, the 'earth' becomes transfigured. 'Those then,' says Heidegger, 'who are at times more venturesome can will more strongly only if their willing is different in nature.' (PLT, 119)

If you do reach the unheard-of centre, you can, through it, open yourself to the 'Open' and allow this 'breath' to spread up through you like a 'song' into the world. 'Song is existence,' says Rilke. This is nothing like the impersonal fate that takes over the unwilling ecstatic and forces its way into our world. Nor is it the kind of political and ruthless 'will to power' that characterises 'will' in the normal sense of the word. This is 'singing' as 'poetry', as the unsayable coming through the words that the poet says, because the poet is turned towards another kind of hearing and living from the unheard-of centre. Poets are more venturesome, 'more daring by a breath', because they allow (freely will it so) something beyond their own consciousness to conspire with their saying and attach itself to their breath, so that the 'poem' is more than anything they ever could have done or said on their own – it is 'more daring by a breath' because it incorporates the unsayable from the unheard-of centre. Rilke spread himself fully to become the sound-box for this 'organing impulse'.

The world of the 'Open', which is also the 'order of angels', is a place of paradox. If we imagine life and death to be two sides of the same coin, then this 'place' is situated on the edge of that coin, where both realities are ever-present.

Angels (one says) often are not sure if they
move among living or dead. The eternal torrent
hurls all ages along through both realms
forever, and sounds above them both. (D1)

Rilke's first *Duino Elegy* ends with a reminder of the story of Linos, a Greek god, loved for his beauty. When he died, those who had known him were stricken with a 'rigid bleakness'. The void he left behind was itself so shook by the loss that its trembling bemusement was called music. 'Is the tale to no purpose?' Rilke asks. The tale tells the place and the time, the 'position' of those called to the 'order of the angels'. Death is the element that ripens the greenness of our natural life. Those who 'turn' towards the 'Open' (also the place where the dead have been ejected into exterior darkness) allow 'the other side' to illumine the whole of reality, they allow another note to penetrate their song, another breath to breathe itself into their existence. The task is to achieve the balance between the pull of the earth and the vortex of the abyss. Without this balance we can become hypnotised by the void and 'like a child, / one of us will lose himself to it in the stillness / and has to be drawn back. / Or another will die and be it.' (D8)

According to Heidegger, our self-emptying, 'turning' also implies 'that the Open itself must have turned toward us.' (PLT, 122) Something from the outside touches us and 'when we are touched ... the touch goes to our very nature and the will is shaken by the touch so that only now is the nature of willing made to appear and set in motion. Not until then do we will willingly.' (PLT, 125) This last quote I find particularly important as an explanation of the meaning of 'will' for Heidegger, and also a key to the difference between the Heideggerian and the Nazi motivation. Will is the motivating force, the dominating energy in all our lives. The will to power is perhaps the mechanism of the universe as we find ourselves in it. But this is only because willing is the way we think we have to be, the way we crave to be, because it is the motor-force that pushes us towards fulfilment. We are condemned to search for happiness, for what we perceive to be the complete fulfilment of our being. Conversion occurs when we are stopped in our tracks, the tracks laid down by our habitual way of perceiving our destiny. Something 'touches' us and this is the beginning of our 'conversion', which is essentially a transformation of the nature and the movement of willing. All of which must occur in a place – though not a geographical one. Being 'rooted' for Heidegger is a mystical metaphor: we are talking about the 'inner domain of the heart' and 'the conversion of consciousness and that inside the sphere of consciousness'. (PLT, 127)

The mystery of the union of two wills is the kernel of the mystery of inspiration. *In Wahrheit singen, ist ein andrer Hauch. / Ein Hauch um nichts. Ein Wehn im Gott. Ein Wind.*[9] ('Really singing issues from a different breath. A breath from nowhere. A draft in God. A wind.') Something more has entered the work.

So, there is a space between, a difference between, Being and willing on the one hand – no foreign force invades and takes over my powers and faculties – but also between the two kinds of consciousness that such 'conversion' makes inevitable: 'The inner domain of the heart is not only more inward than the interior that belongs to calculating representation, and therefore more invisible; it also extends further than does the realm of merely producible objects.'[10] This is 'uncustomary consciousness', a new way of being conscious.

> Our customary consciousness lives on the tip of a pyramid whose base within us (and in a certain way beneath us) widens out so fully that the further we find ourselves able to descend into it, the more generally we appear to be merged into those things that, independent of time and space, are given in our earthly, in the widest sense worldly, existence. True this presence too, like that of the customary consciousness of calculating production, is a presence of immanence. But the interior of uncustomary consciousness remains the inner space in which everything is for us beyond the arithmetic of calculation and, free of such boundaries, can overflow into the unbounded whole of the Open.[11]

If we pursue these paradoxical metaphors of boundaries overflowing and unbounded, we can follow Heidegger and Rilke to a place within ourselves which is 'heart' rather than 'mind', where 'existence beyond number wells up'. Here, in 'the depth dimension of our inner being … this imaginary space … the widest orbit of being becomes present in the heart's inner space'. This is 'the innermost region of the interior'.[12] Rilke is the poet of this dimension, but the philosopher is also necessary, because, according to Heidegger, 'Rilke gives no thought to the spatiality of the world's inner space; even less does he ask whether the world's inner space … is … grounded in a temporality whose essential time, together with essential space, forms the original unity of that time-space by which even Being itself presences.' Whatever it is, Heidegger is aware that it is the most interior region that has ever yet been reached, and this can only increase the reality of humankind itself.

And this is where the philosopher is important and where a certain kind of critical endeavour is most helpful. In order to manifest 'the widest orbit of the open' through the most intimate interiority of the poet, Heidegger takes it upon himself to 'meet the poem halfway in thought' and to 'draw on other poems for help'. (PLT, 131) The poet speaks from this innermost interiority and the poetry, or what the poet says, 'speaks not only from both realms, but from the oneness of the two, insofar as that oneness has already come to be as the saving unification'. (PLT, 133) The order of the 'angels' is the unification of the two realms: 'The Angel is in being by virtue of the balanced oneness of the two realms within the world's inner space.' (PLT, 135) The conversion of 'turning' is the transformation of our inmost interior into that 'equalising of space', that spirit level which 'gives space to the wordly whole of the Open'. (PLT, 136) It is a changeover 'from the work of the eyes to the work of the heart.' (PLT, 138) The poet becomes a singer from the heart rather than a composer from the mind, and song is the breath from that inmost interior: 'Song is existence,' which means that existence is that 'saying' between Being and ourselves, because 'in the song, the world's inner space concedes space within itself'.

From our side of this duet, in terms of human nature, this transformation is best accounted for in terms of will. The 'self-assertive' person is one who wills in the covetous fashion of the merchant, calculating from our perspective the vision of things and the goal of all activity. Such willing is calculated towards productivity of the most useful and profitable kind. On the other hand, 'the more venturesome' or 'those who say in a greater degree, in the manner of the singer', are those 'whose singing is turned away from all purposeful self-assertion. It is not willing in the sense of desire. Their song does not solicit anything to be produced.' (PLT, 138) And yet 'the more venturesome will more strongly in that they will in a different way from the purposeful self-assertion of the objectifying of the world. Their willing wills nothing of this kind. If willing remains mere self-assertion, they will nothing.' (PLT, 140)

Dimensions of interiority have been unearthed that supersede the comparatively superficial dimension within which subjectivity is the beginning and end of its own meaning and activity. The 'nothing' beyond the false self-sufficiency of humankind, which leads many theologians to the philosophical deduction of creation 'out of nothing', leads Heidegger to a further dimension, which is 'the track into the dark of the world's night'. (PLT, 141) This dimension can never be recuperated for humanity by the covetousness of subjectivity. It is as though the 'heart' in our natural self-assertive order is concave, whereas in the 'order of angels' it becomes convex. The convex attitude of the heart is a conversion of all the natural covetous shapes and gestures into an attitude that accomplishes rather than produces 'a song whose sound does not cling to something that is eventually attained, but which has already shattered itself even in the sounding, so that there may occur only that which was sung itself'. (PLT, 139)

Heidegger recognises that in the major poetry of Rilke 'only that which was sung itself' has occurred. This means that Rilke is not entirely responsible for what has occurred, nor can he completely name it or appropriate it. Heidegger is not a poet; he is a thinker. He must undertake the appropriate kind of literary criticism: 'Thinking is perhaps, after all, an unavoidable path, which refuses to be a path of salvation and brings no new wisdom … It has already renounced the claim to a binding doctrine and a valid cultural achievement or a deed of the spirit.'[13] These last two, the deed of the spirit, which becomes a cultural achievement, are the works of the poet. But they are not original to the poet, in a way that might allow the singer to either contain or control the origin of the song. A singer is one who allows the breath of existence to find its way through. It is a 'middle voice' whose reality is neither within nor without. Heidegger became a servant to this kind of song, at one remove from the singers themselves. His commentaries on Rilke are tentative and tremulous, a far cry from *Mein Kampf*. The kind of literary criticism that can provide some exegesis for the song that is existence must be 'a step back from the thinking that merely represents – that is, explains – to the thinking that responds and recalls'. (PLT, 181) He hopes, but does not 'know' that Rilke, who is 'poetically on the track of that which, for him, must be said', is one of those 'sayers who more sayingly say … a saying other than the rest of human saying'. (PLT, 140)

In fact, his final word about Rilke is in the conditional mood: 'If Rilke is a "poet in a destitute time" then only his poetry answers the question to what end he is a poet, whither his song is bound, where the poet belongs in the destiny of the world's night.' (PLT, 142)

This is difficult thought. It took me a very long time to understand something of what it is saying. However, it is necessary to do so. Heidegger is saying that we cannot afford not to read poetry, not to understand poetry, because poetry is our only detectable contact with Being.

Our culture, according to Heidegger, has been founded on a lie, and Christianity has helped to promote and sustain that lie. And the lie is this: that it is possible to work out in our heads a logical system that will give us access to ultimate truth, to Being. The name of such a system is philosophy and the particular branch of that 'science' which deals with Being and places it within our intellectual grasp is metaphysics. Christianity borrowed that system, refined it and inserted into it the geometry of the God who had been revealed in Jesus Christ. Those who were very gifted intellectually and who had the time could master this intricate system and could become masters of metaphysics. They could then teach some very gifted disciples. The rest would acknowledge that the mystery was too deep for them, would be thankful that there were masters who actually did understand the meaning of such intricate designs, would humbly accept crumbs of popularised penny catechisms, or would chew on jawbreaking terminology to eventually anaesthetise their curiosity.

Heidegger climbed to the top of this mountain and came back down to announce that there was nothing up there – the place was empty. His first work was designed to show that – and how – the history of philosophy had been one long self-induced amnesia. It is the story of the King's New Clothes told over twenty centuries. Not only had our culture lost all real contact with Being, but it had substituted an alternative on the inside which was as convincing as the most intricate and true-to-life artificial flowers – the ones you have to smell and touch before you can tell that they are false.

The only real contact with Being, the only ontological language left in our culture, is poetry of a certain kind. Not just any poetry. There are good poets and bad poets, there is poetry for decoration, for propaganda, for entertainment; there is poetry for lovers, for mourners, for magicians. But, according to Heidegger, there is also a metaphysical poetry – poetry that takes upon itself to give utterance to Being. Such utterance can only be done in words, can only be about the world around us. Our only access to Being is through the things and beings that surround us, even though none of those things is actually Being itself. Anything you can know or see is a 'being', a thing. These are all we have to work with. These include trees, dreams, mathematical formulae, music or hydroelectric dams. Nothing in this world is not a thing. A thing *has* its being but *is* not Being. Being is not any one of these things. Nor is it something hidden in any of them. It is a no-thing. Nothing in our language, no word that we can invent, corresponds to Being as such.

And yet, each one of us, from our earliest childhood, is aware of Being; it is like the air we breathe, it is always at the back of our minds. Metaphysical poetry, or 'great' poetry, opens our eyes to what we had always already known. It makes us see what we were insensitive to, what was always there but we had never adverted to. It is a revelation of Being, an epiphany that shows us in the ordinary things and the everyday world that surrounds us the transfiguring and translucent light of the Being that energises them all, even while it always remains invisible and absent from the palpable world we graspingly inhabit.

The poet who says more is the one who dwells in that place

within, which is in contact with this reality, and so allows the breath of Being to be caught on the sprocket of each word and thus secrete itself into our culture as a luminosity or phosphorescence that coats the poem as it emerges with its tang and its fragrance.

Great poets dwell in the secret places of the earth and their essential heartwork is production of honey from these rocks. They are what Rilke refers to as 'bees of the invisible'. Their poetry is language drenched in the moisture of Being. The object of metaphysics is never present, it is not there. Metaphysics has no object, in fact. So, the process whereby we 'do' metaphysics – which is the 'doing' of poetry – is one 'which at all times must achieve Being anew', as Heidegger says.

But, whenever we have a sense experience, whenever we touch something, smell something, hear something, see something, we always and at the same time have a secret experience at another level. There is always this delicate shimmering gossamer around every experience, which we, in our day-to-day commerce, our rush through the business schedule, fail to notice and invariably ignore. This second-level experience of Being, which is not something added like a coating or an undercarriage but something 'present' in its reticent presentation of the thing to our notice, is something we have to reactivate and examine. It is almost as if we have to go back into the darkroom of our experience and develop its implications from the negatives of the day-to-day photo call. It is because this second-level experience of 'Being' transcends our sense experience that we have to invent nets that can collect this phosphorescence, entrap this fragrance, filter this fine dust that always arises from our contact with reality, but which disperses and gets lost in the process of harvesting what we normally feed ourselves with. It is not the content of what we glean from this harvest that gives us access to Being, it is not the ideas we contain in our heads. It is the actual contact, the meeting with reality, that creates these sparks, which we need to recover if we are to accede to the dimension of Being – the reality of what is – which escapes our immediate attention as life passes by. This is what essential poetry tries to do.

Rilke describes this very beautifully to his wife Clara in a letter he wrote after he had seen the exhibition of Cezanne's paintings in Paris in 1907:

Surely all art is the result of ... having gone through an experience all the way to the end, where no one can go any further. The further one goes, the more private, the more personal, the more singular an experience becomes, and the thing one is making is, finally, the necessary, irrepressible, and, as nearly as possible, definitive utterance of this singularity ... Therein lies the enormous aid the work of art brings to the life of the one who must make it –: that it is his epitome; the knot in the rosary at which his life recites a prayer ... for the utmost represents nothing other than that singularity in us which no one would or even should understand, and which must enter into the work as such, as our personal madness, so to speak, in order to find its justification in the work and reveal the law in it, like an inborn drawing that is invisible until it emerges in the transparency of the artistic.[14]

But in order to really develop these negatives and invigorate the experience with absorptive intelligence, a combination of critical thought and poetic transmission is recommended. This work engaged Heidegger in the last years of his life. He believed that unless we 'dwell poetically' on this earth, we are strangers here.

Throughout this book, the notions of 'poetry' and 'art' have been almost interchangeable. In fact they both describe that process which we invent to capture the evanescent reality that underpins everything, and yet is unavailable to the categories of science or the language of ordinary discourse. Such 'art' or cunning is whatever form we can create that will capture the truth we are stalking, or pin down the essence of our obsession. In the context of the following chapters, such 'poetry' or 'art' can be articulated as a novel, as a poem or as a play. It is not the variety that matters, it is the intensity, the depth and the scope of the exploration.

CHAPTER FOUR

Philosophy and the Feminine: The Novels of Iris Murdoch[1]

A distinguished professor of philosophy always recommended Iris Murdoch's *The Sovereignty of Good* (1970) to his students with the wistful aside that she could have been a great philosopher if she hadn't wasted her time writing novels. The point of view being defended in this book is that she wrote novels because they could achieve what philosophy could never do: penetrate the mystery of particularity. Philosophy can only lead us to the threshold of art. D. H. Lawrence berated the philosopher, who, because of a superior capacity for thinking, decides that nothing but thought matters. There is more to truth than thought. The novelist is one of those who, according to Lawrence, can get the 'whole hog'.[2] Iris Murdoch in her novels tries to get the whole hog.

The title of her first novel, *Under the Net* (1954), describes why she uses this 'form' of writing. The net is a favourite image of Wittgenstein, for example, to describe the process of conceptual thought. Through the medium of the novel, Murdoch gets beneath this ungainly mesh and manipulates instead the more subtle skein of her own novelist's web. In one of her purely philosophical works,[3] she describes a weakness of Sartre as novelist: 'an impatience, which is fatal to a novelist proper, with the stuff of human life'. Sartre is essentially a philosopher with 'a passionate desire to analyse, to build intellectually pleasing schemes and patterns'. This is the net under which Murdoch's novels trawl. The 'stuff of human life', the business of her novels, the thing that escapes Sartre's impatient and overwrought netting, is 'the absurd irreducible uniqueness of people and of their relations with each other'.

Philosophy was invented – by men for the most part – to create a universal discourse on the essence of reality, a conceptual framework within which to discuss what is common to humanity. Art can stalk the zaniness of private behaviour by inventing a bugging device to trace the craziness of individuality, the unpredictability of singularity.

The Murdoch novels (there are twenty-six of them, dating back to 1954) are always very funny, dealing with a fairly narrow segment of society, usually educated middle to upper class with (to my taste) a fascinating blend of character study and dialogue that is witty, fresh, perceptive, plausible. At the level of conversation and character, an Iris Murdoch novel resembles Newman's 'Idea of a University', where 'a multitude ... keen, open-hearted, sympathetic, and observant ... come together and freely mix with each other and are sure to learn one from another, even if there be no-one to teach them; the conversation of all is a series of lectures to each, and they gain for themselves new ideas and views, fresh matter of thought, and distinct principles for judging and acting, day by day'.

This is at the surface level of the narrative – what E. M. Forster calls the 'backbone' or the 'tape-worm' of the novel, which we can 'isolate from the nobler aspects through which it moves' and 'hold out on a forceps – wriggling and interminable'.[4] This Forster calls 'the naked worm of time'. Here we can point to themes and topics that Murdoch's various novels contemplate and explore – art, love, myth, sex, ideas, religion, passion, etc., – and deal with in a way that is masterly and convincing: 'not a dull page or a slipshod sentence', as one reviewer puts it. But it is the 'nobler aspects through which these move' that provide the intriguing ambiguity, the multi-dimensional treasure.

Each novel is framed and penetrated by archaeological, geographical and mythical references and is studded with images and symbols that submerge us to a depth of suggestive incomprehension. These lead us into quite another set of correspondences, which seem to sneer at our facile following of the surface plot. Such time bombs set beneath the linear surface generate a nervous excitement, as do dreams and irrational behaviour patterns, usually associated with the symbols in mythologically significant places. We realise that the surface we are treading is landscape covering a maze of underground tunnels and that a whole life is being lived in the dark warrens into which now and again we see people and places disappear. Whether it be the Axle stone on the ley lines under the Roman road in *The Book and the Brotherhood* (1987), or the hot spring with healing properties where pre-Roman goddesses might have been worshipped in *The Philosopher's Pupil* (1983), conspiratorial access to another world makes the reader examine each fact, each item, each event, like a hologram, in case it is a secret agent of this other world.

When Caroline Spurgeon produced her study of *Shakespeare's Imagery* in 1935, it revolutionised critical appraisal of his work:

> It enables us to get nearer to Shakespeare himself, to his mind, his tastes, his experiences, and his deeper thought than does any other single way I know of studying him. It throws light from a fresh angle upon his imaginative and pictorial vision, upon his own ideas about his own plays and the characters in them … It seems scarcely necessary to say that the images form, when thus collected, a world in themselves, for they mirror the richest experience and the most profound and soaring imagination known to man.[5]

In a similar way, it seems to me, the novels of Iris Murdoch have something of a life of their own at the level of imagery. This dimension adds much more to the 'philosophy' within them. Such a study of the Murdoch imagery has not yet been undertaken, as far as I know, and so I am left with a corpus of work that, if it were meant to be a fruitcake, would be one of those disastrous ones where all the fruit has sunk to the bottom. But since it is not meant to be a fruitcake, it leaves me (as reader) with the task of maintaining the connection between the top and the bottom, the layer of narrative (cake) and the layer of imagery (fruit) – an experience I have found enriching and tantalisingly pleasurable. I

had always imagined that at some stage – in a future novel of
Murdoch's, or at a future time in myself – a perspective would
emerge and the two layers would become aligned in a way that
would allow me to participate in the Murdoch 'message'. With
each novel, I felt myself nearer to that goal. It was as if the
philosopher were inviting her pupils to take up the invitation
issued through *The Message to the Planet* (1989):

> I don't know where you are in your thoughts – but you
> should write it down, I don't mean solving it, but just stating,
> writing it in plain rigmarole, as it were, with all the knots and
> inconsistencies showing. I know you see it as a sort of cosmic
> game of patience which would one day come out, and per-
> haps it will. But meanwhile you ought to write about the
> state of the game, about the kind of muddle and confusion
> you're in.[6]

The later novels harp on similar patterns, and the feeling given
is that they are either prologues to the swelling act or that the act
itself has been performed secretly at the deeper level of symbol,
while the narrative hums away plausibly as a decoy. The overwhelming tremulation tangibly felt by at least this particular
reader is that she, Iris Murdoch, in herself or in her work, holds
some key, does have an understanding of the mystery of life,
which it would benefit us to hear.

In *The Philosopher's Pupil*, for instance, 'John Robert died because he saw at last, with horrified wide-open eyes, the futility
of philosophy. Metaphysics and the human sciences are made
impossible by the penetration of morality into the moment to
moment conduct of ordinary life: the understanding of this fact
is religion.' The death of this philosopher/philosophy is the
birth of the novel, whose task is precisely to elaborate the horri-
fying vision that killed off John Robert: the rehabilitation of
Christianity as something essentially beautiful, something essentially sexual, something to do with ritual, symbol and art.

How far Christianity is and has been from these criteria is
portrayed in *The Bell* (1958). Here is described a ghastly lay
community living beside a contemplative monastery. A fresh,

natural, ordinary girl, Dora, seeks out her husband, who has gone to stay in this community. When she arrives, they gently and sweetly try to get her to 'embrace' their way of life. The novel has to be read to taste the smug suffocating superficiality of their goodness. Dora flees to London to an art gallery where she experiences the contrast between the hostile censoriousness of the community life at Imber, derelict and dusty 'like the aftermath of amateur theatricals', reminding her of school, and the 'authority, the marvellous generosity and splendour' of the paintings. Here, at last, was something real and perfect:

> The pictures were something real outside herself, which spoke to her in kindly yet in sovereign tones, something superior and good whose presence destroyed the dreary trance-like solipsism of her earlier mood … She looked at the radiant, sombre, tender, powerful canvas of Gainsborough and felt a sudden desire to go down on her knees before it, embracing it, shedding tears … She must go back to her real life, her real problems. And since, somewhere, something good existed, it might be that her problems would be solved after all. There was a connection; obscurely she felt, without yet understanding it, she must hang onto that idea; there was a connection. [7]

This is the connection that we are encouraged to hang onto as we follow Iris Murdoch's journey as an artist through the second half of the twentieth century. The contrast in *The Bell* between the silly, cosy, grasping and greedy 'religious' life that is lived with grinning ruthless fascism by the lay community, and the 'contemplative' monastery, which exists (in hazy unscrutinised idealism) beyond the lake, is the one between religion, as most imagine it, and religion as it was intended to be. In the passage quoted we find the words 'sovereign' and 'good', which make up the theme of Murdoch's lectures on Plato. In the novel we are surrounded by an enriching jewellery of symbolism, such as water and the eponymous bell.

What the novel seems to be reaching towards is the vision of some overwhelming beauty: 'Something we have seen with our own eyes, that we have touched with our hands: the Word, who is life – this is our subject. That life was made visible' (John 1-2), as an earlier artist tried to put it into words. This intuition was that Christianity began in thraldom; that the earliest disciples were literally bowled over by the sheer beauty of a man and the unaccountable way in which this presence would compel you to adore. It is a way that was also understood by Plato, as it is by every human being who for the sake of beauty has agreed to become a lunatic. This is the lesson of great art, according to Iris Murdoch:

> [It] teaches us how real things can be looked at and loved without being seized and used, without being appropriated into the greedy organism of the self ... Beauty is that which attracts this particular sort of unselfish attention ... The direction of attention is, contrary to nature, outward, away from self, which reduces all to a false unity, towards the great surprising variety of the world, and the ability so to direct attention is love.[8]

The religious community in *The Bell* is a false community. It reduces life to the small-minded perception of non-life – turn the old drawing-room into an oratory and turn life into a diluted vicarious substitute, a shoddy remould. But the sound is wrong and this is the essence of *The Bell*, it can only be authenticated in the sound of its singing. If it doesn't ring true, it is nothing.

Iris Murdoch's major intuition is about love. So, what is the 'love' that can direct the 'attention' outward and away from self toward 'the great surprising variety of the world?' The only method capable of describing such a movement and such an object is the flexible cardiography which is the novel.

The Message to the Planet (1989), as I read it, forms part of a pattern and moves within an identifiable orbit. To situate these I shall refer to it and the three novels that precede it, *The Philosopher's Pupil* (1983), *The Good Apprentice* (1985) and *The Book and the Brotherhood* (1987). In all four, men, rather than women, are the major protagonists. In all cases, one male is the centripetal focus around whom the plot and the players move.

In chronological order, he is the philosopher; the fertility god, Jesse Baltram, who lives in a magical world guarded by three women; the (dangerously attractive) writer of The Book; and the visionary mystic Marcus Vallar, who is giving birth to The Message to the Planet. In all cases we are surrounded by mysteriously healing underground springs, where water plays a role in the subterranean rite being suggested, and the settings are archaeological remains, which imply that powerful mythological influences are embedded in the psychic memory of such places.

All these men are irretrievably and hilariously inadequate. They are domestically inept and dependent, psychologically deficient to the point of being dangerous, and spiritually indolent. They all have at least one male disciple, a sorcerer's apprentice who is more or less the Boswell to their Dr Johnson (and here the similarities of character and biography are many). They also have at least two or three female attendants who are helpless victims and playthings of their volatile temperaments and demanding genius. Above all, they are fruitless. In the first case the writing is drowned in the bath with the almost murdered philosopher; in the third, 'the book' is written but the reader never gets a glimpse of it after the author's suicide and his disciple's resentful literary executorship; and in the last, the suicide of the visionary after so many chapters of expectancy gives us the feeling (described in another context in this novel) of having been present at 'a secret liberating ritual of some scandalous sort, a shedding of blood, like a magic rite involving the beheading of a cock'.

In all cases, Iris Murdoch is trying to get to the source, to hear the sound of the bell. Many of her most beautiful and pertinent pages are about music, singing and the genuine human voice. But the world in which she lives and has her philosophical being is a world of men. If she is to speak the truth, it has to be as ventriloquist, through 'the philosopher' in her own and the Western archetype. And so these later novels share something of a rite of exorcism – a cutting off of a 'head' of 'a cock'. The cerebral, masculine bias of all discourse on truth has to be laid to rest before the still small sound of the bell can be heard. And this process demands not just the beheading of the philosopher, but also the destruction of the master-pupil syndrome, which dictates that the lover must be one person and the letter-writer another. To tell us that love, which is the ability to direct our attention away from self and outwards to the great surprising variety of the world, Iris Murdoch somehow feels obliged to seek out the professional love-letter-writer, usually (as in Garcia Marquez's *Love in the Time of Cholera*[9]) the most self-righteous, pompous, sleazy, indolent, smug and opinionated male.

The place where Murdoch comes nearest to 'the source' for me is the passage (in both senses) in *The Philosopher's Pupil* where Tom, 'in the state of restless obsessive nervous energy', goes down to the bottom of the Ennistone baths: 'I must find the source, I must get there' he says and there is a brilliantly symbolic description of his 'going down', which ends with the soliloquy:

> 'Why am I here? There must be a reason. I have got to do something, I have an aim, a task, I must go on down. I've come so far I can't give up now … I've got to find *the place*. I've got to see it, the real source … I must get there and … and touch it.

This very young, naïve male is the one who gets nearest to where Iris Murdoch is trying to reach through her army of flocculent 'philosophers'. And his capacity in this regard is essentially connected with his youth and almost child-like recklessness, abandon and trust:

> He came back, stood a minute as if in prayer, and touched the wet concrete floor like a child touching 'base'. He said aloud, 'I did my best', then hurried back to the stairs.

So, after many attempts to get the men to yield up some truth, we seem to be caught in a somewhat predictable and sterile pattern. Iris Murdoch seems to be giving advice to herself when the narrator in the last chapter of *The Philosopher's Pupil* says:

> I lately expressed the hope to Stella that now that life has become (it seems) more predictable she should stop regarding George as full-time occupation, and consider harnessing her

excellent mind to some coherent and developing intellectual study. She says that no doubt she will, but 'not yet', that perhaps she will 'write something'. I am afraid that at present she is more concerned about George's mind than about her own.

To search out the source, to speak the love, name the passion, resurrect the religion that would make a welcome message to the planet in the evening of an ugly century, we needed *The Good Apprentice*, Iris Murdoch herself.

In 1992, over forty years after she began teaching philosophy at Oxford, using her own voice and speaking the language of philosophical discourse, she gave us her own views on *Metaphysics as a Guide to Morals*.[10]

The book is written for everyone. It is courageous, generous and plainspoken. She engages in dialogue over fifty highly intelligent men who have devoted their lives and their considerable genius to the questions on her agenda. Hannah Arendt and Simone Weil are the only two women quoted amid the galaxy of philosophical talent from Ayer to Wittgenstein. It is a world of muscular masculine thought, not unlike the one inhabited by many of the characters in her novels. It is the world of 'The Philosopher' as he presides self-importantly over the history of Western philosophy. Murdoch acts here, not as ventriloquist but as no-nonsense referee. 'Philosophers,' she says, 'are supposed to clarify, and should attempt to write in ordinary language and not in jargon.' Where they lack this competence, she supplies for them, telling us clearly what they are trying to say to us confusedly. Because 'everyone is involved in this fight, it is not reserved for philosophers, artists and scientists'. As author, Murdoch identifies with 'everyone'. Her hope is to establish the connection between philosophy, art, religion and morality. She could present herself as either an artist or a philosopher but eschews both titles. She is one of the ordinary folk who have a right to understand what these people (mostly men) are saying. She gives each protagonist time to say his bit and gives the odd clip on the ear when they are being too long or too short: 'Wittgenstein elegantly shuns explanation,' she quips, 'Sartre is all explanation.' Her fear is that 'philosophers' have made their subject seem so difficult that we are put off using the only power we have for shaping the world as we would want it to be. 'We cannot see the future,' she admits, 'but we must fear it intelligently.' This is what philosophy should help us to do. 'The world is not given to us "on a plate," it is given to us as a creative task.' Without philosophy we are doomed to narrow-minded and prejudiced egoism that shields us from reality. 'Learning is moral progress, it provides deeper, subtler and wiser visions of the world ... [which] alter our instinctive movements of desire and aversion.' Our ordinary everyday consciousness is full of illusion: 'All human activity,' she declares, 'except that of exceptional and original persons, is based on networks of uncriticised assumptions and deep unconscious drives and patterns.' As an antidote to such limiting normalcy, 'it is very important that Western Philosophy, with its particular tradition and method of imaginative truth-seeking and lucid clarification, should not fail us here'. Her book is a brilliant presentation of the best in that tradition.

However, it is still not 'the book' that her writing to date had been promising: even as a text it has a hybrid flavour. At its worst it becomes a concatenation of quotations and lecture notes, at its best an evocative use of metaphor to scale metaphysical heights. On the two important questions about art and religion, there appears to be an almost puritanical mysophobia and minimalising tendency that I find disappointing. These shortcomings seem attributable to her uncompromising and unbalanced adulation for Plato in the overall picture of Western philosophy, and for Wittgenstein on the smaller canvas of the twentieth century. Both these thinkers allow her to remain entrenched in a Monophysite world as far as art and religion are concerned, a world that is belied by much of her work as a novelist.

She is clear and specific. In her view, geniuses are few in both art and philosophy, and only geniuses have the right to make innovative and adventurous reappraisals of tradition. Only geniuses should invent languages or coin new terms. What they, and we, are trying to do is to ascertain whether or not there are any 'deep structures' in our lives, and to articulate these as clearly and helpfully as possible. 'Our very small number of philosophical geniuses have suggested structures that have dominated and guided centuries of thought, not only inside philosophy but in science, in theology, in morality, and in the most general sorts of worldview held by unreflective people. Philosophy, it may be said, collects and formalises new ideas which, at various times, for various often mysterious reasons, are hanging about in the air, sensed by thinkers of all kinds.'

Artists also tap into this spirit of the times and 'art does register or picture, sometimes prophetically, the movement of the *Zeitgeist*. The way we grasp the world changes, and the artist knows first, like the animals whose behaviour foretells an earthquake.' So art, 'in its intimate and unspoken relation with the *Zeitgeist*,' and philosophy, in its attempt to articulate this relationship, are both ways of being in touch with the 'deep structures' of our lives, and therefore in touch, as far as we are capable of being so, with reality or whatever is beyond ourselves. 'We work at the meeting point where we deal with a world which is other than ourselves. This transcendental barrier is more like a band than a line.' This band or line is what metaphysics should be about: the 'deep structures' that unite us with and divide us from what is other than ourselves. Religion, art and philosophy all concern themselves with this line. Philosophy claims to approach it exclusively from the point of view within which we are irretrievably embedded.

Where religion and art are concerned, Murdoch remains fastidiously on this side of the transcendental barrier. She has nothing less than a horror of invasion from the other side. She does believe that 'great' poetry is language from and about the 'deep structures' and the transcendental frontier, but she refuses any possibility that it could be more than the breath, the voice, the inspiration of the poet. Poets write poetry. There is nothing more to it than that. However much their sensitivity may be enlarged or heightened by their privileged intimacy with the frontiers, they never escape from the limitations of their human-hood, and they never become vehicles or mediums for some extra-terrestrial reality.

Wittgenstein remains for Murdoch the major philosophical spokesperson of the twentieth century. She sees Heidegger as a dangerous charlatan proposing a dehumanising relationship with what is other than ourselves. Heidegger's 'Being' is to be repudiated:

> Heidegger's idea, adorned by references to (poor innocent) Holderlin, of a sort of return of the gods or a new undreamt-of renewal of the sacred and the holy, is a piece of poetic metaphysical melodrama. The concept of 'Being', used as a substitute for 'God' or 'Absolute', is of dubious value; and in the thinking of late Heidegger becomes a sinister historicised Fate, a posited entity about whose future 'structure' or 'in-tentions' we may speculate. (A player of games.) Heidegger's search for a universal language, or fundamental basis of lan-guage, in the language of poetry is also, whether we regard it as metaphysics, or 'science', or literary criticism, a false path, a search for 'deep foundations' where there are none. (Poetry is written by poets, there are not many of these, poetry is very difficult.) If one does want to believe in what is 'deep' in the form of the old God then let this belief be kept mysterious and separated and pure, and not mixed up with dubious history, or indeed with any history.

What we are dealing with here is a relationship between time and eternity, between transcendence and immanence, between the same and the other. Murdoch would seek to place herself firmly in the tradition of total separation of these two – the Jewish tradition, the tradition of Martin Buber and Simone Weil: There are two worlds whose very definition separates them from each other. There can be no commingling. Religion as a link can never become a filter. Transcendence is of the essence of God who must remain 'mysterious, separated, pure'. The philosophy of Heidegger is tantamount to rape, to invasion of our territory.

I find this condemnation too indiscriminate and partisan. I also sense a fear in it that fuels its virulence. But here my contention is that in her own 'poetic' writing, Iris Murdoch belies what she is stating here in prose. Her own writing as an artist is one of the best examples of what Heidegger is trying to articulate about such 'poetry'. For example, in her novel *The Unicorn* (1963), she describes what it might mean to be a poet of the transcendental frontier:

> 'You see' he said laboriously, if only he could a little play for time, the vision might announce itself quite simply through his speech, … 'you see. You see. You see, death is not the consummation of oneself but just the end of oneself. It's very simple. Before the self vanishes nothing really is, and that's how it is most of the time. But as soon as the self vanishes everything is, and becomes automatically the object of love. Love holds the world together, and if we could forget ourselves everything in the world would fly into a perfect harmony and when we see beautiful things that is what they remind us of.'
>
> 'I think he's delirious. That's just a garbled version of something Father …'
>
> 'I see what you mean, Effie, go on.'
>
> 'It can't be quite as simple as that, Effingham.'
>
> He was sure these were the right words. He felt that it was all fading and that he was going to forget it after all. He would be left with an empty description, the thing itself utterly gone from view. He tried to repeat the words again, like a prayer, like a charm.
>
> 'It's automatic, you see, that's what's so important. You just have to look in the other direction –'
>
> But he no longer believed what he was saying.[12]

Even in the novelistic asides of *Metaphysics as a Guide to Morals*, Murdoch quotes a passage from Henry James's *The Golden Bowl*, where Maggie Verver realises that her husband is enjoying a long-standing love relationship with her best friend:

It was not till many days had passed that the Princess began to accept the idea of having done, a little, something she was not always doing, or indeed of having listened to an inward voice that spoke in a new tone. Yet these instinctive post-ponements of reflection were the fruit, positively, of recognitions and perceptions already active; of the sense, above all, that she had made, at a particular hour, made by the mere touch of her hand, a difference in the situation so long present to her as practically unattackable. This situation had been occupying, for months and months, the very centre of the garden of her life, but it had reared itself there like some strange tall tower of ivory, or perhaps rather some wonderful, beautiful, but outlandish pagoda, a structure plated with hard bright porcelain, coloured and figured and adorned, at the overhanging eaves, with silver bells that tinkled, ever so charmingly, when stirred by chance airs. She had walked round and round it – that was what she felt; she had carried on her existence in the space left her for circulation, a space that sometimes seemed ample and sometimes narrow; looking up, all the while, at the fair structure that spread itself so amply and rose so high, but never quite making it out, as yet, where she might have entered had she wished. She had not wished till now – such was the odd case; and what was doubtless equally odd, besides, was that, though her raised eyes seemed to distinguish places that must serve, from within, and especially far aloft, as apertures and outlooks, no door appeared to give access from her convenient garden level. The great decorated surface had remained consistently impenetrable and inscrutable. At present, however, to her considering mind, it was as if she had ceased merely to circle and to scan the elevation, ceased so vaguely, so quite helplessly to stare and wonder: she had caught herself distinctly in the act of pausing, then in that of lingering, and finally in that of stepping unprecedentedly near. The thing might have been, by the distance at which it kept her, a Mohammedan mosque, with which no base heretic could take a liberty;

there so hung about it the vision of one's putting off one's
shoes to enter and even, verily, of one's paying with one's life
if found there as an interloper. She had not, certainly, arrived
at the conception of paying with her life for anything she
might do; but it was nevertheless quite as if she had sounded
with a tap or two one of the rare porcelain plates. She had
knocked, in short – though she could scarce have said
whether for admission or for what; she had applied her hand
to a cool, smooth spot, and had waited to see what would
happen. Something had happened; it was as if a sound, at her
touch, after a little, had come back to her from within; a
sound sufficiently suggesting that her approach had been
noted.[13]

I give this rather lengthy quote in full because it provides both
the locus and the text for what I am trying to express about Iris
Murdoch herself. First of all, it is from the great novelist who has
been described as 'so refined that an idea never crossed his
mind'. His is the kind of expression that is most adequate to the
task of elaborating the deepest truths. 'How we proceed here,'
she says, commenting on this text, 'can be a matter of our deepest thoughts. We recognise this dialectic, these levels, these differences of style and image, in our own thinking as we understand a writer and as we are at other times led to reflect upon
what the stuff and quality of our consciousness is.' Henry James
is the master of this style, this capacity to articulate 'the mess of
actual consciousness' as opposed to 'the philosophical problem
of consciousness', which is always 'set up … with ulterior mot-
ives'. And, for both James and Murdoch, we don't know what
'the stuff and quality' of this consciousness is, until we catch
ourselves doing something that reveals it to us. The novel is the
sufficiently versatile and elastic medium that can follow with accuracy the doing of such thought. And for Iris Murdoch herself,
this 'doing' is her novel-writing itself.

So, Murdoch is rejecting philosophy as adequate to the task
of capturing the subtle 'stuff' of consciousness, which is too
unique for generalised concepts, and is proposing Henry James

as a model of someone with the artistic genius capable of articulating this reality.

This passage from Henry James is also a description of Iris Murdoch's own situation in her last novel, *Jackson's Dilemma* (1995). Here she is doing what Maggie Verver was doing in relation to 'what is "deep" in the form of the old God'. She recognises, in and through the 'doing' of this novel, that Heidegger has been having a long-standing relationship with her best friend, or vice versa. *Jackson's Dilemma* is, in fact, Iris Murdoch's dilemma. It hovers over that line or band that separates the two worlds. However, what she 'does' in this novel, which is all about opening doors, building bridges, crossing over divides, leads her to discover that God is, in some frighteningly mysterious way, 'mixed up with dubious history'.

This novel is the articulation of what Heidegger was trying to point towards in his later philosophy, both in what it articulates – especially through the different levels and the interplay of imagery – and in the way it leads Iris Murdoch herself, through its own words, through the mysterious power of language, to articulate a reality that she had expressly repudiated in the 'philosophical' work of three years before.

At the level of narrative, it is about a man (Benet) who lives alone in a particular place or territory, and who is writing a book about Heidegger. 'However, he found it difficult to plan the work and to decide what he really, in his heart, thought of his huge ambiguous subject.' This, it would seem to me, is the situation for Iris Murdoch also. Like Maggie Verver in the Henry James novel, she finds herself doing this 'thought' in the form of a novel, in an art form that incarnates the thought as 'poetry'. 'Heidegger, the greatest philosopher of the century? But what was Benet thinking somehow so deeply about when he turned his mind to that remarkable thinker? It seemed to him that after all his philosophical reflections, there was a sound which rang some deeper tremor of the imagination. Perhaps it was his more profound desire to lay out before him the history of Heidegger's inner life ...' 'Benet found himself accusing himself of being fascinated by a certain dangerous aspect of Heidegger which was in fact so deeply buried in his own, Benet's, soul that he could not scrutinise or even dislodge it.'

The only way to do either or both is to let it deliver itself into the novel. And so, at the second level, the imagery concerns places – two territories divided by a river. The places are forever being locked, barred, bolted, and are connected by bridges. 'The gate, sometimes locked, was now fortunately not locked … [There was] a scarcely perceptible right of way running steeply down to the River Lip at a place where there was a shaky little wooden bridge. After the river she had left Benet's territory and entered Edward's territory. (They still feuded about the bridge.)' Those living in both territories are aware of just how tenuous, difficult and dangerous are the territorial ties between them. Part One of the book lands us in the middle of an attempt to solve this relationship in the most 'natural' and 'romantic' way by arranging a match. This is so predictable and 'heavenly'. There is a fourteenth-century church on Benet's side of the river, where this wedding is to take place the following day. It is as if the Gods have arranged it all, but more especially the ancestral ghosts of Penndean in the person of Uncle Tim (called after Timaeus Patroclus to keep us in the true Graeco-Roman tradi-tion). The night before the wedding 'Benet had firmly laid hold of Edward (the bridegroom owner of the 'other' territory), seiz-ing his sleeve … "Edward, if only Tim were here we would really be in heaven. Well, of course now we are in heaven anyway! I've longed for you to marry that girl."' A guest suggests that it is 'like the end of the Paradiso', but Benet insists: 'not the end … it is the beginning'. After which 'they moved back into the house'. In moments like these, 'and such strange moments sometimes came', Benet 'felt the spirit of Uncle Tim descending upon him, clothing him as it were, and breathing his breath'. This is the spirit of place, the tribal spirit of possessiveness that drives to-wards the consolidation of earthly ties, natural kinship between the peoples.

Well it is not to be so. The 'Marian' solution is definitively sabotaged when Maid Marian herself says no at the last minute. And so, the complete cast, in Part Two, is thrown out of paradise into 'hell'. Benet retires to his territory 'for some sort of quietness or solitude', and there, once again, is his book on Heidegger and 'Heidegger's central concept of truth or unconcealment'. It all begins according to a lecture that Heidegger gave in 1943 with a certain kind of wonder. 'Wonder first begins with the question, "What does all this mean and how could it happen?" How can we arrive at such a beginning?' ... Benet paused, well what does it all mean, he thought, and why on earth do I go on with it? ... Could one forgive Heidegger or be interested in him ... No, he was just a curious romantic pseudo-historian. He would rather spend his time reading Holderlin than Heidegger. Really he loved pictures not thoughts.'

And so we are led into the real business of the novel – Jackson's dilemma – Benet's relationship with Jackson, and Jackson's connection with history, which is Iris Murdoch's 'picture' of what Heidegger really meant by 'truth'.

Benet is forever trying to lock himself into his house. At the end of Part Two, 'he went round and locked the doors and bolted and chained them'. Then 'he decided to go to bed and to sleep'. The house itself is acoustically ambiguous. 'Those strange sounds were there again: a crackling sound of something on fire, an almost inaudible little wailing sound as by a small creature in pain, then a sharper brief sound not unlike a knock. Of course it was all nonsense, these were familiar noises, he heard them all the time, the natural murmurs of an ageing house, its little secret wounds, wood rotting, tiles slipping ... His ferocious concentration upon Heidegger had for a brief time distracted him.' But, despite his decision and his will to go to bed and lock himself securely within his own territory, 'suddenly he found himself prowling around the house and reflecting upon quite a different matter which now increasingly distressed him. It was Jackson.'

'Jackson was his servant.' 'The legend was that Benet had discovered Jackson curled up in a cardboard box late one night.'

In terms of territory, he had first met Jackson in 'that area

near to the river' which 'had been, ever since Benet could remember, some sort of gathering place'. But 'Benet himself was
not at all sure ... how exactly it had *begun*. Had he really seen
strange eyes looking at him in the dark? ... The idea 'it is fate',
was taken up later by Mildred. Had Benet, much earlier, unconsciously, seen those eyes? *Can* it be that one particular person,
sent by the gods, is singled out for another particular person?'

It certainly had to do with trying to find your way into your
own home and then hearing a voice, 'a soft voice', 'a cool calm
voice', saying 'May I help you? Perhaps I can help you.' 'I can do
many things.' 'Benet had not heard or dreamt of hearing this
voice. The voice was hard to place.' He is becoming aware 'that
he was not alone.' 'He turned round, annoyed, then alarmed, by
the silent unknown figure ... He was troubled by the stranger's
silence, and wished he could find somewhere to shake him off.'
The novel is a series of attempts to 'shake him off'. 'At last Benet
... turned round abruptly to survey his curious partner. He in-
stantly felt something pass through him, as of an electric shock.'

Getting into his house, finding no light in his house, 'the man
was there. Benet said, "Do you know anything about electricity?"
"Yes." "Come in". That was how it began.'

That was how what began? We are talking again about relationship with what is 'beyond', about the 'deep structures',
about the source. We are working through someone who is trying to find his way into his own homeland, his territory, in such
a way that he can claim it as his own, accurately delineate it and
then secure himself within it, locking it up, barring and bolting
the door. But he cannot even find his way in, his way around inside, without the 'help' of 'someone else', a 'voice'. It is a question of finding a key, of electricity, of light, even within his own
territory.

It is as if nothing works, nothing is possible, nothing exists,
without some contact with the territory beyond, with the outside of the house, the space between. Jackson's dilemma is how
to pick up the pieces after the apparent disaster occasioned by
the explosion of the romantic solution, how to establish another

kind of contact, generate another kind of electricity, that would
not be the endlessly stereotypical one of the marriage bond. The
non-event of this marriage in the church of the Arch-Angel
Michael and All the Angels is characterised as almost an anti-
sacrament: 'How *weird* it was, and *terrible*, what an *extraordinary*
scene as if some great ceremony were being performed.' The
italicised words emphasise the numinous dimension of the second sacrament, which was taking place by default. And
Rosalind, who is Marian's sister, becomes the only witness of the
secret return of the bridegroom as a kind of post-resurrection
apparition awaiting the arrival of the new dimension: 'She saw
something, somebody, just visible from where she stood now …
a man, sitting upon the flat top of a tombstone and looking
down.' Where she stood now, is the place and the time arranged
by Jackson. 'Thank you so much for lending us Jackson, he fixed
the thing in no time.'

So, who is this Jackson who is able to fix 'the thing' in 'no
time'? He is 'our dark angel', Ariel (who, according to Benet,
was not an angel), to 'run along the rooftops delivering messages,' Caliban, 'who really knew the island, the animals and the
plants', the Fisher King in disguise? He is whatever or whoever
is able to establish contact between the Gods and ourselves. He
is 'of the angel order'. He is God's illegitimate son, as Caliban
was Prospero's by the witch Sycorax. He is 'Benet's illegitimate
son': in both cases, quoting Shakespeare: 'This thing of darkness
I acknowledge mine.' Throughout the novel, we all eventually
recognise that 'however it may be, in Jackson I recognise my
brother'.

He is 'one of us' and, at the same time, he is beyond us. He
belongs to the space between our two territories. 'He walked
across in the dark and looked down into the garden below.
Jackson lived there, in the little house of his own which Benet
called "The Lodge". The light was on in the lodge.'

In other words, the novel is a description of the relationship
between us and God, or 'the gods'. All its imagery of territories,
spaces, places, houses, etc., is describing a kind of mysticism

that architecturally enunciates the 'deep structures' of our lives, the line or the band between us and the 'other' world. The river is the most picturesque analogy for that band. It is called 'Lip' as both the edge and the faculty with which we can achieve that 'kiss' which Meister Eckhart describes as the sublime contact with the 'Other'. Rosalind, as Marian's sister, is the other possibility of relationship once the Marian convention has been courageously refused. 'A less courageous person would have felt it was already too late, they would have been ashamed, they would think … I'm so involved now I'll have to put up with it.' So that, when Benet goes to visit Rosalind in her 'third floor flat', the imagery of doors, locks, above, below, windows, inside, outside, can be understood in this way:

> He pressed open the front door and began to climb. He heard Rosalind's door opening above – and the pain now came back and the fear, the *awfulness* of the situation, its bottomless void … He heard her door opening above and thought, I will recall this. Rosalind held the door open, then when Benet entered, shut it and leaning against it they hugged each other with closed eyes. Then Benet, holding her by the wrist, led her over to the window where a long seat covered with cushions gave a view down the busy little street dusty with sunshine and a narrow glimpse of the great Catholic Cathedral.[14]

The space between, the door between, which has to be pressed upon, opened from inside, is the place of that new kind of relationship between God and humankind. It is a dark place, an 'awful' place: *Terribile est locus iste*, as every mystic has experienced. In the middle of the passage just quoted, Benet tells us 'he knew that beyond these particular matters there was a dark horror which he must not, and indeed could not, thrust away … Suddenly something out of Shakespeare, the dreadful peril of the bard himself.' This concern, this comparison, this suggestion that Shakespeare has known this situation, echoes a previous passage where we hear Benet suggesting that Heidegger also was in possession of this terrible secret: 'Heidegger, the greatest philosopher of the century? His … desire to lay out … the *history* of Heidegger's *inner life*, the nature of his *sufferings*: the man who began as a divinity student and became a follower of Hitler, and then –? Remorse? Was that the very concept which sounded the bell? What had that pain been like … A huge tormented life? Was Heidegger really Anti-Christ? "The darkness, oh the darkness," Benet said aloud.'

This novel is an attempt to articulate such a dimension. And to 'do' the fearful possibility that this is what relationship with God must mean after the times we have been through. Jackson is the personification of such relationship, of such a possibility. 'On the occasion of the key he had refused money, he had, to make this clear, actually reached out his hand, laying it on Benet's hand – his fingers touching the back of Benet's hand. He had touched Benet. Well, what did that mean – a gesture of love? Impossible! He had been closer then than now. Well, Benet's emotion – was there emotion – had soon passed! Yet perhaps the emotion had built up later on: the dream, the return to the river.'

Having tried to escape from this relationship, having dismissed Jackson, in fact, Benet tries to return to normality, but 'he struggled as if against a power to which he must soon succumb'. This power has all the outward signs of a hypnotic sexual attraction. This possibility goes through Benet's mind: 'It was also possible, and this occurred to Benet later in the episode, that the fellow was gay and thought that Benet was! He decided that this was unlikely …' And we, also, who have followed Iris Murdoch through her novels, are aware that she is more aware not only of this possibility but of the almost inevitable connection between it and mysticism. A. S. Byatt comments that in *The Bell*: 'both Michael and Dora are real and unexpected individuals; Michael as a type, ineffectual homosexual idealist, school-master cum priest, we may have met often enough before, but such a character can rarely have been treated with the completely non-sentimental respect and the patient understanding which Miss Murdoch affords him.'[15]

Both Benet and Jackson could be such characters if Murdoch wished them to be. But they are not. Although, again, this ambiguity is part of Jackson's dilemma and there are times when Benet's 'visions' and 'apparitions' seem to have the homoerotic flavour of some of Thomas Mann's stories, especially 'that curious stroke in Venice' which immediately preceded his first real interview with Jackson. And when eventually he and Jackson meet up and decide to remain together, it does appear as though either or both of them are 'cruising' along the bridge over the Thames. However, this is not the kind of relationship that the novel is presenting, even though it might have been the preliminary to it or the occasion of it, which is not stated, but which corresponds with certain Platonic ideas about erotic love, which Murdoch explains in her *Guide to Morals*:

> Plato envisages erotic love as an education, because of its intensity as a source of energy, and because it wrenches our interest out of ourselves. It may be compared with the startling experience in Zen (perhaps a literal blow) which is to bring about enlightenment. (p. 345)

Whatever ambiguities may pervade the context of, or the lead up to, the eventual meeting between Benet and Jackson which seals their fate as committed partners to one another, the actual event, as described in the novel, delineates a specific kind of relationship with the Other, which involves reaching the deep structures of the self and opening that self to the Infinite. Benet first goes to 'the house where he used to live and where Jackson had first spoken to him'. He walks down to that part of it which is beside the river. 'He felt a curious impulse to knock at the door. In fact he knocked, but no one answered.' He goes to the railway station intending to take the train home. 'Why am I here,' he asks himself, 'oh God forgive me, except that I don't believe in God.' Just beyond was the river Thames. At one moment he was in the railway station about to get on a train, but 'then he found himself standing at the foot of the steps leading up to the railway bridge; automatically he began to mount. Why was he doing this, he felt so tired and so senseless. At the top of the steps he paused. He thought, I am nobody now. He was the beginning of nobody. Now it was dark. The Thames below was full and quiet. It was dark on the bridge ... Benet ... set off slowly toward the other side. Near the centre of the bridge a man was leaning upon the rail, looking down the river ... Nearing, the hideous idea occurred to him of simply *passing by* ... How this had occurred to him seemed later incredible – certainly it was not contempt or hatred – it was *fear.*'

Despite the ambiguities: it could be that either or both of them have gone there to pick up a partner or to commit suicide, the imagery and the thrust of the novel lead elsewhere. Jackson is the bridge. His dilemma is how to entice us to the centre. Once the connection has been made, at the end of Part Nine, the two men 'walk back towards the station' together, and to do this, we are told, 'Jackson detached himself from the bridge'.

Jackson is the Murdoch version of Heidegger, the reality of the Spirit in our world, the space, the bridge, the pontifex, between us and God, who is not an impersonal fate, but a personal servant. The novel walks us towards the centre of that bridge, which had been philosophically identified in the *Guide to Morals*:

Personal love exists and is tried in impersonal contexts, in a real large world which transcends it and contains other goals, other values, other people. We love in the open air, not in a private room. We know, and this is one of the things we know most clearly of all, which is indeed a knowledge that is 'forced upon us', that the energy of Eros can be obsessive, destructive and selfish, as well as spiritual, unselfish, a source of life. 'Falling in love' may be our most intense experience, when the world's centre is removed to another place. It is difficult to be unselfishly in love, and the lover who lovingly surrenders the beloved may serve as an image of virtue, of the love that 'lets go', as in Eckhart: emptying the soul to let God enter and even, for God's sake, taking leave of God. Eckhart was loved by Schopenhauer and also influenced Heidegger. Heidegger's concept of *Lichtung* (as portrayed earlier while man was still the Shepherd of Being), a clearing, an opening of space to allow Being to be, expresses Eckhart's denial of self. (p. 345)

Iris Murdoch's last novel, *Jackson's Dilemma*, written as Alzheimer's disease was about to make all such writing impossible for her, exudes another energy which takes over and allows the novel to describe the process by which the Spirit intervenes in human lives. The second last paragraph of the book is almost prophetic if one sees it as describing Iris Murdoch's own situation at the time of writing:

> He (Jackson) breathed deeply. Sometimes he had a sudden loss of breath, together with a momentary loss, or shift, of memory. So he was to wait, once more, forgetfulness, his and theirs. He thought, my power has left me, will it ever return, will the *indications* return? ... He had forgotten where he had to go, and what he had to do ... How much now will I understand. My powers have left me, will they return – yet my strength remains, and I can destroy myself at any moment. Death, its closeness. Do I after all fear those who seek me? I have forgotten them and no one calls. Was I in prison once? I cannot remember. At the end of what is necessary, I have come to a place where there is no road. (pp. 248-9)

In an earlier interview, Murdoch had said: 'One can only write from one's own mind, within the limit of one's own understanding of human life. This will be marked by your history, where you've been ... What's interesting about the novel is that all kinds of things that you know and feel and think, a great variety of things, are elicited by the art form, so in a way writing a novel is a process of self-discovery – you know much more than you think ... The unconscious mind is the great source of the power of art, and all these things will emerge if you wait for them and summon them.' This last novel must have been written very largely from the unconscious, with the discipline and the habit of years of writing helping her to battle against the onslaught of Alzheimer's.

'You have to explore and extend your limits. This is why reading is so important ... another world is pulling you out of yourself, and to get out of yourself is the great thing ... I'm very interested in dreams. We are accompanied by a dream world, the unconscious mind teems with strange things. And a work of art is a place where you can formalise and present some of these strange things which are just outside the focus of your ordinary consciousness.'[16]

Iris Murdoch's last novel, written as the curtain of conscious memory was descending, provides us with one of the most remarkable testimonies to the haunted inkwell. Jackson in the novel is the Holy Spirit, son of 'This Jack, joke, poor potsherd, patch, matchwood' that ultimately 'Is immortal diamond'.[17]

CHAPTER FIVE

Wole Soyinka and the Fourth Stage

Is African intelligence, as Léopold Sédar Senghor suggested,[1] different in kind from European logical intelligence, and does it require the elaboration of a black epistemology? Is it true that black people are the end-product of a long process of adaptation to the African environment and that such a process has determined an inner disposition and worldview?[2] Does this make the African relate to Being in an idiosyncratic way, and is it possible for us to learn this way of truth?

This was the view of some of the philosophers of the movement known as 'Negritude', which was summed up in 1962 by Léopold Senghor as 'the sum total of cultural values of the Negro world'. Such a point of view has been severely criticised and denounced in recent years as 'racist', 'condescending', or 'romanticism that is mawkish and strikes a pose'. But it has to be admitted that, as a movement at a certain time, Negritude had the political effect of helping to develop African nationalism and a broader black consciousness, while at the artistic level it spawned a generation of creative works, which in themselves would vindicate its value as a provocative stimulus, whatever about its validity as a concrete reality.

In 1991, the Nigerian sculptor Ben Ewonwu declared his indebtedness, and that of his generation of artists, to the inspiration of this movement.[3] Asked by an interviewer where the 'freedom' of his later style emerged, he replied: 'At the point of Negritude. At the point of African independence, when Zik (Nnamdi Azikiwe) and other nationalists whipped up the political consciousness that infected us all.'

So, at the levels of politics and of art, there can be no doubt that Negritude was a reality that had a historical and, in many ways, beneficial effect. But at the level of philosophy, what is its intrinsic and lasting value? Does it constitute a different way of being and, if so, can this be shared?

In June 1932 the movement was launched in Paris by a group of young French West Indians. Their journal, *Légitime Défense*, although it lasted for only a single issue, was the originating impulse.[4] The name of the movement came from a poem by the French-speaking poet from Martinique, Aimé Césaire,[5] but the 'philosophy' of the movement, if such there be, was mostly articulated by Léopold Senghor. Senghor, although essentially a poet, was educated in Paris and was prominent in intellectual and political life in West Africa throughout his life. He was installed as first President of the Independent Republic of Senegal in 1960.

Perhaps the most influential connection for him in the realm of philosophy was his meeting with Jean-Paul Sartre, whose essay of introduction to Senghor's *Anthologie de la nouvelle poésie nègre et malgache* (1948), called *'Orphée noir'*, provided both Negritude and Senghor with an intellectual audience and direction that neither might otherwise have taken, or taken to, on their own.

Sartre interpreted Negritude within the parameters of his own philosophy, seeing it as 'an historical phenomenon – a contingent stage in a total historical process. It is simply an articulated moment in the movement of the black consciousness breaking through the bounds of its historical and sociological determination towards the recovery of its original existential freedom.' In other words, Sartre incorporated this philosophy into the dialectic of his own blend of Marxist existentialism.

The Pan-Africanist C. L. R. James saw at the time that Sartre's explanation 'of what he conceives Negritude to mean, is a disaster'. However, Negritude came to be identified with Pan-Africanism also, which was just as misleading. This latter was essentially a 'British' movement with specifically political goals, the idea being to achieve a united Africa in a way somewhat similar to the present political movement towards a united Europe.[6]

One of the most devastating and comprehensive critiques of Negritude comes from Wole Soyinka.[7] He begins by acknowledging the 'vision' of Negritude and its achievements, which 'should never be underestimated or belittled'. However, he then attacks and condemns it because it became 'the contrivance of a creative ideology' which rested on a 'falsified basis of identification with the social vision'.[8] The condemnation involves two levels of judgement: the first against Sartre; the second against the whole movement in terms of its ideology.

Soyinka objects to the 'racism' that would distinguish black people from the rest of humanity in any way that would make them qualitatively different. They are not different. They are human in exactly the same way and with all the defining properties and identifying characteristics of every other human being. He further castigates the 'difference' that this 'racist' ideology implies as the hallmark of black people. According to the Negritudinists, black people think differently from other races – European reason is analytical, whereas African reason is intuitive. Soyinka reduces this idea to the basic syllogism that supports it. His use of the syllogism here has all the mischievous irony that makes his criticism as sharp as it is stinging:

(a) Analytical thought is a mark of high human development
The European employs analytical thought
Therefore the European is highly developed.
(b) Analytical thought is a mark of high human development
The African is incapable of analytical thought
Therefore the African is not highly developed.

These syllogisms were the bases for colonialism and the white racism that underpinned slavery and apartheid. Negritude, according to Soyinka, leaves this essentially racist and European syllogism intact and replaces the second one with an amended version:

(c) Intuitive understanding is also a mark of human development
The African employs intuitive understanding
Therefore the African is highly developed.

Soyinka repudiates such complacent and ingratiating submission to European megalomania. He accuses Senghor of turning himself into a black poodle in the court of imperialistic French rationalism. He denounces him as a naturalised European bourgeois who returns to Africa to persuade his countrymen to glory in the demeaning position they are asked to assume in the hierarchy of French prejudice. He quotes Senghor disparagingly as saying that 'emotion is completely Negro as reason is Greek' and denounces the whole philosophy of Negritude, because:

> It accepted one of the most commonplace blasphemies of racism, that the black man has nothing between his ears, and proceeded to subvert the power of poetry to glorify this fabricated justification of European cultural domination.[9]

Negritude was Uncle Tom's Cabin converted into a fully furnished basement flat.

My own point of view is that, whereas this caricature of Negritude might be justifiable in terms of the movement as a popular philosophy, or in the version perpetrated by Sartre, it is not an adequate presentation of Senghor's vision. It is important to distinguish between Negritude as political philosophy, as black epistemology, as anthropology, and as metaphysics. It is as this last, expressed in the mature work of Senghor, that I am considering it here. Even if it is tried and found wanting in every other capacity, it could still provide important insights into African philosophy today.

Most of the arguments against the movement are levelled against Sartre or against the attempt to erect it into a totalitarian anthropology embracing every black person in the universe. Neither of these is essential to the later vision of Senghor; nor are the various political philosophies that have come to be identified with Negritude.

My argument is that Negritude should not be identified with

a political movement; that it need not be applied to every generic African or to any group of people anywhere in the world; that it should not be irretrievably linked with the socio-historic background of any of its spokespersons; that it should not be treated as a comprehensive account of the anthropological structure of any given race. Like any other philosophy, it should be read and understood in the writings of a particular philosopher. Just as most twentieth-century European philosophers have refused the label 'existentialist', which historians of philosophy have used to categorise them, so, too, should we be careful to examine the clichés that cluster around categories such as Negritude.

The famous witticism that Wole Soyinka used to laugh this movement out of court, namely that tigers should not have to go round shouting about their tigritude, is a case in point. The question is not about generic identification; it is about specific difference. Senghor is not saying that black means true-blue human, sterling silver, carat gold, etc. He is not waving the flag of Negritude as a certificate proving membership of whatever class of humanity. He is declaring his vision, describing a relationship with Being. In other words, he is undertaking the kind of 'intentionality analysis' that many contemporary philosophers regarded as a new direction in philosophy, and one that could only be conjugated in the first person singular, present tense. In this sense, he can be seen as part of a movement in contemporary thought that parallels the 'thinking' presented in Chapter Three of this book. These philosophical movements are essentially destructive of philosophy itself, and they deny that 'thinking' happens 'between the ears' or that 'analytical thought' is necessarily 'a mark of high human development'. On the contrary, as Senghor says in an essay on 'Negritude and Marxism', which echoes much of what has been said earlier in these pages:

> It will be remembered that the First World War had, in the view of the most lucid minds in Europe, marked some degree of bankruptcy of civilisation, through its absurdity, as well as the spiritual and material ruins in its wake. How has

this been possible, they asked themselves, when recovering their wits; is this our Reason, our Science, our Christian Morality? And then philosophers, writers, artists, and even scholars once more brought the old charges against them, those already listed at the end of the 'stupid nineteenth century'. But this time they went right down to the roots of things. Their criticism became radical and extolled the rehabilitation of intuitive reason and the collective soul, of archetypal images rising from the abysmal depths of the heart, from the dark regions of the groin and the womb, in a word, the rehabilitation of primordial rhythms in accord with the very pulsations of the cosmos.[10]

This is not saying that Negritude spells a difference between Africans and other human beings. It is saying that Europeans, who had forgotten these depths, were forced in the early part of this century to rediscover what the Africans had never lost: 'primordial rhythm in accord with the very pulsation of the cosmos'. This is surely a far cry from any sanctioning of Soyinka's syllogism. Senghor is recording the major defeat and repudiation of analytical thought and especially 'scientific inventiveness', which Soyinka equates with the subject of the major premise of his syllogism.

When Senghor goes to America and says of New York: 'At first I was confused by your beauty … So shy at first before your blue metallic eyes, your frosted smile', he is acknowledging the superficial beauty and attraction of 'high human development' in terms of sky-scrapers, bridges and all the accoutrements of 'scientific inventiveness', but by the last verse of his poem he is rejecting these:

New York. I say to you: New York let black blood flow into your heart
That it may rub the rust from your steel joints, like an oil of life,
That it may give to your bridges the bend of buttocks and the suppleness of creepers.
Now return the most ancient times, the unity recovered, the

reconciliation of the Lion, the Bull and the Tree
Thought linked to act, ear to heart, sign to sense,
There are your rivers murmuring with scented crocodiles
and mirage-eyed manatees.
And no need to invent the sirens.[11]

This is not an invitation to a symbiotic human culture – the black
leaven in the white metallic loaf, as Soyinka suggests. This is declaration of a purer, more human, more ancient way of being. It
is a way of being which Senghor himself embodies. His embodiment of it is essentially linked to his being as an African. This
being involves hereditary components without thereby being
racist; it is moulded by geographical environment and climatic
conditions; it is endowed with access to the collective unconscious, to 'the ancestors', the spirits, the gods. It is this way of
being that constitutes Negritude as a philosophy, and not the
other way round. It explains why Africans retained what
Europeans lost.

At just the moment when European philosophers and artists
were acknowledging their bankruptcy, their 'forgetfulness of
being' and the flight of the gods from their temples, others – outside the influence of the all-pervading totalitarianism of 'analytical thought' – had preserved real contact with Being. This is
what, as I understand it, Senghor claims for himself. He acknowledges that this vision derives from his being African. He pre-
sumes that, as such, it is available to those who share this kind of
being-in-the world, no more, no less.

It seems to me that to dismiss this possibility because of
someone else's version of it, is to cut ourselves off from a potentially valuable source. Prescinding from all slogans and smears,
it is worth our while examining what Senghor himself has to
say, especially in his later and more developed articulation of
his 'philosophy'.

According to at least one commentator: 'Senghor successfully
transformed Negritude from a series of public gestures to a lonely
confrontation with the self.'[12] This would change completely the
context and the location of our critique. It is also indisputable

that Senghor's thought changed and developed during his life-time:

> I have to admit that our pride was quickly transformed into racism. Even Nazism was acceptable to us as it bolstered our refusal to cooperate ... At that time we had the sincerity of youth and of passion. Everything that had anything to do with white Europe was insipid to us ... The triumph of Nazism and the Second World War were to bring us to our senses. We finally understood that racism was hatred and violence and war ... And then, we also had become conscious of the fact that racial purity was a myth.[13]

In the form which he later expressed and endorsed, Negritude is connected to being black simply because the physiology of those who are born in the tropics is more directly absorptive of reality. Warmth and humidity produce a heat-and-sweat physiology and a radiation physics that impinge upon the nervous system and intensify sensibility. These are ecological effects. They apply to any warm-blooded creature living constantly in such conditions. One of these effects on the human organism is a more immediate contact between sensation and stimulus, between the person and 'the things themselves'. These are the geographical and physiological facts. Also the notion of rhythm is pivotal. The physiology derived from the barometrical pressures of equatorial zones allows for smoother insertion into the circumambient world. This is what Senghor calls an 'organic sense of rhythm'. Rhythm is the 'architecture of being ... the system of waves which it sends out towards others'. It is in this context that he describes himself as living the other by dancing the other. Dancing does not mean mindless gyration. It is communication through a wavelength more immediate and intimate than concept or discourse. All of which amounts to his famous formula: 'Classical European reason is analytical and makes use of the object. African reason is intuitive and participates in the object.' Participation here implies an abridgement of the gap between knower and known, a foreshortening of abstractionist protocol, a compression or telescoping of the epistemological apparatus.

Far from confirming the hegemony of analytical reason, this dismantles the whole scaffolding of consciousness and advocates direct access to reality, immediate artistic awareness.

Artistic expression is the privileged medium of such participation. Rhythm expresses itself through 'lines, surfaces, colours, volumes in architecture, sculpture and painting; accents in poetry and music, movement in dance'. Understanding of Being, as described by Senghor, is less an act of the person than an event that happens in and through the person – a mystical participation. This last phrase could, of course, be vague romanticism, hazy gouache glorifying sentimental gush. Many critics imply as much when they suggest that 'even in his theorising Senghor remains the poet'.[14] Sartre reinforces the suspicion when he comments that 'Negritude ... finds expression only in poetry' because it is no more than a moment in the dialectic of history, 'a tension between the nostalgic past' and a future that has not yet been realised. In other words, Senghor's poetry is the expression of a reality not yet accomplished or achieved. The final dismissal comes with the accusation that Senghor's is actually European poetry in disguise: 'French verse interlarded with African allusions.'[15]

These arguments fall short of the point at issue and prevent us from encountering the works that make this point. Senghor is essentially a poet. Far from making him less capable of articulating his vision, this gift makes him, in the view of poetry presented in this book, more capable of doing so. Not that the expression has to be clearer on this account, but it will be nearer to the reality it seeks to enunciate. His being as poet also implies that his own translations of this vision into prose, into discursive language, are secondary discourse and not the definitive word. When he says in, perhaps, his most extended analysis in prose, *Les Fondements de l'Africanité*, that his response to reality (and he is identifying himself with the 'psycho-physical constitution' of the African) is a specific intentionality – a 'spirituality rooted in his sensuous nature' so that he penetrates through sensuous perception to its very essence – he is echoing similar expressions of that 'epiphany' of Being recorded by many artists and philosophers of this century, and his testimony should be examined in depth and in detail.

One of the most idiosyncratic and important aspects of Senghor's vision is his understanding of a collective consciousness shared by Africans and the extension of this to the realm of the ancestors. It is as if, for him, subjectivity is not autonomous, self-contained, hermetically sealed identity, but rather a filter placed within a field of forces extending into dimensions of space, time and consciousness, which transcend most categories of Western philosophy:

> Listen to the voice of the Ancestors of Elissa. Like us exiled
> They did not wish to die, to lose their seminal flow in dust.
> Let me listen too in the smoky hut for the phantom visit of
> propitious souls
> My head glistens on your breast like a kuskus ball smoking
> out of the fire
> Let me breathe the smell of our Dead Ones, let me recall and
> repeat their living accents, let me learn
> To live before I go down, deeper than the diver, into the deep
> darkness of sleep.[16]

Dance is one of the ways to open out this unconscious area. It is also the way to dwell on this earth, in the place of the here and now, in contact with that part of oneself which can provide access to the world of the Spirit. In so doing it gives access to the deepest dimensions of the self. This opening is also available to all that is beyond the immediate confines of everyday consciousness. It can allow the ancestors, the spirit of others, the Spirit of God, to have access to the space created by the dancer of this metaphysical kind. This is true in many religious and cultural traditions all around the world. Within the Christian tradition, the Shakers believed that dance was connected with the Holy Spirit; that dancing was self-emptying exultation that imbues one with the elation of worship.

Such dance can be used, of course, as a magic to seduce God into appearing – a kind of manipulation, or pedipulation. In the case of the Sufi whirling dervishes, it induced a trance through physical exertion. It can become a kind of spirit 'possession', as has been reported in the Bori spiritualist cult in Nigeria.

Dance can be used to dehumanise – to induce a trance-like state allowing us to abdicate control of ourselves. But dance of its very nature is not such. It is a sign of the spirituality of matter and shows the spiritual potential of human nature precisely as body. It can be a way of moving beyond our normal conscious-ness, of extending that awareness, without thereby losing our identity. Wole Soyinka explains that when the great dancers of his tribe are making way for the gods, they are not being invaded by totalitarian powers, or abdicating the role of their conscious minds. It is not a question of withdrawing from conscious reality; on the contrary: 'consciousness is stretched to embrace another and primal reality'. We are dealing with a very subtle distinc-tion here: 'Within the mystic summons ... the protagonist ... re-sists ... the final step towards complete annihilation ... He ... emerges ... as the mediant voice of the god, but stands now as it were beside himself, observant, understanding, creating.'[17] It is a way of being at the edge of consciousness. One French philoso-pher suggests that 'to dance one's life is to place oneself at the heart of things, at the point of bursting forth of the future which is in process of being born and to participate in its discovery'.[18]

Wole Soyinka himself is an artist whose work is at the meet-ing point where we deal with a world that is other than our-selves. In some ways his archaeology of the deep structures of our lives might be compared with that of W. B. Yeats, even though he himself has characterised the 'vision' of the latter as 'dotty excursions into a private nevernever land'. I compare them insofar as they both use the theatre to articulate the deep structures and they both draw upon a native culture to provide the mythological backdrop to the metaphysics they unearth. The Celtic and Yoruba cultures from which they draw inspiration have at least one belief in common: there is an in-between world, where the dead who have gone before us dwell. It is not so much an Otherworld as an undercarriage to this one. Ant-hills in

Nigeria and fairy forts in Ireland are like openings into this space of the dead, the ancestors. Just as the later plays of Yeats are attempts to make present the spatio-temporal structure of this invisible world that is contiguous to our own, so several of Soyinka's plays are metaphysical liturgies based upon traditional Yoruba rites and ceremonies. Many purists in both traditions would deplore this translation of an essentially religious act into what they would consider to be the degrading and trivialising medium of commercial theatre, regarded as mere entertainment. Neither of these playwrights would view their own art in this light. Theatre for them is a privileged space that allows room to dimensions and structures of human existence otherwise buried in the everyday.

Most of Soyinka's plays are presentations of historical events or recognisable human situations, which act as sacramental carriers of another space and another reality. The stage itself is usually carved into architecturally distinct areas, at least one of which is the preserve of that in-between world which is always there in every situation but which needs the instrument that heightens perception at every level in order to make it available to sensibilities untutored to the detection of its presence. There is a symbolic quality to everything in the Soyinka play. It is as though each character, situation, event, stage property, were the tip of another reality, which we only see from the surface, and are inclined to read as a coherent, contiguous pattern, whereas the full significance of the configuration can only be gleaned by holographic penetration to the in-depth dimension that each one assumes in its relationship to a hidden centre, rather than in its superficial narrative connection with the other pieces in the play.

So, the author's note to his supposedly 'historical' drama *Death and the King's Horseman*, which is based on events that took place in Nigeria in 1946, warns:

The Colonial Factor is an incident, a catalytic incident merely. The confrontation in the play is largely metaphysical, contained in the human vehicle which is Elesin and the universe of the Yoruba mind, the world of the living, the dead and the unborn, and the numinous passage which links all: transition.

Death and the King's Horseman can be fully realised only through an evocation of music from the abyss of transition. Music is the element best able to incarnate the hidden mystery that the play is there to evoke. Soyinka's plays are passages which attempt to make visible the line or band that connects this world that we inhabit with the one inhabited by the dead and the unborn.

In *Dance of the Forests*, the play first performed as part of the Nigerian Independence Celebrations in October 1960, and *The Swamp Dwellers*, both the forest and the swamp on the stage represent that 'other' world, out of which can come those who are capable of making the 'transition' to our world. In *The Swamp Dwellers*, 'the scene is a hut on stilts, built on one of the semi-firm islands', which is a mirror-image of the world we inhabit, if we could only be sensitised to the fact that we are not living on the ground floor with nothing under us except *terra firma*.

In his 1965 play *The Road*, 'this symbolic feature is the numinous passage, the narrow ridge, the no-man's land between the land of the living and the abode of the dead'. This play is an enactment of the actual transition ('Agemo is simply a religious cult of flesh dissolution') from one dimension to the other. As music is the idiom of *Death and the King's Horseman*, so dance is the essential dramatic function in this representation of *The Road*: 'The dance is the movement of transition … Agemo, the mere phase, includes the passage of transition from the human to the divine essence.'

Theatre, for Soyinka, is the X-ray machine that allows us to observe the bone structure of the universe. Every item on the stage makes up, at one level, a two-dimensional map on plane surface, which, when loosened out and untangled by the artistic rhythms of music and dance, reveal their potential as markers on a deeper-laid topographical contour map. This is even more pertinent in the performance and the creation of some of the characters in each play, who are spokespersons or incarnations of the deeper world of the abyss. In *Death and the King's Horseman*, Elesin is the human vehicle who embodies 'the world of the living, the dead and the unborn'. So, too, in *The Road*, the mute Murano, who cannot speak in the idiom or the words of the workaday world, is a dramatic embodiment of that hypostatic union between the two worlds that occurs in the person of the artist. Dumb in the context of this world, Murano also limps. He is a lost soul whose real homeland is elsewhere. He is aware of the essence of death, which the Professor is groping to understand, but he cannot communicate it. However, the play is set in the Yoruba masque idiom, which involves a certain kind of possession on the part of those singled out to represent the other world:

> It is believed that the spirit of the deceased may be evoked to enter into the masquerader during the dance. At the height of the dance every true *egungen* will enter into a state of possession when he will speak with a new voice.[19]

In the play itself, the Professor, who is seeking to understand these realities from our side of the transitional line, gives the following exegesis of the role of Murano in the play, which is the role of the artist in our world.[20] Asked where he found Murano, he says that he found him 'neglected in the back of a hearse and dying'. He nursed him back to life and 'set him to tap palm wine' (which is another metaphor for the way in which artists connect with their truth):

> Deep. Silent but deep. Oh my friend, beware the pity of those that have no tongue for they have been proclaimed sole guardians of the Word. They have slept beyond the portals of secrets. They have pierced the guard of eternity and unearthed the Word, a golden nugget on the tongue. And so their tongue hangs heavy and they are forever silenced … When a man has one leg in each world, his legs are never the same. The big toe of Murano's foot – the left one of course – rests on the slumbering chrysalis of the Word. When that crust cracks my friends – you and I, that is the moment we await. That is the moment of our rehabilitation.

The meaning of life and the rehabilitation of society will take place through the word enunciated by the artist, who is the birthplace of the saving word. Such people must belong to the *Strong Breed*. In his play of this name, Soyinka describes a family whose task is to carry the evils of the village to the river in ritualised ceremony once every year. The old man describes to his son the kind of people who are capable of performing this task:

> Other men would rot and die doing this task year after year. It is strong medicine which only we can take. Our blood is strong like no other. Anything you do in life must be less than this, son … Your own blood will betray you, son, because you cannot hold it back. If you make it do less than this, it will rush to your head and burst it open. I say what I know my son.

The image of blood here does not imply mere heredity, which could invoke racist overtones. The artist is a kind of person who belongs to no family or tribe. Like the estranged characters who haunt most of Soyinka's plays, the artist has a displaced quality, which prevents citizenship of a purely human kind. The kind of being which the artist is, in the understanding of Soyinka, can be glimpsed through the *abiku*, a feature of African life and culture which has haunted him from his earliest youth. This term describes a child who is born to die, who belongs to the other world and who slips in and out of this one with almost heartless regularity, destined to be reborn several times.

A culture which experiences a large infant mortality rate and which believes in reincarnation would almost naturally put these two elements together and imagine that families can be afflicted with something in the nature of a hoax child, one who only comes to wring your heart and then disappears back into the world which is its indigenous environment. Several different cultures describe this same reality by different names. At least two Nigerian poets, Soyinka and J. P. Clark, have written poems on the abiku, which are often juxtaposed in anthologies and poetry textbooks. Whereas Clark takes the more conventional and understandable attitude in his poem, bemoaning the inhuman carelessness of the wandering child and sympathising deeply with the suffering mother, Soyinka takes the part of the abiku and defends its way of being as a necessary and legitimate alternative. Such children have to be and have to be allowed to be. He identifies with such a child. 'I am Abiku, calling for the first/And the repeated time.'[21]

In his autobiographical account of childhood, *Ake: The Years of Childhood*, Soyinka gives much consideration to this phenomenon. One of his playmates was known to be an abiku. 'Amulets, bangles, tiny rattles and dark copper-twist rings earthed her through ankles, fingers, wrists and waist. She knew she was abiku. The two tiny cicatrices on her face were also part of the many counters to enticements by her companions in the other world. Like all abiku she was privileged, apart. Her parents dared not scold her for long or earnestly ... Looking at her, I wondered how Mrs B. coped with such a supernatural being who died, was re-born, died again and kept on going and coming as often as she pleased. As we walked, the bells on her anklets jingled, driving off her companions from the other world who pestered her incessantly, pleading that she should rejoin them ... She was so rare, this privileged being who, unlike Tinu and me, and even her companions in that other place, could pass easily from one sphere to another ... It made me uneasy. Mrs B. was too kind a woman to be plagued with such an awkward child. Yet we knew she was not being cruel; an abiku was that way, they could not help their nature. I thought of all the things Bukola could ask for, things which would be beyond the power of her parents to grant.'[22] It is clear from the rest of this account that the Soyinkas were 'plagued with such an awkward child'.

An artist in the family is a difficult number. Most of the poignant tension and humour in the book are conflicts arising from the claims of artistic originality and individuality and the demands of family life and community insertion. Incidents throughout suggest that Soyinka himself always felt incursions into his life from another world and seems to have been haunted by the possibility that he himself was abiku. In an essay in *Before*

Our Very Eyes, the tribute to Wole Soyinka on his winning the
Nobel Prize for literature in 1986, his friend Olumuyiwa Awe
has this to say:

> Wole has been preoccupied with the mystery of the abiku for
> a long time now … The Yoruba have a saying that a person
> ceases to be an abiku only after he/she has survived his/her
> parents. In that sense, Wole could no longer be regarded as
> an abiku after April 1983 when his mother, Eniola Soyinka
> died. His father, S. A. Soyinka, had died earlier in January
> 1973 … Having now successfully crossed the line which sep-
> arates the abiku from the rest of us, here is wishing him many
> more fruitful years in the fields of literature and drama
> where he has earned recognition, worldwide.[23]

Whereas I would agree that the actual possibility of being an
abiku may have been dispelled by the events here described, I
still do not accept that Soyinka has 'crossed the line which separates the abiku from the rest of us'. That is the line which the
artist is called to straddle. Its existence and the fact that some of
the Strong Breed are called to the privilege of resting there, 'on
the slumbering chrysalis of the Word', will always separate
Soyinka and other great artists from the rest of humanity. In
other words, the physical reality of the abiku becomes a symbol
of the state of the artist. Like the actor in ritual drama, the artist
'becomes the unresisting mouthpiece of the gods, uttering
sounds which he barely comprehends, but which are reflections
of that transitional gulf, the seething cauldron of the dark
world'. This last quotation comes from the first essay in *Myth,
Literature and the African World*, Soyinka's major attempt to articulate his metaphysics in prose.

Commonly recognised in most African metaphysics are the
three worlds we have already discussed – the worlds of the ancestors, the living and the unborn. Less understood or explored
is the fourth space, the dark continuum of transition where the
inter-transmutation of essence-ideal and materiality occurs. It
houses the ultimate expression of cosmic will. In one of his earliest essays, included as an appendix in the work just quoted,

Soyinka makes his most comprehensive attempt to describe what he calls 'The Fourth Stage'. There is a great abyss or gulf between the world of the gods, the world of the living, the world of the dead and the world of the unborn. Bridging and lessening this gap is the work of salvation for the socio-political world of the living. The artist is the one who must plunge into that transitional space. 'This is the fourth stage, the vortex of archetypes and the home of the tragic spirit.' The past belongs to the ancestors, the present to the living, and the future to the unborn. The deities stand in the same situation to the living as do the ancestors and the unborn, obeying the same laws, suffering the same agonies and uncertainties, employing the same masonic intelligence of rituals for the perilous plunge into the fourth area of experience, the immeasurable gulf of transition. Its dialogue is liturgy, its music takes form from humankind's uncomprehending immersion in this area of existence, buried wholly from rational cognition. The source of the possessed lyricist, chanting hitherto unknown mythopoeic strains – this source is residual in the numinous area of transition.

Three things should be noted about Soyinka's fourth stage: 1) He is quite aware of similar proposals in Western European philosophy, starting with Nietzsche. He sees the truth of Nietzsche's analysis and repudiates the racist implications: 'Ironically, it is the depth-illumination of Nietzsche's intuition into basic universal impulses which negates his race exclusivist conclusions on the nature of art and tragedy.' 2) He does not have any of the neurotic hang-ups that afflict Europeans in the presence of such ideas because of their similarity with those that preceded and gave birth to National Socialism and the rise of Hitlerism in Germany. 3) He is not proposing an invasion and abdication of the conscious mind:

> To think, because of this, that the Yoruba mind reaches intuitively towards absorption in godlike essence is to misunderstand the principle of religious rites, and to misread, as many have done, the significance of religious possession ...
> The actors... are the communicant chorus, containing within

their collective being the essence of that transitional abyss.
But only as essence, held, contained and mystically expressed.
Within the mystic summons of the chasm the protagonist
actor … resists … the final step towards complete annihilation … He, the actor, emerges still as the mediant voice of the
god, but stands now as it were beside himself, observant, understanding, creating.

Soyinka is suggesting that European commerce with this dimension of religious experience has been perverted, mostly because
those availing themselves of this source, such as Freud and Jung,
were dealing with people who were neurotic:

Jung, begetter of so many racist distortions of the structure of
the human psyche, interchangeably employs ritual archetypes and images of the psychotic … Those who directly and
healthily are in touch with the religious origins of such ritual
archetypes are described as having a 'primitive mentality'.
The psychoanalyst, meanwhile, makes a living from trying to
sort out this imagery which has uprooted itself and slipped
into a hostile and dislocated environment.

The artist is one, therefore, who withdraws into an inner world
from which he returns communicating a new kind of word. This
does not mean that such a communicant 'withdraws from conscious reality, but rather that his consciousness is stretched to
embrace another and primal reality'. The poetry and art that
emerge from this embrace are speech and gesture raised to a
greater level of intensity. Not anyone can be such an artist:

Only one who has himself undergone the experience of dis-
integration, whose spirit has been tested and whose psychic
resources laid under stress by the forces most inimical to individual assertion, only he can understand and be the force
of fusion between the two contradictions. The resulting sensibility is also the sensibility of the artist, and he is a profound artist only to the degree to which he comprehends and
expresses this principle of destruction and re-creation.

This last quotation from an early essay reads almost as a prophecy in terms of Soyinka's later experiences. In 1967 he was imprisoned by the Federal Military Government of Nigeria on the grounds that he was supposed to have helped the secessionists during the Biafran war. His experiences in prison have been most graphically and movingly described in his book *The Man Died*, which was published in 1972. In the course of describing all the injustices, cruelties and horrors of prison life, he also describes his own attempt to 'reach that point where nor mind nor body of me can be touched, move beyond the capacity of small minds to soil my being or reach towards it'. He achieved this purpose by a kind of mental asceticism, which led him to reach the deepest structures of his own being and to touch that transcendent line which divides his being from the abyss or void which is the beyond, the world outside his being. He describes it with all the power of his inimitable self-articulation:

> In the beginning there was Void. Nothing. And how does the mind grasp it? As waste? Desolation? Nothing is cheaply within grasp from what was. But as the fundamental nought, the positive, original nil? As the immeasurable drop into pre-thought, pre-existence, pre-essence? But then, the mind that will conceive this must empty inwards from a lifetime's frame of accumulated references, must plunge from the physical platfrom into primordial abyss. Within which, alas, lie the creative energies which 'abhor a vacuum' even more than nature.[24]

The person who reaches the transcendental barrier remains free to relate with whatever is to be found there. The hermit who said 'I need nothing. I seek nothing. I desire nothing', fascinates Soyinka, 'but that hermit', he continues almost wistfully, 'did not speak in void and his words were spoken to a living soul'.

The place of meeting is also the place of creation out of nothing, and so, he surmises, 'creation is admission of great loneliness'. This is as much a statement about God as it is about the artist. It leads to an art that is 'ritual empathy with the gods, the eternal presence, who once preceded him in parallel awareness of their own incompletion'.

Nigeria became independent in the 1960s. Forty years later, Wole Soyinka is fiercely critical of what Nigeria became. If it had allowed the artist to guide its steps from the beginning, its present corruption and alienation from its spiritual roots might not have been so obviously debilitating.

One of the earliest attempts to express this mysticism and metaphysics is *The Interpreters*, Soyinka's first novel. A first attempt in a new artistic medium can induce a recklessness and originality that make more visible the source and the musculature of the inspiration. As compared with the play, a novel can also be more comprehensively explicit and provide more discursive intelligibility.

The surface plot is set in Nigeria in the 1960s, where a newly independent country is trying to establish for itself a 'social scene'. Five main characters are examining this attempt critically, and are trying, at the same time, to forge or maintain links with another, more ancient ambience – a 'spiritual' world, which risks obliteration in the newly constructed one that society at large is obsequiously entertaining. The five characters also act as a filtering pentagon, a prism through which the banished world can shed its rays. Their contact with this other dimension unsettles them and heightens the critical faculties with which they 'interpret' the society around them. They act as go-betweens, interpreters for another world, to which most of their contemporaries, of a professional class in an urban society, in which most of the novel situates itself, would be oblivious.

The novel divides into two parts. In each there is a narrative thread that unfolds the story and connects the two. However, the more powerful energy of the work is conveyed through imagery and character study. It is as though the five characters are fingers of a hand reaching further than the world of the story and exploring areas of human feeling and awareness beyond the recognisable plot. The novelist, through a kaleidoscope of connecting imagery, loosens the sides of the world we are in and gives access to a wider, more ominous and encircling world beyond.

In the first part, the perspective would seem to be within the world we recognise and inhabit. Our view of this 'normal' world is jaundiced by the disruptive behaviour and critical conscious-ness of the five main characters who become our guides. Every now and then they provide glimpses of another dimension, which captures their attention and dismantles concentration on the ordinary everyday world.

The second part describes the same scene, but as if from a frontal viewpoint, 'outwards from the black edges of the move-able proscenium'. These are the words used by Soyinka himself to describe the last scene in the novel. They speak in the idiom of the playwright. Extending them further, we might say that in the first part of the novel, we are on stage with the characters, some of whom are acting out a visible and plausible drama, while others, especially the five protagonists, are reaching up-wards, backwards and outwards from that illuminated cube which is the world of the stage, towards the darkness of the real-ity surrounding it.

In the second part, the reader is placed in an auditorium, with a lateral view of a cross-section of both these worlds, be-cause from the new vantage point 'some bones on that stage were bared, sandbags and transverses, collapsible platforms bil-lowing black drapes on the two sides'. The reader is allowed to glimpse the surrounding 'aura' of the other world, not just as a dark vacuum beyond the ordinary, but as an imaginable contin-uation of the quotidian with which it is constantly engaged in some kind of heteronomous interpretation.

In part one, the eponymous interpreters hint at the other real-ity, and we infer its existence through various excesses in 'nor-mal' behaviour that evoke the possibility of a world beyond. The social world that the characters inhabit has the glamour and superficiality of an over-lit cocktail party, thrown unwittingly on the side of a volcano from which it is 'separated only by the thigh-high bamboo wall giving the so-called "party privacy"'. Meanwhile, through the leaking sides and roof, rain and night-time pour.

Each of the five protagonists has some privileged access to this world outside. Sekoni, the scientist-cum-engineer, is, perhaps, nearest to it as a source of energy and power, but he has little capacity to express it, articulate it, or give objective manifestation to it in this world of ours. He has a stutter, a symbolic impediment of speech. His attempts to translate the energy into 'neat geometric patterns', to close his palm 'cradling the surge of power' by constructing at Ijioka a small experimental power station, are dismissed as junk by the expatriate expert: 'a wasteful expenditure, highly dangerous conditions, unsuitable materials, unsafe for operation'. Sekoni is the first to pass from the scene in this world to the other realm when he dies in a car accident at the opening of the second part. He leaves behind a sculpture of a wrestler, which is much admired. It is a portrait of himself wrestling to give expression to his intuition above the stutter, the hic-cups and the cobbles.

Sagoe is a journalist. The natural excess that aligns him with the 'other world' is drink. His drink lobes put him in touch, as he explains whenever he is drunk: 'Everyone is born with them, but you have to find them you see. You get to know them when you become professional. Then it gives a delicate trill and you know you're there. The first time, it is like confirmation … a truly religious moment.' One of the first times we meet him, he is waking up with a hangover in the bedroom of his girl-friend's apartment. The room becomes an image of the world we live in, and access to the other world occurs through the presence within that space of a wardrobe, which fills him with horror: 'The room tightened further and in utter gloom, Sagoe found his gaze would drop to the repellent skin of the wardrobe.' Eventually, the wardrobe opens and an array of people, long since dead, enter the room.

Kola is the artist. His art is the power that gives him access to the other world, but in a way that remains firmly rooted in this one. His art is to find substitutes, facsimiles, impersonations of the gods. The work that he is engaged in throughout the novel – completed in the final chapter – is a painting of the complete pantheon, in which each god is represented through the portrait of one of the characters, whether major or minor, whom we have met in the course of the story. Kola's job is to recognise them as potential incarnations of the god and then to reconstruct each on his canvas in the transfigured approximation of that divinity. Kola 'can record intimations of all these presences', all of which have been too 'momentary', and so 'they come in disjointed fragments'. However, he does succeed in the end in piecing together the fragmented deity.

Egbo's intimacy with and proximity to the 'other' world is achieved through sexual ecstasy. From the first pages of the novel, we are absorbed in his attraction to water, to darkness, to the vortex, which 'he acknowledged finally' was 'a place of death':

> and admitted too that he was drawn to it as a dream of isolation, smelling its archaic menace and the violent undertows, unable to deny its dark vitality.

This mysticism, which makes him 'incessantly drawn to the pattern of the dead', is an eroticism that finds its unquenchable thirst temporarily slaked in sexual ecstasy. But the face of the void, momentarily masked by that of a woman, remains 'the black Immanent' of those 'nymphomaniac depths'. His mother and father were both drowned in the waters of a creek under mangrove arches. He would spend hours of childhood listening at the edge of the water, 'convinced that my parents would rise from the water and speak to me … I expected they would appear wherever the conditions were right … So night after night I went and called to them and placed my ear against the water, on the line of water against the bank.'

Egbo is the nearest to the 'other world'. His ear is tuned to that fine line between the two. He has found a place in the forest where the meeting with the gods can occur at night-time. 'He felt night now as a womb of the gods and a passage for travelers.' The place is, significantly, adjacent to a railway bridge. 'Always, for Egbo, the god expanded through the forest … his colossal feet thrust through the soft underbelly of earth.' It is a place 'untainted by human breath'. This discovery, he tells us, is 'like waking in the morning and feeling in me a great gift, accepting it without seeking to interpret. I come here often to draw upon that gift and be reprieved.'

The character of Lasunwon is not part of this group, except as a hanger-on who provides the viewpoint of one definitively relegated to the domain of 'this world'. When Egbo, at the beginning of the novel, 'looked around the club seeking an object to frizzle and be warmed in turn by energies he had aroused', we are told that 'there was only Lasunwon the politician-lawyer. He dogged their company always, an eternal garbage can for such sporadic splurges, and uncomplaining.' Lasunwon is the 'common man', the neutral and uncomprehending witness from the common-sense world, guardian of the principle of non-contradiction, the law of reason and the interests of commerce. He does not form part of the promethean pentagon.

The fifth character, who acts as a base or rather a hinge in the swinging of this door between two worlds, is Bandele, the recognisable prototype for Sekoni's sculpture of 'the wrestler' with his 'taut sinews, nearly agonising in excess tension, a bunched python caught at the instant of easing out, the balance of strangulation before release, it was all elasticity and strain'. At all times in the novel, he provides the hospitality for the other characters, even the most undesirable and unwelcome. He also provides the intentionality of the plot. 'It was like Bandele to insist although motiveless.' He is described as 'a timeless image brooding over lesser beings', and at the end of the novel he places himself apart from the others 'old and immutable as the royal mothers of Benin throne'. He seems to represent the original godhead before fragmentation, and typifies the description of Obatala given elsewhere by Soyinka:

> We now turn to Obatala, a gentler sector of the arc of the human psyche (to keep within that cyclic image of Yoruba existential concepts). Within his crescent is stored those virtues of social and individual accommodation: patience, suffering, peaceableness, all the imperatives of harmony in

the universe, the essence of quietude and forbearance; in short, the aesthetics of the saint.[25]

Although he welcomes all and accepts everything that happens, he is removed and distant, holding everything in place, and yet refusing to influence in any way. In his role as 'hinge' to the doorway between two worlds, 'Bandele fitted himself, wall-gecko, into a corner'. When, towards the end of the novel, Egbo turns angrily on Bandele and asks him: 'What are you getting out of it?', the latter replies, taking up the title of the novel itself: 'knowledge of the new generation of interpreters'. It is as if the gods, too, are waiting to see what combination of complexity is going to establish itself in the relationships between the two worlds struggling to achieve some equanimity in interpenetration.

In the beginning was the resurrection. The second part opens with the sacrifice of the sky bull and ends with the sacrifice of the black ram. Sekoni is killed by the sky bull, and from the black ram 'a thin streak of blood marked Bandele across the shirt' … and 'even Bandele smiled, remembering that this, after all, was also for Sekoni'. Ressurrection means sacrifice, sacrilege and apostasy, in order to achieve a hitherto unheard-of modality of being.

From beginning to end of this second part, we are bombarded by imagery of light and darkness. We travel through every shade in the spectrum from black to white and back again. This imagery underpins the mythic copulation taking place between two essentially different natures and spheres. The colour spectrum is paralleled by the gamut of sexual differentiation. It is as though the openings through which interpenetration can occur are the spaces between these differing shades. Minor characters from the first part become major symbolic figures in the second: the albino girl Usaye 'appeared to him a near divine intervention, colour and features achieving his perfect image'. Like the imagery of swamps, 'bridges of squelching planks' and 'sluggish semi-canals of lagoon seepage', which describe the porous landscape giving access to the inhabitants of 'the underbowels of earth', so, too, the albino represents that element in the human make-up which allows access to the unnatural gods, like 'a new laid egg when the shell is not full hard … or the pulsing soft centre of a baby's head'.

This play of imagery between black and white, light and darkness, heaven and the underworld, carries the burden of movement that characterises the novel's attempt to capture that interpenetration of worlds, which is resurrection, a combination of movement up and movement down by trapeze artists ready to break each other's fall.

In the second part of the novel, as in the pantheon of Kola, Egbo fuses with the god, Ogun, that 'reluctant leader of men and deities':

He is 'lord of the road' … representing the knowledge-seeking instinct, an attribute which sets him apart as the only deity who 'sought the way', and harnessed the resources of science to hack a passage through primordial chaos for the gods' reunion with man. The journey and its direction are at the heart of Ogun's being and the relationship of the gods and man.

The novel is essentially about the possibility of such relationship in Nigeria after the 1960s. It carries us to the brink of a new possibility. This new Nigerian society could be as false and as 'colonised' by imitation European culture as the plastic decorations in the Faseyi drawing-room. However, if some of the new generation are prepared to open themselves to the possibility of relationship with the gods, and it must be remembered that in the 'geocentric bias of the Yoruba' it was 'the gods who needed to come to man, anguished by a continuing sense of incompleteness, needing to recover their long-lost sense of totality', then a completely other kind of society can emerge. Such a society must begin with resurrection – a free rising up in partnership of independent beings.

From the point of view of the gods, 'Ogun it was who led them, his was the first rite of passage through the chthonic realm.' But in this novel, his partner, also representative of the new society emerging in Nigeria, is 'the new woman of my generation, proud of the gift of mind and guarding her person from violation'. She was the first and the only one with whom Egbo/Ogun had intercourse, in an act of sacrilegious apostasy on 'a burial-ground of gods'. When he hears that she is pregnant, he makes a decision, an act of will, which is like 'a choice of a man drowning ... only like a choice of drowning'. He must commit himself.

In a lecture that Soyinka gave in Ibadan in 1991, the first in a series on religion, which he entitled 'The Credo of Being and Nothingness', he began with a description of mysticism of the void and ended with the following precept, formulated by him ten years earlier as one of the seven he had distilled from the wisdom of the Yoruba:

The will of man is placed beyond surrender. Without the knowing of Divinity by man, can Deity survive? O hesitant one, man's conceiving is fathomless; his community will rise beyond the present reaches of the mind. Orisa reveals Destiny as Self-destination.

CHAPTER SIX

James Joyce: Priest and Prophet

'At the very least, James Joyce was an amateur student of the philosophers', Denis Donoghue tells us, but 'his work shows little of that love of wisdom which constitutes the philosophic habit.'[1] This division between 'amateur' and 'professional' thinker, between the 'love of wisdom', which 'constitutes the philosophic habit', and the 'work' of James Joyce, is an anachronistic prejudice which Joyce's 'work' has helped to dispel.

If Joyce is to be examined as a 'thinker', it must be on his own terms. There is no question of Joyce being in any way deferential towards or daunted by the philosophic habit. There doesn't seem to be any area of human endeavour which he felt himself incapable of understanding. Stephen Dedalus, when asked whether he wanted to be famous enough to become part of Ireland's history, replied that Ireland would be famous because she was part of his. Joyce himself might have made a similar reply to the question about his place in the history of philosophy.

There is a popular view that Joyce hated the Jesuits and that he had a particularly rough time at their hands. In fact, both he and his father always had the highest opinion of the Jesuits. They were both snobs and they thought of the Jesuits as 'the Gentlemen of Catholic Education'. To quote James Joyce directly: 'I don't think you will easily find anyone to equal them'.[2] When, in June 1891, John Joyce was forced, by straitened circumstances, to withdraw his son from Clongowes, he sent him to the Christian Brothers school in North Richmond Street. Not only is this fact not mentioned in *A Portrait of the Artist as a Young Man*, it was a source of shame to that artist and one that he took certain pains to obliterate from his biography. The Christian Brothers were, in his father's phrase, 'Paddy Stink and Mickey Mud', and, however unflattering a picture emerges from Joyce's description of his sojourn in Clongowes, it is at least regarded as worthy of mention. In 1895, after James had won two exhibitions in the Intermediate examination, the Joyces were approached by the Dominicans, who offered James free board and tuition at their school. By this time James had been reassigned to the Jesuits in Belvedere College, thanks to a happy meeting between John Joyce and the former rector of Clongowes, Fr Conmee, who had been appointed rector of Belvedere and who was anxious to help out his former student, fallen on hard times. When the offer came from the Dominicans, John Joyce left the decision to his son. James declared without hesitation, 'I began with the Jesuits and I want to end with them' (Ellmann, 47).

Harriet Shaw Weaver wrote to Joyce about the Nausicaa episode of Ulysses, saying: 'You are very good for the soul, I think, medicinal, you are so unflattering to our human nature: So, though you are neither priest nor doctor of medicine, I think you have something of both – the Reverend James Joyce, S.J., M.D' (Ellmann, 475). And Joyce himself once corrected Frank Budgen by remarking, 'You allude to me as a Catholic. Now for the sake of precision and to get the correct contour on me, you ought to allude to me as a Jesuit' (Ellmann, 27).

I reproduce these anecdotes to emphasise the influence that the Jesuits had on the mind of James Joyce, not just as educators but as archetypes. As educators they taught him, in his own words, 'to arrange things in such a way that they become easy to survey and to judge' (Ellmann, 27); as archetypes they provided the framework within which the portrait of the artist was eventually to emerge. It seems quite likely that Joyce could have been persuaded to become a Jesuit, but for one essential element in his personality which precluded this possibility. Quite early in the career of Stephen Dedalus, as unfolded in *A Portrait*, we are given several indications about his sense of vocation. It is quite clear that the director of Belvedere College questioned him very seriously on this score, and the whole movement of *A Portrait* carries the soul of Stephen Dedalus along 'two paths, the path of the priest he might have been and the path of the artist he is to become.'[3] Boys of his intelligence and sensitivity were often coaxed into the Order. One early commentator says 'it is in fact rather in the direction of intellectual curiosity than of single piety that he is different from other boys, but it is precisely out of such material that priests are made – and heretics' (Golding, 55).

The one element in his personality that prevented this possible outcome was his unusually precocious sexuality. For a boy of sixteen in a Dublin day school, he seems to have had considerable sexual experience. His sexuality formed the warring partner in the struggle towards his ultimate destiny. He realised that the call to the priesthood meant the complete eradication of this vital aspect of himself. He saw the Catholic Church as a call to a certain kind of perfection, which demanded emasculation and evisceration.

A Portrait of the Artist as a Young Man describes the bitter and lonely struggle between these two warring elements in an almost unbearably sensitive youth. The famous sermon on hell was the final blow to the possible vocation to the priesthood. 'Before the rector had delivered himself of his last word, the developing priest was slain in Stephen Dedalus; the developing artist, like a waiting animal, stared watchfully and did not move' (Golding, 56).

Joyce decided to remain true to his own nature and to reject the way of life proposed to him and endorsed by all who surrounded him. This involved him in the three famous rejections of family, faith and nation. Around the age of twenty-one, his mind began to 'feel its way towards some comprehension of the actual nature and dimensions of the work imposed upon him by his own nature and qualities' (Golding, 35).

From the beginning, Joyce thought of himself as a poet. His first artistic attempts were poems, which he later published in two volumes: *Chamber Music* and *Pomes Penyeach*.[4] It is also clear from a reading of these works that he was a mediocre poet and that some of his poems are weak and syrupy, others no more than doggerel. However, as Louis Golding perceptively pointed out as far back as 1933, these poems still hold the key to Joyce the artist. As his first attempts to undertake his work as an artist, they incarnate the purest and deepest of his longings in this regard. In his life as an artist, Joyce tried every form of artistic literary expression, and if he ended up by having to invent his own, this was because he realised that he could never be an adequate poet and yet he could not renounce his aspirations towards a creativity that would incorporate his essentially lyrical impulse. It is Golding's contention that the intensely fearsome struggle that Joyce underwent as a boy in a Jesuit boarding school not only burnt out of him any aspiration towards a priestly vocation but also cauterised any possibility of his becoming a poet. In this regard it is interesting to note how many of the poets of Ireland were educated and brought up in a Protestant atmosphere. The ethos of Catholicism in Ireland at this time was bullying and insensitive. It is the perspicacious and irrepressible Buck Mulligan who explains this secret to us in one of his more serious descriptions of Stephen in *Ulysses*:

> They drove his wits astray, he said, by visions of hell. He will never capture the Attic note. The note of Swinburne, of all poets, the white death and the ruddy birth. That is his tragedy. He can never be a poet. The joy of creation ...[5]

By the end of *A Portrait* it is clear that Stephen's education has made him a rebel:

> I will tell you what I will do and what I will not do. I will not serve that in which I no longer believe, whether it call itself my home, my fatherland or my church: and I will try to express myself in some mode of life or act as freely as I can and as wholly as I can, using for my defence the only arms I allow myself to use, silence, exile and cunning.

Lieutenant-Colonel P. R. Butler, an exact contemporary of Joyce in Clongowes, recalls that

> each pupil had to make a recitation chosen for its real or fancied

appositeness to his own character. Butler's piece was "The Charge of the Light Brigade" while Joyce's was "Little Jim", which begins,

> The cottage was a thatched one
> its outside old and mean,
> but everything within that cot
> was wondrous neat and clean.

and ends with the prayer of the dying Jim's parents,

> in heaven once more to meet
> their own poor little Jim.

The mawkishness was not lost upon either the scornful listeners or the embarrassed reciter' (Ellmann, 31).

This 'little Jim', who was shattered and paralysed by the grim world in which he found himself, was the poet that Joyce could never become. Artistic life became the creative attempt to pick up these pieces and give expression to the survivor. His poetry contains the secret of this fundamental aspiration. But this secret never found adequate expression in the medium of poetry for reasons that are sensitively analysed by Louis Golding:

> I say of poetry that it is the exercise of the subconscious mind, because, whatever the source of it, the element of irresponsibility is stronger in poetry than in any other forms of aesthetic composition in words, even though the conscious mind may quite scientifically, throughout the whole process, organise the technique of its expression. That Stephen Dedalus did not give up all hope that he might some day exercise in poetry the subconscious mind is proved by the pathetic retention of the scraps of verse which constitute *Pomes Penyeach*. It is as if he hoped that by muttering them over to himself he might some day suddenly, in the fortunate coincidence of kabbalistic syllables, find that the iron doors opposed to him had drawn apart. (Golding, 20)

The loss of Joyce the poet gave birth to Joyce the artist. He had to consciously set about constructing a way of expressing himself, and this detour forced him to become one of the most important artificers of our century. If he could not be a poet, he could, at least, describe the contours of this paralysis and, in so doing, perhaps release himself from the cocoon. Clive Hart suggests that Joyce's works are all in the nature of self-purgations, and that each of his books is

> the expression of a sensibility haunted by emotional conflicts requiring the most powerful symbolic exorcism. This personal – often uncomfortably personal – art was the only kind Joyce could create or understand ... As soon as the personal experience had been externalised ... the drives and conflicts temporarily evaporated and interest dissolved ... Whenever the need for artistic purgation arose again, fresh techniques were necessary; the same magic could not be made to work twice. On each occasion a more potent exorcism was called for, involving greater complexity, more difficult labyrinths from which to escape, and, above all, the objectification and rationalisation of more and more personal involvement.[6]

Whatever about Joyce's poetry, his novels are hailed as masterpieces of that art form. Some would claim that Joyce is the greatest novelist of our time and that *Ulysses* is one of the outstanding novels of all time. Be that as it may, it was not really what interested Joyce. He was a novelist by default, and some would say that this period of his artistic career was no more than the necessary therapeutic interval that allowed him to resume his original poetic impulse in his final work, *Finnegans Wake*. To the connoisseurs of the aesthetic form of the novel, this last work is an aberration. It marks eighteen years of senile decay during which the novelist of our time wasted his talent and his time concocting a huge labyrinthine joke in bad taste.[7]

To take such a point of view is to misunderstand this particular artistic project. Joyce was not interested in art for art's sake. Art, for him, was the indispensable medium through which he could give expression to himself. The fact that he was an incomparable master of the technique of the novelist did not allow him to bask in the glory of such virtuosity.

Joyce's work must be seen as a whole. It is a life of search for the word: not the word of incarnation which would allow his word to be made flesh in the most satisfying and aesthetically pleasing form, but the word of resurrection – his flesh made word and restored to life. For Joyce, the word was life and the problem which haunted him and which made him change so often his literary forms was how best to become consubstantial with that word. This is the theme of the famous Hamlet discussion in *Ulysses*. It is the theme of creativity, not as causality but as paternity.

In 1949 Louis Gillet, a friend and contemporary of Joyce, suggested that 'the problem of paternity ... is the essential basis of the Joyce problem, the one that explains in *Ulysses* ... the long meditation of Stephen and Mulligan on the subject of Hamlet. In fact this fragment is the key to the book ... (It can never be sufficiently emphasised to what extent this astonishing play constitutes the real source of Joyce's work ... even, prefigured by the scenes of humour and lunacy, the monumental madness of *Finnegans Wake*)'.[8]

Paternity, for Joyce, means not only the relationship between father and son but also the relationship between the artist and his work. Such a relationship finds its aesthetic paradigm in Shakespeare's *Hamlet* and its supreme analogy in the word of an all-powerful creator. Joyce's own creativity had no less an analogy in view. His only rival in the field was Shakespeare, his only possible superior, if he existed at all, was the God of creation. These were the lions he was proud to hunt.

Joyce's aesthetic was far nearer to that of Thomas Aquinas than is generally allowed by most commentators. This is not because the words he uses are borrowed from 'the bulldog of Aquin', but because the context in which he uses them implies a similar preoccupation. The famous definition of beauty in terms of *integritas, claritas* and *consonantia*, which have been removed from their original context and developed into a supposedly thomistic aesthetic, were never originally intended as such. St Thomas would have been amazed to find this particular aspect of his reflection transformed into the cornerstone for a philosophy that hardly concerned him at all. The point that Aquinas seeks to establish is a theological one: an image or *similitudo* is beautiful if it perfectly represents another being ... the Son in a very special sense must be conceived of in our minds as having a special, if not exclusive, title to the divine name: beauty.[9]

These remarks of Aquinas on beauty occur in an argument for the suitability of applying to the person of the Son in the uncreated Trinity a particular attribute or name.[10] The beauty of the Son as the Word of God is his capacity to embody, to represent, to incarnate his originating principle. The beauty of Joyce's work would be its capacity to realise the perfection of itself as work of art and its author as haunted artist. Thomas Aquinas combines the two strands of art and fatherhood in his presentation of the mysterious relationship that exists between the Father and the Son (the uncreated principle and the consubstantial word). Thomas was aware of all the heresies that threatened the fullness and the subtlety of so delicately balanced a mystery. Of these, the two most representative would be Arianism and Sabellianism, both of which feature constantly in Stephen's thought in *Ulysses* and *A Portrait*. The first denies the possibility of fatherhood in God. The son was very similar and 'of like substance' (*homoiousios*) but could never be 'consubstantial' (*homoousios*) with God. This implied, from Joyce's point of view, that any word, or creation of his own, could never be the perfect form of himself. He was more attracted to 'the subtle African heresiarch Sabellius who held that the Father was Himself His own Son' (*Ulysses*, 18). This heresy, sometimes called Modalism or Monarchianism (that to preserve the prerogatives of Divine Monarch it is necessary to present the son as no more than a ghost, or a modality, of the Father) is dramatised in Shakespeare's *Hamlet*. It is this Sabellian notion of creativity that is represented by Stephen in *Ulysses* and it is only after the odyssey of this work of art that a new definition of fatherhood is achieved in the person of Leopold Bloom.

This apparently abstruse theological argument is important in that it situates the source and the goal of Joyce's art outside the realisation and perfection of that art in and for itself. Joyce's life and work were a dedicated search and struggle in another order. It also shows that no work of Joyce can be understood as an isolated entity. To say that *Ulysses* was the best and only really great work that Joyce ever produced and to discard the rest on this account may be permissible in the domain of aesthetic criticism, but it is impossible in the context of art as access to Being.

Of course it is important to appraise the role of Joyce the novelist, but not before situating this novelist within the wider context of an artistic odyssey, which begins with *Chamber Music* and culminates and finds its fulfilment in *Finnegans Wake*. However 'good' the other works may or may not be, they are episodes on the way towards the only really important thing. This important thing is *Finnegans Wake*, which is the same thing as *Chamber Music*, except that, here, that original urge has become word made flesh. As Samuel Beckett in his famous essay on *Finnegans Wake* tells us: 'Here form is content, content is form. You complain that this stuff is not written in English. It is not written at all. It is not to be read – or rather it is (not) only to be read. It is to be looked at and listened to. His writing is not about something; it is that something itself.'[11]

Nobody, at the time, among his friends, his family, his critics, his admirers, approved of, or understood, what he was doing in *Finnegans Wake*, this *Work in Progress* as he called it, until the day when its secret title was revealed. All of Joyce's life was a work in progress. This last was the culmination of that lifetime's odyssey and holds the key to any understanding of Joyce's mind.

Harriet Shaw Weaver, on whom Joyce depended so ignominiously and ruthlessly, was completely disenchanted by this work. Joyce took great pains to explain to her the importance of it and in the end succeeded in bludgeoning her into submission. His brother Stanislaus was quite clear that 'I for one would not read more than a paragraph of it, if I did not know you.' He suspects that 'the drivelling rigmarole' in the 'nightmare production' is written 'with the deliberate intention of pulling the reader's leg.'[12] H. G. Wells spoke for most as follows:

Now with regard to this literary experiment of yours. It's a considerable thing because you are a very considerable man and you have in your crowded composition a mighty genius for expression which has escaped discipline. But I don't think it gets anywhere. You have turned your back on common men, on their elementary needs and their restricted time and intelligence and you have elaborated. What is the result? Vast riddles ... So I ask: Who the hell is this Joyce who demands so many waking hours of the few thousands I have still to live for a proper appreciation of his quirks and fancies and flashes of rendering?[13]

Ezra Pound, who might have been the person most likely to understand Joyce's art, has this to say after reading a typescript of one chapter: 'Nothing would be worth plowing through this, except the Divine Vision – and I gather it's not that sort of thing.'[14] So, in fact, he was alone in his struggle during the eighteen years that it took him to compose his final work.

The questions of Pound and Wells: 'Who is this Joyce? What is this vision?' are still the important ones to answer before finding our way through the labyrinth.

There must be many people who read James Joyce for pleasure and this is obviously one very good reason for doing so. I have never found him easy or pleasurable to read. I read him because I have to, because I believe that, as Richard Ellmann says in the opening line of his biography: 'We are still learning to be James Joyce's contemporaries.'

If the poet Milton felt called upon to explain the ways of God to humankind, Joyce felt obliged to explain the ways of humankind to God. Having rejected the orthodoxy of the Catholic Church, he embraced with passion and rigour the orthodoxy of humanity. In a letter to Stanislaus in 1906 he says:

... if I put a bucket into my own soul's well, sexual department, I draw up Griffith's and Ibsen's and Skeffington's and Bernard Vaughan's and St Aloysius' and Shelley's and Renan's water along with my own. And I am going to do that in my novel (*inter alia*) and plank the bucket down before the shades and substances above mentioned to see how they like it: and if they don't like it I can't help them. I am nauseated by their lying drivel about pure men and pure women and spiritual love for ever: blatant lying in the face of the truth'.[15]

He realised that there was more to humanity than Jesuit philosophy had ever dreamed of, and he was determined to explore that dream. In this sense he was a contemporary in spirit of the Surrealists, of Proust, of Freud, of Jung, of Rilke and of those who sensed the new dimensions that were opening up to humanity. Not that he was in anyway appreciative of his contemporaries. He despised Freud and Jung, for example, referring to them as Tweedledum and Tweedledee. He felt that they were pillaging a reality that artists alone were capable of expressing, and exploiting it for their own particular practical needs. They were reducing it to the limited categories of their own minds and training, whereas he was opening himself and allowing this reality to spread through him so that every organ, channel, category, or compartment, was flooded.

The reason why Joyce had to use the style he eventually forged for himself in *Finnegans Wake* is because 'one great part of every human existence is passed in a state which cannot be rendered sensible by the use of wideawake language, cut-and-dry grammar and go-ahead plot', as he wrote back to Ezra Pound. Lionel Trilling held that 'James Joyce, with his interest in the numerous states of receding consciousness, with his use of words which point to more than one thing, with his pervading sense of the interrelation and interpenetration of all things, and, not least important, his treatment of familial themes, has perhaps most thoroughly and consciously exploited Freud's ideas.'[16] This is not to imply that he was directly influenced by Freud's writings. As Lionel Trilling again points out: 'We must see that particular influences cannot be in question here but that what we must deal with is nothing less than a whole *Zeitgeist*, a direction of thought.' When Freud was hailed, on the occasion of his seventieth birthday, as 'the discoverer of the unconscious', he corrected the speaker and refused the title: 'The poets and philosophers before me discovered the unconscious. What I discovered was the scientific method by which the unconscious can be studied.'

And it was precisely this scientific method that Joyce rejected when facing the unconscious. He dismissed psychoanalysis because its symbolism was mechanical, but this was surely because, as Ellmann suggests, 'Joyce was close to the new psychoanalysis at so many points that he always disavowed any interest in it.' He was in fact working along the same lines himself at an artistic level and was disdainful of the plodding scientists who were tapping the same sources in a much less direct and revealing way. Art was the only appropriate medium for Joyce. Medicine and science were half-measures that were even less satisfactory than the religion he had rejected. Talking about psychoanalysis, he said to his friend Ettore Schmitz, 'Well, if we need it, let us keep to confession' (Ellmann, 472). But, at another level, the level of coincidence, corresponding to the suggestion of Trilling about the *Zeitgeist*, which influenced him to an extent that has not yet been fully appreciated, he realised that his work was very definitely connected to that of both Freud and Jung.

What is it that all these people were discovering? The answer is an inner continent, the discovery of which had greater significance and repercussions than the discovery of the 'New World' by Europeans in the fifteenth century. The difference between Joyce and the psychoanalysts, for instance, was that he was discovering it as an artist and therefore sought to express this reality in all its originality, subtlety and polyvalence, whereas they, as scientists, sought to conquer it by reducing it to the machinery available to their limited fields of competence. 'In *Ulysses*, I have recorded, simultaneously, what a man says, sees, thinks, and what such saying, seeing and thinking does, to what you Freudians call the subconscious – but as for psychoanalysis, it's neither more nor less than blackmail' (Ellmann, 524). Joyce described *Finnegans Wake* as written 'to suit the esthetic of the dream, where the forms prolong and multiply themselves, where the visions pass from the trivial to the apocalyptic, where the brain uses the roots of vocables to make others from them which will be capable of naming its phantasms, its allergies, its illusions' (Ellmann, 546).

His search was in a similar direction and dimension to that of the doctors and scientists, investigating the inner world of dreams and of the unconscious. What he disliked was their methodology. When asked by the Danish writer Tom Kristensen to provide some help in the interpretation of his *Work in Progress*, Joyce referred him to Vico. Kristensen asked him if he believed in the *Scienza Nuova*. Joyce replied: 'I don't believe in any science, but my imagination grows when I read Vico as it doesn't when I read Freud and Jung' (Ellmann, 693).

Such remarks are important for an understanding of precisely how writers and thinkers influenced Joyce's work, stressing a difference between scientific and artistic discovery. The first has its identifiable and identifying equipment with which it can harness the new reality. This equipment is a fixed immovable third term between the scientist and the object of science. The pre-cast forms into which the new reality is required to pour itself, have not only a sterilising effect upon it but they also ensure that the scientists are never threatened, to the extent of total transformation of their own reality, by any newness that may confront them. Artists have no preconceived forms or approaches. They have to give themselves totally to the newness that they sense, and then invent the forms which alone can give that reality concrete expression.

Joyce rejected both religious and scientific pretensions to monopoly in the area of human understanding. This new world that had been discovered required a new form of understanding, one that he, as an artist, was capable of imagining. Not, indeed, that he ever had total confidence in his ability. It was not as though he had a hidden blueprint of the plan he was devising. Like most great artists, he had to feel his way towards that technique which would allow him to do justice to each moment and each part of his artistic odyssey as it occurred.

Assessing Joyce's role as a novelist, within the context of his total journey as an artist, is still such a vast and intricate topic that I must approach it selectively. Not that the novels are very numerous, but their versatility and range is enormous.[17]

Joyce turned to the novel as a substitute for poetry, as the only other artistic medium available to him. Although he was exceptionally gifted in this art form, he did not respectfully submit to the established canons of 'the Great Tradition' in novel writing. On the contrary, having abandoned religion and science as methods of self-expression, he was hardly likely to find anything satisfactory readily available. The reason he turned to art was precisely because it afforded him the opportunity of recreating the forms necessary for expressing his originality. In the field of novel writing he found exactly the same weaknesses and prejudices he had found in the world around him. He not only revolutionised the form of the novel, but he exploited this medium for the purpose of displaying the paralysis that enveloped every aspect of life in Ireland, including art itself. His project was to exorcise himself from the impossibilities of becoming a poet by expressing in the most perfect form these very impossibilities.

The major weakness of the novel, from Joyce's point of view, was that it had turned itself into a kind of science. The text was a highly controlled story which both the reader and the writer were able to dominate. The form that imposes this pattern of meaning from beginning to end is the narrative. Here the reader is aware that the author is telling the story and forcing the reader to submit to this guiding hand. The text is the perfectly predictable third term between the reader and the writer and it is governed by a series of conventions that prevent any unnecessary straying on the part of the reader.

Obviously, the author introduces voices other than his or her own into the text. But these are carefully cordoned off between inverted commas, which Joyce regarded as 'perverted commas', and thus prevented from assuming any life of their own. The real language of the text is the narrative proper, which is impregnated with the meta-language of a smug and all-pervading commentary by the author, who speaks directly to the reader and removes all the threat and the obscurity from the other discourses, which are quoted as mere illustrations of his/her basic text. This domination of the author is the tyranny of the father-figure, which precludes any active participation of the reader outside the carefully controlled manipulation of the narrative. It removes all responsibility, in the sense of creative and personal reaction. It reduces the reader to a dull passivity. It also deprives language of its own specific life. It forces it into a linear strait-jacket of predetermined meaning. It allows the author to use both language and the reader as lifeless robots.

The revolution of the word which Joyce achieved was the liberation of both language and the reader by his renunciation of any dominating vantage-point as author of the text. When we read *Dubliners*, for instance, we are never able to establish the identity of the subject who is telling the story. 'It has been argued that the general strategy of *Dubliners* is the refusal of the production of a privileged discourse against which to read off the other languages of the text. This refusal forces the reader to experience the discourses of the characters as articulation rather than representation; in short to experience language.'[18]

'Both *Ulysses* and *Finnegans Wake* are concerned not with representing experience through language but with experiencing language through a destruction of representation ... Joyce's text disrupts the normal position assigned to a reader in a text and thus alters the reader's relation to his or her discourses.'[19] Joyce is trying to alter the established relationships between an author and a reader through the material vehicle of words. The confident 'I' of the author is silenced to allow something else to speak. This something else is the mystery of language itself. The word ceases to be a transparent nonentity through which the reader is made aware of another, exterior and 'real' world, and becomes a reality with a life of its own.

The revolution of the word was not just undertaken for its own sake. It was necessary for Joyce himself. As author, he had no self-confident self that could act as privileged narrator of his text. Allowing language its freedom opened for him the possibility of finding his own voice rather than imposing it from the outset. In fact there were several voices in him, all of which achieve articulation in the deconstructed narrative, which becomes a tapestry of interlocking discourse. The attempt to locate Joyce himself in all of this becomes even more difficult when, for instance, we are faced with the much-quoted paradox that he was supposed to have told Frank Budgen that everything in *A Portrait of the Artist as a Young Man* was autobiographical, whereas Stanislaus maintained that his brother was a creative artist and that, therefore, this and his other works were fictional. In fact, both these statements are true in their own way. All the material that Joyce uses is more or less based on the material furnished him in his own life. One of the exceptional aspects of his make-up was a phenomenal memory. However, this does not mean that his works are slavish recordings of his own life history. On the contrary, the use he made of this autobiographical material was free from any such preoccupation. His creative project was not to record but to express himself and to effectuate the exorcism that would allow him to grow towards the fulfilment that the text prefigures. In other words, 'Joyce is the writer who is writing the text so that the text will produce the writer who can write the text.'[20]

In his famous essay on *Ulysses*, Valery Larbaud claims that the title of *A Portrait of the Artist as a Young Man* 'indicates that it is also, in a certain sense, the story of the youth of the artist in general, that is to say of anyone gifted with an artistic temperament'.[21] This does not seem to be the case. Although the name Stephen Dedalus is symbolic, this does not make it universal. The book is a portrait of the artist, the unique artist who was able to produce *Ulysses*. It is of interest to note that *Ulysses* was originally meant to be another story in *Dubliners*. However, the much more extended work that it later became is both the result and the recording of the exorcism that *A Portrait* achieved in Joyce. The central character of *A Portrait* becomes one point in a triangle in *Ulysses*, each of these points being a different coagulation of colour on the James Joyce spectrum.

The first three episodes of *Ulysses* could be a continuation of *A Portrait*. But then comes the real Odyssey for both writer and reader. Each episode from here on in *Ulysses* is apportioned a specific part of the body as its presiding organism, whereas the first three deal specifically with Stephen. The real paralysis of Stephen Dedalus the artist is not one that is imposed upon him by his surroundings. It is his disembodiment. He is a disconnected spirit. The attempt to make of him a poet is doomed to failure because there is nothing creative in him at all. The matrix of creation is absent. He wanders through the world as a ghostly soul that cannot adhere to anything and cannot, from the inside, release itself from itself.

There is an ironic retrospective glance in *Ulysses* at the artistic pretensions of Stephen in *A Portrait*: 'Fabulous artificer, the hawklike man. You flew. Whereto? Newhaven-Dieppe, steerage passenger. Paris and back. Lapwing. Icarus. *Pater, ait*. Seabedabbled, fallen, weltering. Lapwing you are. Lapwing he' (*Ulysses*, 199). The Stephen who, on the last page of *A Portrait*, goes 'to encounter for the millionth time the reality of experience and to forge in the smithy of my soul the uncreated conscience of my race', has become aware of his own impotence. The lapwing is a forger or faker, a bird who leads you away from its nest by bluffing and leading you on.

The last line of *A Portrait* was 'Old father, old artificer, stand by me now and ever in good stead.' This had not happened. In the present quotation from *Ulysses*, Stephen has become identified with both the father (Dedalus) and the son (Icarus). He is the father of his own labyrinth and, like the Cretan Daedalus, after whom he is named, he was confined in his own tortuous labyrinth and was unable to escape. The original Daedalus escaped when a natural-born son of his came from outside the labyrinth and released him. Stephen of *Ulysses* is searching for a father who will launch him like Icarus into flight.

There is no question of Joyce identifying with Stephen in his views on aesthetics and creativity as presented in this first part of *Ulysses*. Joyce is presenting Stephen as the Sabellian-Idealist artist who can only be freed from his paralysing cocoon by the process of the novel itself. It is the novel that holds the secret formula of paternity and not any of the personages within it.

After the first three episodes, without presiding bodily organ, we leave Stephen and enter the world of Bloom. These episodes introducing Stephen's opposite number are presided over by one bodily organ for each of the five – the kidney, the genitals, the heart, the lungs and the oesophagus. The next time we meet Stephen is in the ninth episode.

This ninth episode, Scylla and Charybdis, takes place in the library in which the famous discussion about Shakespeare's *Hamlet* occurs. This is the last episode in which we meet the Stephen of *A Portrait*. Now that we have entered into the body of the novel proper, each episode being presided over by some bodily organ, the brain is the one chosen for this episode. Materially it deals almost entirely with Shakespearean criticism and is peopled by a group of very thinly disguised Dublin literati of the time. It records a long Platonic dialogue on the personality of Hamlet and the creative presence of Shakespeare in this play, between Stephen Dedalus, Mr Best, John Eglinton, George Russell (AE) and Quakerlyster (the librarian). It includes some lyrics, a short passage in blank verse, and another in dramatic form, thus encompassing the three forms of literature defined by Stephen in *A Portrait of the Artist as a Young Man*. However, all this is the decoy of the lapwing luring us away from the real significance of the episode, which, as the title of the novel suggests, concerns the odyssey of the twentieth-century Ulysses, Leopold Bloom.

In the original odyssey of the mythological Ulysses, the hero had to choose between one of two perilous routes on his way back to Ithaca. He was advised by Circe not to attempt the passage through the 'wandering rocks', but to take the less dangerous of the two, which was the journey between the sheer steadfast rock of Scylla and the whirlpool of Charybdis.

In Joyce's version of the odyssey these two dangers are symbolically present: 'the beautiful ineffectual dreamer who comes to grief against hard facts' (*Ulysses*, 172). The rock of Dogma, of Aristotle and of Shakespeare's Stratford, is contrasted with the whirlpool of Mysticism, Platonism and the London of Shakespeare's time. The real action of the novel in this episode is the almost breathless passing through of Ulysses. 'A man passed out between them, bowing, greeting' (*Ulysses*, 206). Bloom, as the twentieth-century Ulysses, passes out from the dark gloom of the library into a 'shattering daylight of no thoughts' (*Ulysses*, 203). His actual presence in this episode takes up no more than a few throwaway lines. But each time this presence is felt it builds up the real significance of the novel itself.

Just as the moment when the solipsistic Stephen, influenced by both Berkeleyan Idealism and Sabellian Modalism, is propounding a theory of art and literature which is totally dependent on the author and which leaves absolutely no leeway to the causality of chance, the novel takes over and language disrupts the flow of the episode:

– Bosh! Stephen said rudely. A man of genius makes no
mistakes. His errors are volitional and are the portals of
discovery.
Portals of discovery opened to let in the quaker
librarian, softcreakfooted, bald, eared and assiduous.
(*Ulysses*, 179)

This chance external event heralds the later arrival of Bloom through these same portals of discovery, disrupting Stephen's attempt to compromise the movement of the novel, the odyssey proper.

However, the most important dislocation of the narrative in this episode occurs when we discover that Stephen's whole theory of and reflections on Shakespeare are a red herring. What he is describing is not Shakespeare at all but the real father figure of the novel, Leopold Bloom. During the episode we are examining, the narrative moves into the internal discourse of Stephen's mind. He is musing about Shakespeare and concocting an image of the latter, which is remarkably similar to the character of Leopold Bloom, the father figure for whom Stephen is unconsciously searching. Both Shakespeare and Bloom 'are "over-borne" by women, and are forced to marry by the impending arrival of a girl child'. Both lack the self-confidence to win at romance, are ineffective with distant 'Dark Ladies', both stop mating after the second labours of their wives and lose a son after eleven units of time to be left both fatherless and sonless. Both are cuckolds who do not seek redress though they are preoccupied with the brutes their wives take – they return home despite suffering to achieve contentment. And both are avaricious, incestuous and Jewish – qualities Stephen links together.[22] Stephen says to himself on this occasion, 'He was chosen, it seems to me. If others have their will Ann hath a way. By cock, she was to blame. She put the comether on him, sweet and twenty-six. The greyeyed goddess who bends over the boy Adonis, stooping to conquer, as prologue to the swelling act, is a bold-faced Stratford wench who tumbles in a cornfield a lover younger than herself.'[23] This description corresponds to the key scene of Bloom's courtship with Molly on Howth Hill in which she 'got him to propose' and in which Bloom was 'ravished' by her.[24]

Later in a similar interior monologue, Stephen uses the following very unusual words and images to describe Shakespeare: 'In a rosery of Fetter Lane of Gerard, herbalist, he walks greyedauburn. An azured harebell like her veins. Lids of Juno's eyes, violets. He walks. One life is all. One body. Do. But do' (*Ulysses*, 190). Now this is all taking place in Stephen's inner discourse. But, just to show that the correspondence between Shakespeare and Bloom is not the over-zealous interpretation of the reader, the novel itself makes this connection by repeating, this time, within the very different discourse of the interior monologue of Bloom himself, exactly the same words and also in connection with Shakespeare. In the Sirens episode, Bloom is musing about Shakespeare: 'Music hath charms Shakespeare said. Quotations every day of the year. To be or not to be. Wisdom while you wait.' And immediately after this reference to Shakespeare, he repeats Stephen's words almost verbatim: 'In

Gerard's rosery of Fetter lane he walks, greyedauburn. One life is all. One body. Do. But do' (*Ulysses*, 266).

It is not a question of identifying Joyce with either Stephen or Bloom. 'Joyce creates Stephen and Bloom, juxtaposes them and defines their positions as widely and rigorously separated in order to dramatise a conflict within himself and within humanity which he is unable to reconcile.'[25] This means that *Ulysses*, too, is only a stepping-stone towards something else. As early as 1927 Joyce began to lose interest in it. '*Ulysses*!', he once remarked to Maria Jolas, 'Who wrote it? I've forgotten it' (Ellmann, 590). Even Nora was aware of how relatively unimportant *Ulysses* was when compared with *Finnegans Wake* for a real understanding of her husband's artistic project. After his death she was distressed by the disregard for his last work and said to Maria Jolas: 'What's all this talk about *Ulysses*? *Finnegans Wake* is the important book. When are you and Eugene going to write about it?' (Ellmann, 743).

However, to understand the true significance of Joyce's last work, which was not a novel, it is important to understand the internal conflict that he used the novel form to exorcise in *Ulysses*. Here Sheldon Brivic, who situates *Joyce between Freud and Jung*, gives an interesting interpretation. He claims that at the heart of *Ulysses* is a distinction similar to the one that Jung was making in his *Psychological Types*, which was written at about the same time (1921). The two types are incarnated in Stephen and Bloom and the whole structure of the novel, especially the Scylla and Charybdis episode, is based upon the distinction between body and soul, matter and spirit. For Joyce the sexual dimension is fundamental and defines the being of a character and, at this level, either excessive materialism or excessive spirituality is destructive. 'Stephen's addiction to prostitutes is a mode of sex without love which ultimately contrasts to Bloom's love without sex' (Brivic, 148). It implies that Stephen really loathes and denigrates women while Bloom adores and deifies them (Brivic, 141). Prostitution is an appropriate mode of sex for those who reject the world and devalue their bodies, which explains why the brothel scenes are cluttered with religious imagery.

Freud explains that the wilful cuckold, which describes Bloom, is really trying to recreate in his wife the original way in which he related to his mother, with the necessary competitor playing the part of the father. This means that Bloom is at the opposite pole from Stephen and is making a God out of woman and, in this way, putting her in the place of the father.

These two aspects of Joyce's life are certainly present in his letters and they represent the two dimensions of puritanical religious upbringing and highly developed sexual instinct, which for many people create a particularly 'Catholic' temperament.

Brivic's theory is certainly well documented and it is interesting to note that the following commentary by Stanislaus on *Finnegans Wake* would seem to support such an interpretation:

> In the Tyrone Street episode, for instance, the relation or at least the analogy between the imagination in the intellect and the sexual instinct in the body ... is worked out with a fantastic horror of which I know no equal in literature, painting or music ... It is undoubtedly Catholic in temperament. This brooding over the lower order of natural facts, this re-evocation and exaggeration of detail by detail and the spiritual dejection which accompanies them are purely in the spirit of the confessional. Your temperament, like Catholic morality, is predominantly sexual. (Ellmann, 578)

At this second level with which we are dealing, the movement of the novel is generated towards the meeting of these two opposites and their returning home together to Ithaca, where they are both confronted by the third term of the triangle, Penelope, the earth mother, the Gea Tellus. This movement is the important one which causes the dislocation of the narrative proper and which explains that when Stephen's words turn up in Bloom's monologues or vice versa, 'this isn't a "dropping out of character" but a deliberate dropping of character into some other continuum' (Brivic, 171). It is this 'other continuum' of Joyce's novels that we must now pursue to the third level of the analysis of Joyce as novelist.

If Joyce cannot be identified with any of his characters and if the revolution of the word was achieved by abstaining from any privileged or dominating discourse on the part of the author, in order to liberate the text and the reader, what hope is there of establishing the exact relationship that did exist between Joyce as novelist and his novels as texts?

Brivic, in an article called 'Joyce and the Metaphysics of Creation'[26] claims that, although Joyce rebelled against the idea of God in his youth, he later came to realise that he himself must act as God in relation to his creative works and project himself into them as a similarly transcendent principle. All the violations of established styles and dislocations of narrative discourse which have been outlined in the last two sections are, according to Brivic, 'spiritual manifestations, positive acts Joyce performs as God and these miraculous events in the text are productive of one of Joyce's major kinds of reality'. In other words, the destruction of the novel which Joyce achieved in *Ulysses* was not merely a negative reaction of further disenchantment but was the positive creation of another level of reality beyond the confines of the novel and one which would be again recuperated within a text in his last work.

The mental lives of Stephen and Bloom arch towards each other like flying buttresses on the cathedral of *Ulysses*. In the centre is suspended the totality of Joyce constituted by the combination of their two extremes, the sides of his mind that could never be reconciled. Joyce's first entelechy, his personality, is the principle that regulates the relation between parts in his work, and it is only by seeing his living being in all its depth and complexity that we can understand the organisation of his world and the tonality of his voices.[27]

Brivic would seem to be nearer to the truth when he quotes the work of Jung[28] than when he derives Joyce's creative approach from a study of Aristotle. Whatever can be said about enlarging the notion of causality by reintroducing the disabused 'final' and 'efficient' causes of Aristotelian metaphysics, it seems to me that Joyce's concern was with an a-causal principle of creativity.

In an interview with Beckett in 1957, Ellmann gleaned the following interpretation of Joyce's interest in this regard: 'Joyce's fictional method does not presume that the artist has any supernatural power, but that he has an insight into the methods and motivations of the universe ... To Joyce reality was a paradigm, an illustration of a possibly unstatable rule. Yet perhaps the rule can be surmised. It is not a perception of order or of love; more humble than either of these, it is a perception of co-incidence' (Ellmann, 562). This would correspond almost exactly with Jung's description of a similar preoccupation. In his paper on 'Synchronicity: An A-Causal Connecting Principle', he defines this term as

> the parallelism of time and meaning between psychic and psychophysical events, which scientific knowledge so far has been unable to reduce to a common principle. The term explains nothing, it simply formulates the occurrence of meaningful coincidences which, in themselves, are chance happenings, but are so improbable that we must assume them to be based on some kind of principle, or on some property of the empirical world. No reciprocal causal connection can be shown to obtain between parallel events, which is just what gives them their chance character. The only recognisable and demonstrable link between them is a common meaning, or equivalence.[29]

At this third level of our study of Joyce as a novelist, it could be seen, for example, that the Scylla and Charybdis episode of *Ulysses*, which comes under the organ of the brain, is constantly being lowered from the surface level of narrative causality (and all causality is the idiomatic language of the brain) to another level of synchronicity, which introduces a dimension outside the space, time and causality of the narrative as such. This echoes the thought of Jung in his essay on synchronicity: 'We must ask ourselves whether there is some other nervous substrate in us, apart from the cerebrum, that can think and perceive, or whether the psychic processes that go on in us during loss of consciousness are synchronistic phenomena, i.e. events that have no causal connection with organic processes.' After a lengthy argument he comes to the conclusion 'that a nervous substrate like the sympathetic system, which is absolutely different from the cerebrospinal system in point of origin and function can evidently produce thoughts and perceptions just as easily as the latter'.

If this third dimension is present in *Ulysses*, it is only so as product and not as a total presence. This is why the novel form could not satisfy Joyce. The dimension hinted at in *Ulysses* had to be expressed in a much more positive and immediate way, as presence rather than absence. This takes place in *Finnegans Wake*, where Joyce does not content himself with producing the effects of synchronicity within the time-space continuum of a novel but actually works his way back to the a-causal dimension and expresses it directly.

In his essay, Jung shows what a difficult task such a project is: 'The idea of synchronicity with its inherent quality of meaning produces a picture of the world so irrepresentable as to be completely baffling.' The dimension from which such communication must occur is no longer the 'day-time' of *Ulysses* but, rather, what Jung refers to as 'a twilight state'. In such a situation, Jung wonders whether 'the normal state of unconsciousness in sleep, and the potentially conscious dreams it contains … are produced not so much by the activity of the sleeping cortex, as by the unsleeping sympathetic system, and are therefore of a transcerebral nature'. Such expression would require 'a new conceptual language – a "neutral language" and a modality without a cause' which Jung calls 'a-causal orderedness'. All of which seems appropriate as a description of Joyce's project in *Finnegans Wake*.

Joyce himself is essentially the conflict between certain external pressures and certain internal qualities, which at the particular time in which he lived and with the exceptional gifts with which he was endowed, rose to such a pitch that something had to give way. What eventually did give way was the ground on which both the protagonists were standing. Joyce was forced to find within himself a new dimension, a new reality, for which he then became the sign or token through his enigmatic last work.

Joyce is essentially a provincial poet who was driven by the encroaching limitations of his particular province, or rather city, to dig down to its foundations until he released both it and himself from its narrow confines and connected it to the mainstream of humanity as a universal phenomenon.

The pressures that generated such a violent implosion in this unusually gifted man were many and varied. If any one of the accidental details of his particular biographical circumstances had been absent, it might have relieved the pressure to the extent that it might never have reached breaking-point. The important thing for an understanding of Joyce is to see what led to that breaking-point and to what that breaking-point led.

In the first case, there are a number of sometimes trivial factors, none of which, on their own, could amount to very much, but as an accumulation within the structure of this particular psyche were sufficient to ignite the gun-powder.

The first of these was Joyce's Catholicity, the second his middle-class background. This is an important addition to his Catholicity because Catholicism was taken more scrupulously by the middle classes than by the peasantry or aristocracy. It also means that he had none of the prejudices and awe of tradition and convention of the 'upper' classes of his day (those who would normally have received as extended an education as he received), which would have stifled any intellectual originality, revolutionary ideas, or interest in the obscene. Mahaffy, the famous provost of Trinity College, Dublin, described Joyce as 'a living argument in favour of my contention that it was a mistake to establish a separate university for the aborigines of this island – for the corner-boys who spit into the Liffey' (Ellmann, 58).

The third pressurising element was his precocious and predominant sexuality. This might not have become so poignant and so fanatical if it had not been nurtured, or rather poisoned, in the atmosphere generated by the first two pressurising elements. The fourth element was a combination of his exceptional intelligence and the education and cultural formation he was able to achieve. The fifth would be his artistic gifts and temperament, which gave him the strength and patience to withstand such pressures, and the imaginative ability to escape from the labyrinth. The sixth is what I have already referred to as the *Zeitgeist*: he had the good fortune to live at a time when a whole direction of thought was piercing through the confines of the workaday world as it had been understood and defined for centuries. The great psychological discovery of his century was the night world – though he frowned upon the use of that world as a means of therapy, he received from it support and direction in the pursuit of his own originality.

All of these pressures impinging upon a lesser person would have crushed them. Joyce was able to withstand this pressure and convert it into creative energy for two reasons: the first was his capacity for extraordinary artistic self-expression, the second was his fortuitous and symbiotic relationship with Nora. Any understanding of Joyce must attempt to situate the presence of this woman in his world.

Lastly, and most peripheral of all, there are the various intellectual or philosophical influences that gave some formative and directional guidance. In this last case it is possible to read too much into such influences. Joyce was an unusually self-reliant explorer, who had absolute confidence in his own resources and ability to find his way. He did read widely and voraciously, but what interested him was support for his own intuitions, stimulation for his imagination, or information that would illustrate or increase his findings. His intellectual mentors were chosen for very unscientific reasons and were used as such with the most unscrupulous abandon. Joyce was no one's disciple, and no fellow-worker in the field, of whatever age or importance, was granted either the deference or the homage due to a superior.[30]

So, what did all these internal and external pressures produce in the mind of James Joyce and what did he, in turn, produce from them? The overall impression is of disconnection between the opposite poles of his make-up, and a capacity to behave, under different circumstances, in a way that seems as opposite as Jekyll and Hyde. The most spiritual and lofty aspirations coincide with the most carnal and obscene thoughts and actions. The Jesuit Joyce and the seducer Stephen abide under the same roof. One is petulant and almost prudish about other people using foul language or obscenities in his presence, the other is secretly writing letters to his 'whorish wife Nora', which are among the most scatological in the history of letter writing. Then, at a certain point in his life, this schizophrenia melts away. The obscene passion dies out of him to such an extent that Lionel Trilling, in his study of Joyce's letters, suggests that although 'the substance of the marital correspondence at forty is not different from that of the twenties' there is a change in the quality of Joyce's passion and that this 'devolution from his early egotism of the world to the later egotism of nullity is a biographical event that asks for explanation'.[31] Trilling is so intent upon his cultural theory that Joyce was the man who killed the nineteenth century and, like Samson, had to kill himself in the process, that he forces upon us the conclusion that 'the letters of the years of fame were written by a being who had departed this life as it is generally known ... and has passed from temporal existence into nullity, but still has a burden of energy to discharge, a destiny still to be worked out'. Trilling sees the 'controlling tendency of Joyce's genius' as a progress that moves 'through the fullest realisation of the human, the all-too-human, to that which transcends and denies the human'. I would agree with much of what Trilling says but not the conclusion he reaches.

It is true that the real genius of Joyce was to move 'through the fullest realisation of the human, the all-too-human', which he expressed in *Ulysses*, to that which transcends 'this life as it is generally known'. But that does not mean that he 'denied' the human or that he 'passed from temporal existence into nullity'. It means, rather, that he redefined the limits of humanity and extended temporal existence into another dimension. The biographical event that Trilling demands as explanation for the transformation of the scatology of Joyce's early letters is the eschatology of *Finnegans Wake*.

Jung was probably the first to call Joyce a prophet. 'There are,' he says, 'major and minor prophets, and history will decide to which of them Joyce belongs. Like every true prophet, the artist is the unwitting mouth-piece of the psychic secrets of his time, and is often as unconscious as a sleep-walker. He supposes that it is he who speaks, but the spirit of the age is his prompter, and whatever this spirit says is proved true by its effects.'[32] The other controversial statement that Jung made about Joyce was that, like Picasso, he was schizophrenic. This second remark caused such a furore that Jung had to explain himself in 1934 in a footnote: 'By this I do not mean … a diagnosis of the mental ill-ness schizophrenia … but a disposition or habitus on the basis of which a serious psychological disturbance could produce schiz-ophrenia. Hence I regard neither Picasso nor Joyce as psy-chotics.'[33] The two statements are connected and, in Joyce's case, the schizophrenic gave birth to the prophet. The etymology of schizophrenia describes a cleavage of the mind and a disconnec-tion between thoughts, feelings and actions. That Joyce was tem-peramentally prone to this reaction is probably best illustrated by the fact that his daughter, Lucia, was, in fact, diagnosed on 19 May 1931, as suffering from hebephrenic psychosis, which is a form of schizophrenia characterised by hallucinations, absurd delusions, silly mannerisms, and other kinds of deteriorisation.

Joyce refused to accept that there was anything really wrong with his daughter, declaring that if she were insane then so was he. However, his attitude towards medicine and psychoanalysis changed radically when he was faced with the spectacle of his demented daughter. He even agreed to put her under the care of Jung and came to realise that the night-world that he himself was exploring was probably too harsh for ordinary mortals and that the therapeutic and scientific approaches to it, which he had once disdained, were perhaps the only means of access to it for the majority of people. It is interesting to note that the copy of *Ulysses* that was in Jung's library is signed in 1934: 'To Dr C. G. Jung, with grateful appreciation of his aid and counsel. James Joyce.' Lucia had been under the care of Jung for three months, from September 28th of that same year, when Joyce wrote this dedication. However, Jung was the twentieth doctor to have been consulted and Joyce again refused to accept his verdict and took Lucia back to Paris with him. As a result of this episode, Jung wrote his considered opinion of the two in a letter to Patricia Hutchins:

> If you know anything of my Anima theory, Joyce and his daughter are a classical example of it. She was definitely his 'femme inspiratrice', which explains his obstinate reluctance to have her certified. His own Anima, i.e. unconscious psyche, was so solidly identified with her, that to have her certified would have been as much as an admission that he himself had a latent psychosis. It is therefore understandable that he could not give in. His 'psychological' style is definitely schizophrenic, with the difference, however, that the ordinary patient cannot help himself talking and thinking in such a way, while Joyce willed it and moreover developed it with all his creative forces, which incidentally explains why he himself did not go over the border. But his daughter did, because she was no genius like her father, but merely a victim of her disease. In any other time of the past Joyce's work would never have reached the printer, but in our blessed XXth century it is a message, though not yet understood. (Ellmann, 679)

Joyce believed that Lucia was a clairvoyante, that her ravings were similar to his language in *Finnegans Wake*, all of which is important as an approach to this work.

Joyce's schizophrenic temperament drove his several antagonistic aspects to the furthest limits of his personality, thus forcing him to be a completely different person on different occasions. The obvious example is to be found in his letters. Here, as he says himself, 'Some of it is ugly, obscene and bestial, some of it is pure and holy and spiritual,' but, he adds most significantly, 'all of it is myself.' The cultural and other pressures exercised upon Joyce from his early youth forced him into such a psychic situation – the different parts of him that made up the 'all' of himself

were scattered and diversified. Nora was the only person he
ever met in his life whom he trusted fully. This meant that he
was able to display before her all the most obscene impulses that
had been driven to the frontiers and turned into perversions of
their real meaning by the overbearing ethos of the time.

The discovery of the 'night-world' in the beginning of the
century was such an upheaval for most people that it automatically translated itself into their psychological categories in terms
of schizophrenia. This world had to be mapped out as a world
'under' or 'over' our own, as a 'sub'conscious or 'sur'realist
sphere, to which there could be no direct access. This world had
to be approached indirectly through the mechanical processes of
medicine and science (e.g. the interpretation of dreams, which
was tantamount to placing two interpreters, one from the underworld and one from our own upper one, between the 'patients'
and the other side of themselves). This world, like the face of
Medusa the gorgon, could not be looked at directly, but could
only be sighted indirectly through a mirror forged in our tech-
nological world.

Joyce as prophet became the direct mouthpiece for such a
dislocated reality. Whether by disease or natural genius he was
able to situate himself in a psychic dimension, which is for others
as yet only available in such unconscious states as sleep, and
retain his consciousness sufficiently to allow expression of this
dimension to filter through into a text. Jung calls this 'visceral
thinking' (in which case he points to the presiding bodily organs
in each episode of *Ulysses* as significant) or 'conversation in and
with one's own intestines', which describes a process 'of almost
universal "restratification" of modern man, who is in the
process of shaking off a world that has become obsolete'.[34]

The whole perspective that governs our world in terms of latitude and longitude, outer and inner, conscious and unconscious, past, present and future, dream and reality, is one that
was fashioned by humankind as *spectator to* the universe instead
of *participator in* the universe. The particular gifts of Joyce allowed him to situate himself quite 'naturally' at another place

within himself, from which place the language of *Finnegans Wake* flows. Joyce was not 'consciously' trying to be perverse and to write in a way that was deliberately exotic. He said to John Eglinton about the language in *Finnegans Wake*, 'I write in that way because it comes naturally to me to do so' (Ellmann, 546). Writing at this level, and from this level, participates in the real motive force of the universe. It does not just describe the observed causality of the universe, it participates in the psychic dimension of that a-causal connecting principle which is the real motor force of the world. Jung quotes Sir James Jeans as saying that it is possible 'that the springs of events in this substratum include our own mental activities, so that the future course of events may depend in part on these mental activities'.[35]

This would mean that Joyce was a prophet in the very real sense of having tapped the resources of a language that did not content itself merely with describing the causality of the world from a distant and observational point of view, but actively enmeshed itself in the well-springs of such causality. That Joyce himself was aware of such a possibility is suggested by his remark to Oscar Schwarz in Trieste, 'My art is not a mirror held up to nature. Nature mirrors my art,' and his claim that there were many examples in his work of clairvoyance where future events had borne out predictions carried in his earlier work. This would mean that Joyce had discovered a language the resources and power of which have not, as yet, been imagined.

The teleological genius of Joyce allowed him not to be dislocated and dispersed among the schizophrenic elements of his make-up but to creatively pursue these energies to another apex where they achieved a unity of being that opened up for him, and for us, a new dimension of humanity, a new definition of the 'I', as Hermon Broch wrote in 1949, 'an "I" that is at once the *sum* and the *cogito*, at once the logos and life, reunited; a simultaneity in whose unity may be seen the glow of the religious *per se*' and in which we can sense 'the germ of a new religious organisation of humanity'.[36]

Finnegans Wake is directly connected to the reality it describes in the same way that the dream is indistinguishable from the world of the unconscious to which it gives expression. Here language is not the translation of a reality into a text; it is the immediate textual gesture of that reality itself. The work of the author of such a text is not that of establishing the causal connection between one word and the next, as if words were cut and dried atoms with a quantified quota of univocal sense. Here the author's job is to find within each word the peculiar gesture of itself which will reveal an unsuspected and hidden reality, which will, quite by accident, lead on to the next unforeseen gesture of language. 'For you may be as practical as is predicable,' Shem says of his use of language in *Finnegans Wake*, 'but you must have the proper sort of accident to meet that kind of being with a difference.'[37] This describes the artistic process of *Finnegans Wake*. It is the unconscious as language itself, not the unconscious described by language. The text itself is woven out of the hidden energy sparked off by language whose entirely fortuitous gestures, under the guiding hand of the author, provide a providential similarity of sound or appearance in a word, thus revealing new connections between two or more beings indicated by that word.

Early on in the *Wake*, Joyce advises us to 'stoop' if we are 'abcedminded' (*FW*, 84). Here the use of language is not as an ABC of signals that refer to concepts in a shorthand morse code. Language in the *Wake* is a series of gestures of Being, and the work of the author is to search for the 'nameform that whets the wits that convey contacts that sweeten sensation that drives desire that adheres to attachment that dogs death that bitches birth that entails the ensuance of existentiality. But with a rush out of his navel reaching the reredos of Ramasbatham' (*FW*, 18). This is not the language of the mind, it is visceral language that rushes out of the intestines from a nervous substrate like the sympathetic system, which is quite different from the cerebrospinal system which produces the rational language of ordinary discourse. Language at this level, as a gesture of being, is nearest to, on the one hand, the scatological language of Joyce's letters, used to procure a directly physical effect, and, on the other, to the eschatological language of the sacramental tradition in which Joyce was reared, through whose efficacy was achieved the perfect reality of the thing signified. It was through the powerful medium of such language that Joyce achieved the final unification of these two otherwise contradictory opposite sides of himself. *Finnegans Wake,* far from being the final discharge of energy of a being who had transcended the limits of the 'all-too human' and arrived at the non-human void of nullity, described by Lionel Trilling, is the discovery of language as that gesture of Being which establishes a new dimension of humanity, from which these two supposedly antagonistic principles of the spirit and the flesh can achieve a hypostatic union in the person of a new kind of creative writer.

An interesting parallel, which may help to explain Joyce's use of language in *Finnegans Wake,* can be drawn between his use of words and the use of paint by an artist like Francis Bacon. Bacon says that 'the texture of a painting seems to come immediately onto the nervous system,'[38] that 'the mystery of fact is conveyed by an image being made out of non-rational marks ... that there is a coagulation of non-representational marks which have led to making up this very great image'. The way he works is by making 'involuntary marks on the canvas which may suggest much deeper ways by which you can trap the fact that you are obsessed by'.[39] Both these artists are aware of an a-causal principle, which they call chance or accident, which is the ultimate source of their work. As Bacon puts it, 'One knows that by some accidental brushmarks suddenly appearance comes in with such vividness that no accepted way of doing it would have brought about. I'm always trying through chance or accident to find a way by which appearance can be there but remade out of other shapes ... To me the mystery of painting today is how can appearance be made. I know it can be illustrated, I know it can be photographed. But how can this thing be made so that you catch the mystery of appearance within the mystery of making?'[40]

These descriptions of Bacon's use of paint in accidental brushmarks seem to describe the similar task that Joyce set himself in words in his *Work in Progress*. Language in this work takes on itself a role that it has never before been allowed to fulfil. It is given the freedom and the power to speak the meaning of the humanity, which for so long held it in a subservient role of polite and obedient servant. Like the role of the butler in Barrie's play *The Admirable Crichton*, it becomes the most important character in a situation where the lords and ladies of civilised society find themselves shipwrecked on a desert island. In the new situation, which the accidental course of history imposes upon human society, a new priesthood is necessary to provide the words of salvation which will satisfactorily cope with the lifestyle that has been forced upon us. The discovery of the 'night-world' of the unconscious at the beginning of this century represents such a shipwreck of the values, the philosophy, the worldview of Western civilisation.

Finnegans Wake is an attempt to actuate a new being adequate to the situation, by allowing language to dig up the letter from the dump-heap of the world. A kind of ritualistic or ceremonial attitude towards language is required: 'The ring man in the rong shop but the rite words by the rote order!' (*FW*, 167).

Just as Joyce was prevented from becoming a poet by the education he received and the culture that surrounded him, so the twentieth century is incapable of creating its own meaning until it takes seriously the real source of its possible resurrection – the mystery of the 'root language' that holds 'the keys of me heart' (*FW*, 626). *Finnegans Wake* is European civilisation represented by the mythic figure (Finn), who has died in the twentieth century, restored to a new life (again) but this time a(wake) conscious one, through the regenerative power of language. In this work: 'Yet is no body present here which was not there before. Only is order othered. Nought is nulled. *Fuitfiat!*' (*FW*, 613). The Latin words bespeak the re-creation and resurrection of contemporary mankind, HCE (Here Comes Everybody), who is in the process of shaking off a world that has now become obsolete.

For what was the Western world except a projection of the human mind as both these realities were understood. Now language comes as a tidal wave from the unconscious, not something 'out there' and available for use, like an overcoat or a briefcase, but like an ever-flowing river that runs through us and through all the ages of our history. The river will, if we listen to it, whisper to us the secret of our origins, while at the same time it will wash away the architecture of a world built without adverting to it. The artist of language in this capacity is the guardian and shepherd of Being as it expresses itself through the traces of all recorded human utterance, the anatomy of language:

> ... when the call comes, he shall produce nichthemerically from his unheavenly body a no uncertain quantity of obscene matter ... with this double dye brought to blood heat, gallic acid on iron ore, through the bowels of his misery, ... the first till last alshemist wrote over every square inch of the only foolscap available, his own body, till by its corrosive sublimation one continuous present tense integument slowly unfolded all marryvoising moodmoulded cyclewheeling history ... (FW,185–6)

The artist, 'reflecting from his own individual person life unlivable', creates a text 'transaccidentated through the slow fires of consciousness', which is 'perilous, potent' and 'common to all-flesh' (FW, 613). Language here becomes 'the squidself which he had squirtscreened from the crystalline world' of the subconscious, a history of man's unconscious life.

Part I vii of *Finnegans Wake*, where Joyce gives a portrait of himself as Shem the Penman and provides an apologia for his use of language in the *Wake*, describes the new kind of thinking which is language as the principle of paternity.

In this section there is a retrospective account of all Joyce's writings up to *Finnegans Wake*. *A Portrait of the Artist* is described as a 'wetbed confession', all the stories in *Dubliners* are denigratingly mentioned by name, (FW, 186-7) and *Ulysses* is described as a forgery.[41] This renunciation of his style of writing in the past as 'pseudostylic shamiana ... piously forged palimpsests slipped in the first place by this morbid process from his pela-giarist pen' (*FW*, 181-2) is a prelude to the description of his new kind of writing in *Finnegans Wake*. 'In writing of the night,' he says in a letter, 'I really could not, I felt I could not, use words in their ordinary relations and connections. Used that way they do not express how things are in the night, in the different stages – conscious, the semi-conscious, then unconscious. I found that it could not be done with words in the ordinary relations and con-nections.' *Finnegans Wake* is written 'to suit the esthetic of the dream, where the forms prolong and multiply themselves, where the visions pass from the trivial to the apocalyptic, where the brain uses the roots of vocables to make others from them which will be capable of naming its phantasms, its allegories, its allusions'. (Ellmann, 546)

This attempt to express the 'dark night of the soul' was 'a long, very long, a dark, very dark, an allburt unend, scarce en-durable, and we could add mostly quite various and somenwhat stumbletumbling night' (*FW*, 598). In this 'Jungfraud's Messongebook' (*FW*, 460), we are never quite sure whether the language is 'd'anglas landadge or are you sprakin sea Djoytsch?' (*FW*, 485). Here '[t]he war is in words and the wood is the world' (*FW*, 98). Joyce struggles with language to twist it into shapes ('Imeffible tries at speech unasyllabled') and to crush it into forms ('quashed quotatoes') (*FW*, 183) so that '[t]he silent cock shall crow at last' (*FW*, 473) and a hidden silent world ooze into speech.

Such a use of language allows Joyce to '[p]sing a psalm of psexpeans, apocryphul of rhyme!' (*FW*, 242), which exploits every aspect of the syllables that compose the words. 'Yet to con-centrate solely on the literal sense or even the psychological con-tent of any document to the sore neglect of the enveloping facts themselves circumstantiating it is just as hurtful to sound sense …' (*FW*, 109). This is not a scientific use of language which would translate into clear-cut and unambiguous terms. It is a surpassing of the principle of non-contradiction by a supralogi-cal use of words, each one containing at least 'two thinks at a time' (*FW*, 583). The pun, in Tindall's phrase, is mightier than the word because it uses the referential medium of sound to spark off correspondences simultaneously tangential to those suggested by the shapes. The artist of such a language does not fly in a cerebral fashion over the forest of language, he situates himself in the thick of the jungle and hacks away at the roots of vocables until he reaches that 'root language' which holds 'the keys of me heart'.

The difference between Stephen and Shem is in their attitude to, and their use of, language. Both are 'self-exiled in upon his ego' and 'writing the mystery of himself in furniture'. But Shem has found the way out of the solipsistic cocoon back beyond the confines of his own consciousness. He has learnt to produce 'nichtthemerically' (a word that combines the ideas of 'night-time,' 'nonthematic' and 'numerically') 'from his unheavenly body' what Stephen is trying to unfold thematically from his heavenly body, disconnected from the material world.

It is the same Joyce who creates the two protagonists. As he says himself: 'Yet is no body present here which was not there before. Only is order othered' (*FW*, 613). The order of Being has been othered by the installation of language in the paternal role. Language is the main character in *Finnegans Wake*. Starting with the very particular European city of Dublin and the particular life of an individual author, the generative power of language leads the artist into an underworld of the universal unconscious, much as the entry into any particular subway station will lead down to that network of underground correspondences which connect with every other one.

The *Wake* of this universal dimension requires the sleep of ordinary language and the daytime logic of the cerebrospinal cortex. The 'stomach language' of this 'prepronominal *funferal*, engraved and retouched and edgewiped and puddenpadded, very like a whale's egg farced with pemmican' makes no easy reading. Each sentence has to be 'nuzzled over a full trillion times for ever and a night till his noddle sink or swim by that ideal reader suffering from an ideal insomnia' (*FW*, 120), who has to forget the way he was taught to read, and allow language to become the 'aural eyeness' (*FW*, 623) which will provide the 'keys to dreamland' (*FW*, 615).

The image that Joyce uses to describe the source and the production of this new language is the sepia ink secreted by a squid. The house of Shem the Penman is described as 'the Haunted Inkbottle', wherein 'this double dye' is 'brought to blood heat through the bowels of his misery'. Just as the ink of an octopus is part of its being, so language is 'the squidself which he had squirtscreened from the crystalline world'; it is not a translation, it is the reality itself. It comes from his reflecting upon 'his own individual person life unlivable' and his processing of the various 'scalds and burns and blisters, impetiginous sores and pustules' through 'the slow fires of consciousness'. Its effect is not just an individualistic web of the artist's own making, a predictable, orderly and impotent ego trip. This language creates 'a dividual chaos, perilous, potent, common to allflesh'.

The element in it that creates this escape route is its 'antimonian manganese limolitmious nature', whose 'corrosive sublimation' works itself back through the artist's individual consciousness until it reaches 'one continuous present tense integument', which slowly unfolds 'all marryvoising moodmoulded cyclewheeling history' (*FW*, 184–9).

It is in this sense that language, as the generating third term in the triangles of literature and psychology, becomes the father for whom Joyce was searching. As a corrosive river it can journey back into the deep recesses of the psyche to provide a meeting-place for those antagonistic principles that manifested a conscious state of schizophrenia. In terms of literature, it objectifies a 'general omnibus character', inclusive of all the elements of 'homogenius' humanity, in the shape of a new kind of father-figure, 'the Great Sommboddy within the Omniboss' (*FW*, 415) or 'someone imparticular who will somewherise for the whole anyhow?' (*FW*, 602).

The 'some where' that will summarise the whole of 'cyclewheeling history' is the city of Dublin. The 'general omnibus character' who personifies this totality of manhood is the Earwicker family. Although there seem to be several members of the family and several variations of each member, each one characterises one aspect of the integrated human omnibus. It is also difficult to distinguish them from the topography of the 'anywhere' of Dublin. H.C.E., the original father-figure, is identified with the hill of Howth, Chapelizod and Phoenix Park. He is the masculine principle whose initials spell out his universality in their variation as 'Here Comes Everybody'. His wife A.L.P., identified with the river Liffey, which runs through the city, is the feminine principle, 'annyma' (anima), called Anna Livia Plurabelle. His daughter Issy is-a-belle, who can represent any and every kind of girl, while his sons, Shem and Shaun, are those familiar, age-old warring twins, equal and opposite, who inhabit each one of us in varying combinations. They are the rivals who compose the banks (*rivae*) of the river.

The structure within which their family history is unfolded is provided by Vico and Bruno. The coincidence that Dublin does have a Vico road which 'goes round and round to meet where terms begin', (*FW*, 452) and a bookshop called Browne and Nolan, act as proof of the universal principle that Joyce understood to be a paradigm of reality. Both literature and life were one 'grand continuum, overlorded by fate and interlarded with accidence' (*FW*, 472).

Language, as an alluvial deposit, is both the source and the texture of this grand continuum. 'In the buginning is the woid' (*FW*, 378) is Joyce's variation on the opening to St John's gospel. Language, as father, replaces the monarchical autonomous principle by an anarchical and heteronomous one. The void of the word (woid) is constitutive of language. Although a 'thing-of-words', language is not a 'thing-in-itself', because words, however autonomous they may appear, are always referential, their being is to relate to something else. Language is the fluid principle of continuity between the 'squidself' of the artist-father and the 'squirtscreened' image of his consubstantial son at every level of creation from theology to literature. Far from being an invention of human consciousness to act as mere communication between men, language is an aboriginal source of meaning, which flows through history and humanity, by whose shores the artist, as an alert and zealous beachcomber, is called to read 'the signature of all things'.

This new kind of poetry which is *Finnegans Wake* is a recreation of the myth of European man. It provides a restratification of the order of values as these had been developed at every level from philosophy to art. It introduces a new principle of a-causal orderedness through which art participates in the essentially synchronistic pattern of coincidence, which Joyce understood to be the movement of life. The text of *Finnegans Wake* is an artistic creation of this reality on paper: 'For that (the rapt one warns) is what papyr is meed of, made of, hides and hints and misses in prints' (*FW*, 20), which does not mean that it is a 'riot of blots and blurs', although it 'looks as like it as damn it' (*FW*, 118), for it is the work, as Joyce says of himself, of 'one of the greatest engineers if not the greatest in the world'.[42] When it was finished he wrote to Miss Weaver: 'I have passed 24 hours prostrate more than the priests on Good Friday. I think I have done what I wanted to do.'[43]

CHAPTER SEVEN

Seamus Heaney:
The End of Art is Peace

At the end of forty days Noah opened the porthole he had made in the ark and sent out ... the dove, to see whether the waters were receding from the surface of the earth. The dove, finding nowhere to perch, returned to him in the ark, for there was water over the whole surface of the earth; putting out his hand he took hold of it and brought it back into the ark with him. After waiting seven more days, again he sent the dove from the ark. In the evening, the dove came back to him and there it was with a new olive-branch in its beak. So Noah realised that the waters were receding from the earth. After waiting seven more days he sent out the dove, and now it returned to him no more. (Genesis 8:6-12.)

This is how I see the work of Seamus Heaney at the beginning of the twenty-first century. Our world has undergone a flood of unprecedented novelty and most of what we were accustomed to has been submerged in the deluge. We have two options – to stay in the ark or explore our new surroundings. We have to determine the water level and sound out the earth if we are to enter the promised and promising land that is before us. The spies we send before us need discernment and daring. One of the surest guides for me is Seamus Heaney.

Many of those who dislike or even denounce Heaney's poetry are saying that it is not memorable or sonorous: you don't find yourself spouting out verses when you are drunk or nostalgic, or worked up about some scenery you admire, some love of your own.

Then one hot day when fields were rank
With cowdung in the grass the angry frogs

Invaded the flax-dam; I ducked through hedges
To a coarse croaking that I had not heard
Before. The air was thick with a bass chorus.
Right down the dam gross-bellied frogs were cocked
On sods; their loose necks pulsed like sails. Some hopped:
The slap and plop were obscene threats. Some sat
Poised like mud grenades, their blunt heads farting.
I sickened, turned, and ran. The great slime kings
Were gathered there for vengeance and I knew
That if I dipped my hand the spawn would clutch it.

When this title poem from his first collection, *Death of a Naturalist,* appeared as a text in a public examination in England, there was uproar: exposing our youth at so tender an age to such obscenity. Presumably the objection was to 'farting'.

Others complain that Heaney isn't delivering the right message. He hasn't denounced the IRA; or he hasn't stood up and defended 'the cause'. For the first group his poetry is not pretty enough; for the second not political enough. Both may be correct up to a point, but neither are open to what the poetry actually is in itself, and are bludgeoning it to produce something different, a product of their own expectation. Heaney's poetry is neither pretty 'poesy' nor political propaganda. If you need to put a label on it, 'prophetic' might be nearer to the truth, although the poet himself might wince at the title. However, I am not alone in making this suggestion.

John Wilson Foster, in his book *The Achievement of Seamus Heaney*, makes a distinction between 'a vatic, vaginal poetry' and 'the phallic poetry of conscience, protest, social responsibility'.[1] From the beginning of his poetic career, Heaney has been aware of such distinctions.

When I took up the theme of redress in the Michaelmas Term of 1989, I was … clear … that the theme is in fact an aspect or consequence of my autobiography … The artist, the poet must in some sense set the world free to have a new go at its business. As I said also in that first lecture, if our given experience is a labyrinth, then its impassability is countered by the poet's imagining some equivalent of the labyrinth and bringing himself and the reader through it … But I also intended these lectures to be concerned with the redress of poetry in another sense, where the meaning of redress was 'to set (a person or thing) upright again, to raise again to an erect position … to restore, re-establish' … The work of my chosen writers is a 'vehicle of world harmony'.[2]

The epigraph in his first book of essays is a quotation from W. B. Yeats: 'Coventry Patmore has said "The end of art is peace," and the following of art is little different from the following of religion in the intense preoccupation it demands'.[3]

Heaney is one of my chosen writers as such a vehicle of world harmony. In the ark that is Ireland, ploughing towards new shores, most spiritual guidance of the past has been fearful, disheartening, condemnatory. Those who live by the porthole are grateful for the raven and the dove, who have the strength and skill to fly outside and bring us news from out there.

Although Heaney's poetry is similar in theme to many contemporaries, his manner, his tone, his 'element', are different. He is his own 'somnambulist':

Nestrobber's hands
and a face in its net of gossamer:

he came back weeping
to unstarch the pillow

and freckle her sheets
with tiny yolk.

There is an apology for his own sensitivity: 'its mouth agape / its whole head opened like a valve'. It is the voice of a child-prophet: amazed and almost ashamed of the words he has to speak. Such a sensitivity plonked into the violence of that childhood described in *Death of a Naturalist*, turns him into his own 'Bye-child', 'discovered in the henhouse where she had confined him. He was incapable of saying anything':

Little henhouse boy,
Sharp-faced as new moons
Remembered, your photo still
Glimpsed like a rodent
On the floor of my mind,

Little moon man,
Kennelled and faithful
At the foot of the yard,
Your frail shape, luminous,
Weightless, is stirring the dust.

A feminine sensitivity, aware of itself, afraid, unable to deny itself and yet terrified lest anyone should see it, gives this poetry its endearing texture of self-effacement and humility. It is as though his temperament alienated him from the rough and tumble of life on a farm and made him tell 'The wife's tale' (in the first person):

(He nodded at my white cloth on the grass.)
'I declare a woman could lay out a field
Though boys like us have little call for cloths.'
He winked, then watched me as I poured a cup.

The white sheet of paper that the poet must use to 'lay out a field' is also one 'which boys like us have little call for' and which causes us to wink and watch. It is not malicious. It is admiring. But it makes the poet aware of his being different. This might make some arrogant; it makes this poet guilty. And it makes him anxious not to offend, not to be a nuisance or a spoilsport.

Heaney is an outsider in disguise. His terror is that his cover might be blown. His vulnerability must go undetected. A heightened sensitivity and shame at his own condition make him, perhaps, overly grateful for love and allergic to censure.

When we leave the farm and rejoin him in the world of poetry, we find a replica of the one we have left. Among fellow poets and critics there are those 'who throw words like stones' and who 'spring out from behind hedges' and who use language 'like dogs to bark at my world'.

The situation in Northern Ireland can create a kind of poetry that is 'manly' and 'relevant'. Heaney is forced, once again, into a situation akin to the one he found himself in on the farm, where he has to 'die' as a 'naturalist' because 'on well-run farms pests have to be kept down' and always for Heaney:

> The fear came back
> When Dan trapped big rats, snared rabbits, shot crows
> Or, with a sickening tug, pulled old hens' necks.

The same fear and awe of fellow poets and critics may have prevailed in the new world in which he found himself. The kind of reverence that Piggy shows towards Ralph, the leader of men in Golding's *Lord of the Flies*, or the inherent lack of self-confidence of that 'boy of tears', Coriolanus, in Shakespeare's play, make him over-anxious to please Aufidius, the 'lion' he is 'proud to hunt'.

Of these, it seems to me, Seamus Deane was the prototype. The poem Heaney dedicates to Deane in the second part of *North*, 'The Ministry of Fear', opens with a proud declaration of comradeship:

> Well, as Kavanagh said, we have lived
> In important places. The lonely scarp
> Of St Columb's College, where I billeted
> For six years, overlooked your Bogside.

And there is a note of hero-worship and self-deprecation:

> In the first week
> I was so homesick I couldn't even eat
> The biscuits left to sweeten my exile.
> I threw them over the fence one night
> In September 1951
> When the lights of houses in the Lecky Road
> Were amber in the fog. It was an act
> Of stealth.
>
> Here's two on's are sophisticated ...
> Those poems in longhand, ripped from the wire spine
> Of your exercise book, bewildered me –

Vowels and ideas bandied free
As the seed-pods blowing off our sycamores.
I tried to write about the sycamores …

All the way through the poem there is that 'inferiority complex that dreams were made on', 'those hobnailed boots from beyond the mountain' and an almost pathetic gratitude to the figure who 'made a boarder's life not so bad': the heroic figure in the concentration camp who turned that trembling 'I' into a 'we' and 'all around us, though we hadn't named it, the ministry of fear'.

And the suggestion is that in Heaney's mind at the time, Deane was the 'real' poet, whose poems were 'ideas bandied free' like 'seed-pods blowing' and 'ripped from the wire spine', whereas his own were undeveloped and even undertaken in a desire to imitate or at least to share this interest, yet knowing that if they were there at all, they would have to concentrate on the tree itself.

More importantly, this 'development' involved – certainly since *A Door into the Dark* – a struggle between 'the private county Derry childhood part of myself' and 'the slightly aggravated young Catholic male part'. The articulation of this distinction takes place during an interview conducted by Seamus Deane in 1977.[4] The interview mirrors the relationship I am trying to detect between the two. Deane puts the questions: 'Do you believe that there is a recognisably Northern group of poets … connected with the Northern troubles? Does the fidelity of the poet to his community need to be catered for in a political way, especially in the context of the Northern crisis? Do you think that if some political stance is not adopted by you … this refusal might lead to a dangerous strengthening of earlier notions of the autonomy of poetry?' Loaded questions, especially to a poet who has just left Northern Ireland and come to live down south!

Heaney points to a place in his work where these questions come to a head:

You are touching there the very root and intimacy of the

poet's act. There is a poem in *North* which is a metaphorical consideration of this. I think it is a dangerous poem to have written – a poem called 'Hercules and Antaeus'. Hercules represents the balanced rational light while Antaeus represents the pieties of illiterate fidelity.[5]

Heaney has always been aware of the choice between the more instinctual Antaean forge and the more intellectual workshop of Hercules, a choice, as I see it, between two ways of being a poet rather than between atavism and rationality, instinct and intelligence. The poet is made up of all faculties, both instinctual and intellectual. The 'Antaean' poetry is as much a 'thought' as it is an 'instinctive surety'. The difference is in the use of all these faculties. The Antaean use of intellect is neither authoritative nor autonomous. The intellect here is the receiver of something given. The intellect winnows those instinctive gestures that reveal the source of the poetry. The return to this source and its celebration is what the poetry is about. If there is opposition here between two kinds of poet, two kinds of poetry, it is an opposition between two kinds of consciousness and, more importantly, between two kinds of 'willing'. As Heidegger said, 'The hard thing is to leave the covetous vision of things and to will in a way that is different from the purposeful self-assertiveness which is normal.' If willing remains mere self-assertion then the second kind of poetry, the other kind of being, doesn't happen.

I once followed these two kinds of poetry through Heaney's first five collections,[6] and although I would find some of what I said at that time too schematic and obsessed by the Antaeus/Hercules divide, I still find that the imagery of water, of the rat and of the dark, allied to the 'mould-hugger' as 'water-diviner', expresses the 'song of the earth', which best galvanises 'the secret gullies of his strength'. Water is symbol for what energises this poetry. Heaney compares the convulsion it causes to the way it electrifies a water diviner. Water is the music of the earth; earth giving tongue, uttering its secrets, 'suddenly broadcasting through a green aerial its secret stations'. Water travels through the earth and leaves behind the 'word-hoard' of its singing in

the silt and sound of language. The poet must burrow in that
word-hoard.

> Circling the terrain, hunting the pluck
> of water, nervous, but professionally

> unfussed. The pluck came sharp as a sting.
> The rod jerked with precise convulsions,
> Spring water suddenly broadcasting
> Through a green hazel its secret stations.

> The bystanders would ask to have a try.
> He handed them the rod without a word.
> It lay dead in their grasp till, nonchalantly,
> He gripped expectant wrists. The hazel stirred.

There is a connection between water and the rat. All those things
that used to terrify the child and make him panic have become
his major source of inspiration: as if nature, the soil, the earth
had seized him to examine their most sordid and yet stirring
secrets. The all-encompassing image is 'the dark', the element
this child was called to investigate. 'Dark delivers him hunger-
ing down each undulation.' And, 'I rhyme / To see myself, to set
the darkness echoing.'

Door into the Dark, both the collection and the poem itself, situate 'The Dark' significantly in the forge. The forge is behind
that 'door into the dark', which, at that point in time, was all
Heaney knew. This was the Antaean workshop, with its altar as
an anvil 'somewhere in the centre', 'an altar where he expends
himself in shape and music / ... to beat real iron out'. Towards
the end of this collection, the dark begins to take another shape.
It becomes 'bogland', where 'the wet centre is bottomless'. There
is a digging to be done. 'Trust the feel of what nubbed treasure /
your hands have known.'

There is an ambiguity about the earth as an actual physical
place and as an imaginary space, a dimension of interiority. In
his later collections Heaney explores and defines more accurately
these spaces. His 1991 volume, *Seeing Things*, is flanked on either
side by translations from the *Aeneid* and the *Inferno*, both con-

cerned with journeys 'to earth's hidden places'. These set the tone and the seriousness of the endeavour:

Talking about it isn't good enough
But quoting from it at least demonstrates
The virtue of an art that knows its mind.

Heaney explains later in the first of his 'squarings'. These translations from an old and a new testament of poetry give Virgil and Dante's advice when approaching the underworld. The first suggests that the way into 'these shadowy marshes' is easy enough because 'day and night black Pluto's door stands open'. The real problem is getting back out of it. And here Dante tries to dissuade the tempted poet from entering Avernus, saying that if Charon, 'the ferry-man of that livid marsh', 'objects to you' and says that you should not be making this 'crossing', then listen to him carefully and do not be too anxious to overreach yourself.

However, both accept that some people are 'fated' to make this journey and this inevitable impulse is linked with desire and love:

Still, if love torments you so much and you so much need
To sail the Stygian lake twice and twice to inspect
The murk of Tartarus, if you will go beyond the limit,
Understand what you must do beforehand.

Seeing Things is Heaney's attempt to understand what you must do before making this journey. It is a book of thresholds, half-doors, lintels, windows. The poet, with all the concentrated attention of apprehension, is examining both the threshold and the 'field of vision':

Between two whitewashed pillars, where you could see
Deeper into the country than you expected
And discovered that the field behind the hedge
Grew more distinctly strange as you kept standing
Focused and drawn in by what barred the way.

The first thing you have to do is prepare your hands and your pens. Your fingers will become 'pliable twigs' and you will discover a magic pen ('The Golden Bough'), which, if you are the one chosen for the journey, will recognise you:

Therefore look up and search deep and when you have
    found it
Take hold of it boldly and duly. If fate has called you,
The bough will come away easily, of its own accord.[7]

So, here we have Heaney, marching in procession with these
two august psychopomps, looking and feeling like a charlatan.
At the test of the 'Golden Bough', Heaney finds to his amaze-
ment that it does come easily and of its own accord. He has no
problem about writing: 'His hands were warm and small and
knowledgeable ... they were two ferrets, playing all by themselves in a moonlit field.'

But what of 'the journey back'? This is the first poem of Part I
of *Seeing Things*, where Heaney is visited by Larkin's shade
quoting Dante. Larkin amazes Heaney by seconding the notion
of the two prophets that he should gird himself to face the ordeal
of 'my journey and my duty'. Heaney is still trying to wake himself up out of this mythological nightmare, which is becoming
too serious by the minute. He still hasn't given in and nobody is
going to force him:

Still my old self. Ready to knock one back.
A nine-to-five man who had seen poetry.

Now he has seen what poetry is really all about, but nobody else
knows that he has seen it, so he does not have to make the journey unless he wants to, and for the moment he is going to enjoy
his own old self, who has a part-time interest in the underworld.
And this is where the 1991 book of poetry begins and ends. It is
seeing things, not saying them or doing them (and 'only pure
words and deeds secure the house'); it is talking ambiguously,
equivocally about a poetic 'vocation' too awful to be contem-
plated, too potentially ludicrous to be preached:

So from the back of her shrine the Sybil of Cumae
Chanted fearful equivocal words and made the cave echo
With sayings where clear truths and mysteries
Were inextricably twined.

The first part examines the 'field of vision', the journey, the prospect; Heaney's own unpreparedness, unsuitability, fear; his experience of the Golden Bough in his hands, the undeniable potential in himself and what he thinks the whole 'vocation' will mean from now on: 'Me waiting until I was nearly fifty / To credit marvels'. The second part is Heaney 'squaring' up to 'the crossing', getting himself and the ground into shape. Also preparing us for the next step:

Strange how things in the offing, once they're sensed

Convert to things foreknown;

And how what's come upon is manifest

Only in light of what has been gone through.

In the first part 'we marked the pitch'. Pitch has both connotations of place and tone. 'They marked the spot, marked time and held it open.' The journey to be undertaken concerns the holding open of a space, the passing of a limit. In all of this Heaney's father (Anchises in the prologue) plays an important part. It is as though he has prefigured, symbolised unknowingly, predicted retrospectively, the path to be taken. He is Adam. His ash plant is the silver bough, which prefigures the golden. If we 'catch the old one first', then, through its symbolism, we will catch a glimpse of the one to come: 'Blessed be the detachment of dumb love', it will pass on the message, the tradition, 'like a witless elder'. That is why it has to be seen before it is said. 'Once upon a time' Heaney saw his 'undrowned' father come back from the kind of experience that Heaney must now undertake. He describes it in the third part of the poem 'Seeing Things':

But when he came back, I was inside the house

And saw him out the window, scatter-eyed

And daunted, strange without his hat,

His step unguided, his ghosthood immanent.

The imagery is significant. Heaney was inside the house. His father was outside, without cover, without his hat. 'Everything off balance', he had gone over into a deep whirlpool ... 'all tumbling off the world'. Here was his father, who was totally unprepared and inimical to the kind of journey being proposed, 'a rebuke to fanciness and a shrine to limit', being turned into a kind of prophetic X-ray of the fall being prepared for his son. A kaleidoscope of imagery describes this fall, the vocation, the journey, the crossing. In this poem we are on a boat:

As we went sailing evenly across

The deep, still, seeable-down-into water

Heaney's task as a poet is somehow to go down into this element and either haul something up out of it or allow it to 'foster a heavy greenness' in himself. He 'panicked at the shiftiness and heft of the craft itself'. And 'craft' here can be understood as both the boat and the work of the artist. It is also described as similar to 'booting a leather football/truer and farther/than you ever expected!' or a great catch, which can be a ball or fish. It is also like 'the effortlessness of a spinning reel'. But again there is panic in the boat in case what you catch is too big and danger-ous. In the poem 'A Haul' he describes how:

The hole he smashed in the boat

opened, the way Thor's head

opened out there on the sea.

He felt at one with space,

unroofed and obvious –

This is something like the kind of openness that is required of the poet. It is an openness that goes down into the water and al-lows the water to use it as a filter or a sponge. It is an openness also to the earth. In fact it is to do with dwelling in the earth in a certain way, creating a house, open through the floor to the bare earth, open through windows and roof to total exposure:

I was four but I turned four hundred maybe

Encountering the ancient dampish feel

Of a clay floor …

Ground of being. Body's deep obedience

To all its shifting tenses …

Out of that earth house I inherited …

By the true act and art of poetry, a journey is made that allows earth to be inhabited and space to be recapitulated. We get a glimpse of the 'fall' that such a journey involves in the poem

'Wheels within Wheels', where the poet describes how he 'learned the art of pedalling/(by hand) a bike turned upside down':

Something about the way those pedal treads
Worked very palpably at first against you
And then began to sweep your hand ahead
Into a new momentum – that all entered me
Like an access of free power …

Heaney realises that if he gives himself to poetry in a certain way it could 'sweep your hand ahead into a new momentum' and drag you as would a whale at the other end of the line you so innocently started casting into the deep, the infinite, the open.

Almost to avoid this possibility, Heaney spends time in Part I describing all the things which stand in his way, and yet which bring into focus the invisible infinity – the dreaded 'field of vision' – so that 'the field behind the hedge/grew more distinctly strange as you kept standing/Focused and drawn in by what barred the way'.

In this way of 'seeing things', the pen in your hand becomes 'the pitchfork' (in his father's world it was 'of all implements the one that came near to an imagined perfection'), which can also be an instrument of music or a javelin or a haymaker or a pen. In whichever guise, it is 'accurate and light' because of 'the clip and dart of it'. It is the Golden Bough that can sound the depths:

And then when he thought of probes that reached the farthest,
He would see the shaft of a pitchfork sailing past
Evenly, imperturbably through space,
Its prongs starlit and absolutely soundless –
But has learned at last to follow that simple lead
Past its own aim, out to an other side
Where perfection – or nearness to it – is imagined
Not in the aiming but the opening hand.

The image becomes a symbol. It contains the whole journey to be undertaken. It represents art, music, poetry. In itself it has the mixture of a tuning fork, something pitched at an object and an implement for harvesting. The poem describes the space to be probed and the attitude of the prober. The schoolbag is the 'thing' that represents the poet's education 'so take it for a word-hoard and a handsel'. 'The Biretta' recapitulates the Roman Catholic religion in which the poet was raised. This prevents him from hearing 'vocation' in the acoustic it is meant to reach him now. Here it 'put the wind up me and my generation'. It is only by turning the religion of his youth upside down that it can be of help to him in the religious vocation that is now his as a poet:

> Now I turn it upside down and it is a boat –
> A paper boat, or the one that wafts into
> The first lines of the *Purgatorio*
> As poetry lifts its eyes and clears its throat.

'The Settle Bed' represents his culture, his home background (opposite to 'the wishing chair', 'freshening your outlook/ Beyond the range you thought you'd settled for') – cosy, comfortable securities. In it he is 'cribbed' and his 'ear shuttered up', surrounded by 'its own dumb, tongue-and-groove worthiness and un-get-roundable weight'. These three nets, like the ones Joyce left Ireland to escape, are – as Heaney says in 'A Basket of Chestnuts' – 'what he thought he'd maybe use/As a decoy'. They prevent from getting down to the real business.

Other distractions are the poet's own poor image of himself as a suitable candidate for the journey down to earth's hidden places, or, depending on the special imagery adopted, to its highest reaches, as in mast or mountain-top. Heaney sees himself as a sentry/'Forgotten and unable to remember/The whys and wherefores of his lofty station' … 'That far-seeing joker posted high over the fog' … 'One sound is saying, "You are not worth tuppence".'

> But the others are in the Forum Café waiting,
> Wondering where we are. What'll you have?'

This is where a large part of Heaney would rather be – with the lads in the pub, a democrat in the marketplace. Even though with that other side of himself – the one that is called:

> We climbed the Capitol by moonlight, felt
> The transports of temptation on the heights.

Parts of Heaney's description of himself in 'Glanmore Revisited' are reminiscent of of Dostoevsky's sneer: 'I knew one "fighter for an idea" who told me himself that when he was deprived of tobacco in prison he was so distressed by this privation that he nearly went and betrayed his "idea" just to get a little tobacco! and it is such a man who says, "I'm fighting for humanity!" … How can a man give up his habits, where can such a slave go, if he is so used to satisfying his innumerable needs which he has himself created?' And here is Heaney when 'Lent came in', reminding him of his high vocation and the necessity for self-control, the exercise of will 'and wild for discipline'. Well, our heroic guide to the underworld gave it the two-finger sign and 'taunted it with scents of nicotine / As I lit one off another'. This plea of unworthiness and role of Devil's advocate against himself reaches its most poignant note in the second part of 'Wheels within Wheels', where he claims that not only is he weak, unfit and far too gregarious, but he has used his glorious talent for unworthy purposes.

But enough was not enough. Who ever saw
The limit in the given anyhow?
In fields beyond our house there was a well
('The well' we called it. It was more a hole
With water in it, with small hawthorn trees
On one side, and a muddy, dungy ooze
On the other, all tramped through by cattle).
I loved that too. I loved the turbid smell,
The sump-life of the place like old chain oil

And there, next thing, I brought my bicycle.
I stood its saddle and its handlebars
Into the soft bottom, I touched the tyres
To the water's surface, then turned the pedals
Until like a mill-wheel pouring at the treadles
(But here reversed and lashing a mare's tail)
The world-refreshing and immersed back wheel
Spun lace and dirt-suds there before my eyes
And showered me in my own regenerate clays.

For weeks I made a nimbus of old glit.

Then the hub jammed, rims rusted, the chain snapped.

Not only is all this self-analysis insufficient to excuse the poet from the duty inflicted upon him, it is, perhaps, the reason why he is most suited to perform this task. He has to sink himself into the mud ('To the destructive element submit', as Conrad puts it in *Lord Jim*). The poet as mud addict is required to sink into that element while retaining his consciousness in order to discover the meaning of his own muddiness and at the same time transform the mud! 'He is like a sentry':

A bulrush sentried the lough shore: I had to
Wade barefoot over spongy, ice-cold marsh
(Soft bottom with bog water seeping through
The netted weeds) to get near where it stood
Perennially anomalous and dry,
Like chalk or velvet rooting in the mud.

This task of remaining chalk and velvet while at the same time rooting in the mud is a service rendered to the earth. It is a happy fall (*felix culpa*), which may jam the hub, rust the rim and snap the chain of the bicycle used to achieve it, but it is essential to the earthing of the world. It is the task of opening, of achieving the open.

As if a ladder leaned against the world
And they were climbing it but might fall back
Into the total air and emptiness
They carried on their shoulders.

The poet acts as the lip that allows the earth to 'brim over'. He waits as the flood collects beneath him. He may not feel himself to be the natural inheritor of such a task, but he is its 'fosterling', and the 'immanent hydraulics' of this land have chosen him to be their 'silting hope'. He has to achieve the 'in-placedness' that will produce in him 'that heavy greenness fostered by water':

Evening was dam water they saw down through.
The scene stood open …
They gazed beyond themselves

Some people regard the poet as 'steeped in luck': 'I hear them say, steeped, steeped, steeped in luck'. In fact he is steeped in earth, ground, being, bog, water, humanity, and it is a mixed blessing, as it is an awesome and fearful calling, to listen

And hear the flood too, gathering from under,

Biding and boding like a masterwork

Or a named name that overbrims itself.

Whether Heaney is a great poet, the best poet, the number one poet, is calculation in quite another scale. He will be judged 'in apposition with/Omnipresence, equilibrium, brim'. (And in a court where mere innocuousness has never gained approval or acquittal.)

In the six sonnets of the first part of *Seeing Things*, Heaney returns to Glanmore and there attempts to construct a house for himself that will reproduce all the security and the double-glazed insulation against vocation that was once enjoyed in the womb of the settle bed. This home will be an earth-proof, weather-proof, sound-proof tortoise-shell, and poetry can become the safe and pretty task of painting and decorating its interior.

I liked it low and closed,

Its claustrophobic, nest-up-in-the-roof

Effect. I liked the snuff-dry feeling,

The perfect, trunk-lid fit of the old ceiling.

Under there, it was all hutch and hatch.

In this setting, the poet could be safe from the open, the outside,

And whatever rampaged out there couldn't reach us,

Firelit, shuttered, slated and stone-walled.

The passion, the curiosity, the fecklessness that might prompt a foray into the unknown, the cold or the dark, are shut out, and 'love' is only 'allowed within the rules' of the game of Scrabble played in this house. However, as the poet 'hibernated on behind the dormer', something else in his nature stirred against this executive suite:

Even then, my first impulse was never

To double-bar a door or lock a gate;

And fitted blinds and curtains drawn over
Seemed far too self-protective and uptight.

So the second person in there has his/her way: 'You were the one for skylights.' So the poet becomes one who stares, squints, angles, aims and peeps through doors, half-doors, thresholds, awnings, openings, skylights, windows. And 'when the slates came off, extravagant/Sky entered and held surprise wide open'.

Part II, called 'Squarings', depicts the poet facing up to, getting ready, preparing for his journey. He is still

In a doorway, and on the stone doorstep
A beggar shivering in silhouette.

He still hankers after the security of the battened-down hatches. He advises himself to 'relocate the bed-rock in the threshold' and to 'take squarings':

Squarings? In the game of marbles, squarings
Were all those anglings, aimings, feints and squints
You were allowed before you'd shoot

It is possible to create a security at the threshold, to climb all the way up to the top of the diving board, describing every step of the ladder, and then make a nest there and never dive. This is the point, the angle, the position from which 'You squinted out from a skylight of the world'. But this part of the book describes the kind of dwelling-place that the poet needs in order to achieve his task. The floor must have direct access to the earth (or even water) for 'encountering the ancient dampish feel/of a clay floor'. This is the 'ground of being' which absorbs the 'Body's deep obedience to all its shifting tenses'. The roof or windows of the house must be open or give access to 'unroofed scope'. It must have the double condition of being both 'airy' and 'earthed'. It is in such a setting ('settings' is one of the sections in this second part) that the poet may dwell and be poetically. He is a lightning conductor, and the electrifying moments of his creative existence – 'a phenomenal instant when the spirit flares' – are outlined and X-rayed in geometrical vocabulary.

In earshot of the pool where the salmon jumped
Back through its own unheard concentric soundwaves
A mower leans forever on his scythe.
He has mown himself to the centre of the field
and stands in a final perfect ring

and

Nothing rose to the occasion after that
Until, in a circus ring, drumrolled and spotlit,
Cowgirls wheeled in, each one immaculate
At the still centre of a lariat.
Perpetuum mobile. Sheer pirouette.
Tumblers. Jongleurs. Ring-a-rosies. *Stet*!

These images are seeking *claritas* ('the dry-eyed Latin word') in examples. The poetry seeks to make us 'present there as the smell of grass / And suntan oil', willing the poets 'to dare it to the centre they are lost for …' This centre is like 'three marble holes thumbed in the concrete road' … 'three stops to play the music of the arbitrary on'. What the poet has to do to create a music that would be some proof of God's existence is to let his ear attend 'where the extravagant / Passed once under full sail into the longed-for'. This attention and excruciating concentration from the hub to the circumference, the centre to the rim, is expressed in an anecdote about Thomas Hardy, who lay down flat on the earth allowing his 'small cool brow' to experiment with infinity by making it 'like an anvil waiting for sky to make it sing the perfect pitch of his dumb being'. And, this note having been sounded, it would echo above 'the resonating amphorae' to create ripples of sound-waves on the ether which would last and be lasting for earth:

Outward from there, to be the same ripple
Inside him at its last circumference.

Such is the dreaded crucifixion of the poet
                                        on a promontory
Scanning empty space, so body-racked he seems
Untranslatable into the bliss
Ached for at the moon-rim of his forehead

Who could blame any poet tempted to 'roof it again. Batten down. Dig in' rather than stand 'unroofed and obvious', saying 'A farewell to surefootedness' by awaiting 'a pitch beyond our usual hold upon ourselves'. Such is the torture of allowing one-self to be drawn by language, as Hector was dragged around the walls of Troy, or Savonarola was tortured with ropes hanging him by the wrist:

The open they came into by these moves
Stood opener, hoops came off the world

Who are we, as critics and as fellow human beings, to recom-mend 'the commanded journey', and, in face of this 'ultimate Stony up-againstness', to tell him: 'Shield your eyes, look up and face the music'.

One of the poems in this second part tells how the monks of Clonmacnoise were at prayer inside the oratory, when a ship passing in the air above them got its anchor hooked into the altar rails. 'A crewman shinned and grappled down the rope.' He could not release the anchor.

'This man can't bear our life here and will drown',
The abbot said, 'unless we help him.' So
They did, the freed ship sailed, and the man climbed back
Out of the marvellous as he had known it.

Heaney and the poetry, 'sluggish in the doldrums of what hap-pens', have to be tempted into the marvellous as he has not known it – 'Me waiting until I was nearly fifty / to credit marvels … Time to be dazzled and the heart to lighten'. There can no longer be the great difference and distinction between the life of the monks at prayer in their oratory and that of the ship above them in the air. Either this ferry-man 'crewman' can make the journey up or down and survive it, or we will all drown, as none of us will be able to bear our life here. And indeed we must help him in every way. He is one of the few of our contemporaries for whom 'the bough will come away easily of its own accord', Prosperpina's own special gift, and it is useless to speculate about why it comes away in one hand and not in another. And yet to be chosen by fate does not imply that one has to respond.

What on earth would entice anyone to undertake such a journey? Once again our two flanking elders supply two possible answers, which we hope are sufficient for the one who translated them so effectively. The first is that love torments you so much that you need to sail the Stygian lake and are impelled to 'go beyond the limit'. The second is that:

> they are eager to go across the river
> Because Divine Justice goads them with its spur
> So that their fear is turned into desire.

The question remains: Where is this place, this protectorate of poetry? It has been pointed out that Heaney has moved from 'air' (in *Sweeney Astray*, 1983), through sea ('The whole sea' of *Station Island*, 1984), to earth (in *Seeing Things*, 1991), and that now, as Helen Vendler suggests, everything takes place within the poet's mind: 'Religious and philosophical certainty have been left behind, and transcendence has been reimagined as that which can occur in "psychic space" so as to create a virtual world of both memory and value.'[8] She quotes Heaney commenting on Yeats: 'We are at that thrilling moment when the place of writing shifts its locus into psychic space.' This place, called 'aftermath' in Heaney's poem 'Hailstones' (from *The Haw Lantern*, 1987) is made 'out of the melt of the real thing / smarting into its absence'. And sonnet 8 of 'Clearances' (*The Haw Lantern*) describes a chestnut tree that was planted in the year of Heaney's birth, which has now been felled. 'Its virtual existence in his mind, now that its "real" existence is over, is "a space / Utterly empty, utterly a source".' This 'bright nowhere' of the virtual world is the 'place' we have been waiting for Heaney to reach so that he can speak its existence in poetic language. And this happens in *The Spirit Level* (1996).

The first fact to note about this collection is that it is 'for Helen Vendler'. Has Heaney nailed his colours to the mast and endorsed the Vendler reading of his work to date? I find her influence too narrow-minded and pedantic. I would prefer if she (and he) were more open to 'the marvellous'. In *Sweeney Astray*, for instance, when the revived Sweeney asks himself what the

result has been of his being driven into 'the kingdom of the air',
Heaney's poem says:

Give him his due, in the end

he opened my path to a kingdom
of such scope and neuter allegiance
my emptiness reigns at its whim.

But Vendler cautions and prescribes. She thinks 'neuter allegiance' is 'a position of great psychological danger for a passionate poet', but she accepts that her protegé has to be there as 'it is
the only recourse in the face of solicitations from all sides to betray the accuracy of art in favour of the tendentiousness of argument'. So, one is allowed to remain in the sanitized zone rather
than be tempted by the vulgarity of 'argument'. But Vendler
puts a ban on incursion into the area of 'religion', which is 'following the path of incipient grandiosity'.

When the poet whispers: 'I would restore/the great chambers of Boyne', she is worried about him, because, although he
'fully recognises the elements of hallucination and self-delusion
in the realms of memory and value', he still 'accepts the realm of
imaginative force as one of indubitable emotional and historical
power'. And this causes her to put in a bracket of censure, telling
him that he really should extend the skepticism which they both
share to this area also – having taken for granted that they both
are one in their 'epistemological and religious skepticism'.

Vendler is unsurpassed at pointing out where lines might be
borrowed. When Heaney said in a radio programme; 'I felt that
my first poems were trying to write like stained glass but that I
would like to write a poetry of window glass,' Vendler immediately spots the connection with Herbert's 'The Elixir':

A man that looks on glasse,
On it may stay his eye;
Or if he pleaseth, through it passe,
And then the heav'n espie.

And she does accept that such a poetry is struggling with 'contradictory allegiances ... to the numinous and to the matter-of-
fact', but she is happy that Heaney is sorting all that out within

the precincts of his own psyche. There is no possibility and no permission to explore another dimension to poetry altogether.

I prefer, for my part – 'waiting for the next move in the game' – to read what the later poetry says about such things: 'you are like a rich man entering heaven/Through the ear of a raindrop. Listen now again.' So,

'On you go now! Run, son, like the devil
And tell your mother to try
To find me a bubble for the spirit level

This collection is trying to find that bubble for the spirit level, whether inside or outside of the psyche, is probably impossible to identify. As a bubble, it is a separate and distinct enclosure, a place of its own, a protectorate for poetry, an emptiness accessible only to the defenceless, to those who have emptied themselves: 'my emptiness reigns at its whim'. This is the place 'beyond' our 'psychic space', unattainable unless 'I thought of walking round and round a space/utterly empty, utterly a source/... Silent, beyond silence listened for.'

Heaney has been there. The poetry speaks from there. Each poem is a portent. And that means precisely what Vendler has described so much better than anyone else. ('When it came to gathering, Persephone/Was in the halfpenny place compared to' her.) And, perhaps, he would never have got there without her help. But, whether she likes it or not, he has restored 'the great chambers of Boyne':

So who were we to want to hang back there
In spite of all?
In spite of all, we sailed
Beyond ourselves and over and above ...

There is in this collection what one commentator has called 'the enduring child', the same child we recognise throughout all Heaney's poetry. This time he is on 'a Sofa in the Forties' or on 'the swing' or 'when I was small I swallowed an awn of rye'. The child we've been advising, cajoling, admonishing, castigating, for the last sixty years now! 'Don't go near bad boys/In that college that you're bound for. Do you hear me?/Do you hear me speaking to you? Don't forget!' And he has the same endearing diffidence, shy perceptivity, startling versatility and devastating precision that can, as always, take 'hold like a chain on every bodily sprocket', or 'catch the heart off guard and blow it open'. But something has happened to the child. He has been somewhere in the meantime. From that 'sofa-train' in the forties that carried him into 'history and ignorance', 'like unlit carriages through fields at night', he has been travelling through a tunnel – whether this be represented as a railway tunnel, a deep well, or a door into the dark, it doesn't matter – the darkness, the ignorance, the claustrophobic constriction, the fear, are the same. But 'I can see the sky at the bottom of it now', and his eyes seem 'full / Of open darkness and a watery shine'.

And there has been a 'liberation', an eventual emergence into open space. The tunnels and the wells were a descent into hell. And now he has come out of it. '*Hosannah ex infernis*. Burning wells.'

To have lived it through and now be free to give
Utterance, body and soul – to wake and know
Every time that it's gone and gone for good, the thing
That nearly broke you –

Is worth it all, the five years on the rack,
The fighting back, the being resigned, and not
One of the unborn will appreciate
Freedom like this ever.

All of which is depicted in *The Spirit Level* in terms of 'The Flight Path' and 'The Swing', as a taking off and moving upwards, 'heady and defenceless / Like inmates liberated in that yard.'

The swing is 'a lure let down to tempt the soul to rise'. And 'sooner or later, / We all learned one by one to go sky high.' In 'Two Stick Drawings' we find him there 'as if / He were leashed to it and it drew him on / Like a harness rod of the inexorable.' This poem is followed by a description of his vocation ('A Call') to follow that inexorable 'lure'. 'Hold on,' she said (not Helen Vendler this time), 'I'll just run out and get him.' So, Heaney has been 'got' this time, whatever about reluctance in the past, what-

ever about 'The selves we struggled with and struggled out of',
he has eventually been lured to the wellhead. And 'At the
Wellhead' he must 'wield and slice and poke and parry' until
you 'sing yourself to where the singing comes from.' The source.

> And then this ladder of our own that ran
> deep into a well-shaft being sunk
> in broad daylight, men puddling at the source
>
> through tawny mud, then coming back up
> deeper in themselves for having been there ...

This is the place. But what kind of 'place' is it? Is it a geographical province or a 'space within the psyche'? First of all, it is very
near: it 'spelled promise / And newness in the back yard of our
life.' And then it is also very far:

> When I answered that I came from 'far away',
> The policeman at the roadblock snapped, 'Where's that?'

It is very near and very far. It is 'Beyond where we dumped our
refuse and old bottles' (and therefore beyond 'The Circus
Animals' Desertion', the 'foul rag and bone shop of the heart').
Beyond psychology. In fact, so far 'beyond', that it constitutes
'the bright rim of the extreme', and we can only follow it 'as far
as the eye can see / To where it can't until he sketches where.'
And he sketches 'where' in these poems through 'the sway of
language and its furtherings'. Language is what gives form to
'where his head had been'.

> Then I entered a strongroom of vocabulary
> Where words like urns that had come through the fire
> Stood in their bone-dry alcoves next a kiln
>
> And came away changed, like the guard who'd seen
> The stone move in a diamond-blaze of air
> Or the gates of horn behind the gates of clay.

The words of these poems, the language, carry us to 'The Spirit
Level' and introduce us to the 'gatekeeper / Of the open gates
behind the brows of birds':

> Eleven in the morning. I made a note:
> 'Rock-lover, loner, sky-sentry, all hail!'

This is a journey you make on your own. 'We all learned one by one to go sky high' ... 'To the hermit's eyrie above Rocamadour.' It consists of 'everything intimate / And fear-swathed.' 'If I do write something, / Whatever it is, I'll be writing for myself.' It is inside yourself, at the most intimate space of your interiority. 'Intimate and helpful, like a cure / You didn't notice happening.' But it is also 'outside'. He is 'inside / His cell, but the cell is narrow, so / One turned-up palm is out of the window ...'

A part of him is 'inside' and a part of him is 'outside' when he reaches this 'centre'. In fact, he is 'high-sterned' and 'splay-bottomed': the 'high' part, 'a crook-necked one – to snare the highest briars', the other part forming 'the little pyramid / At the centre every bit as hollow / As a part of me that sank because it knew / The whole thing would go soggy once you launched it.'

And the two parts are equal, 'Equal and opposite' – the high part 'winking ahead of what it hauls away', while the other is 'Widening far back down, a wake through starlight.'

And now it is – both where I have been living

And where I left – a distance still to go

Like starlight that is light years on the go

From far away and takes light years arriving.

And what is 'It' or 'the Thing' that the poetry is saying? 'The Thing' is a kind of 'locus', it is the focus of the 'gathering' forces of the Symbolic in its effort to domesticate the Real: 'the thing that nearly broke you'. And here we are at the level of Vendler's 'third act' of criticism: assessing how the poet's imagination works in symbolic form. Heaney is searching for 'the Thing', as Lacan also calls it,[9] which is the core of human activity in the midst of a forest of desires. Something always tantalisingly out of reach, something lost. 'As lost object, the Thing is what the subject lacks, therefore wants, hence it is the object-cause-of-its-desire.' The lost object leaves a void in the emerging subject that Lacan calls 'its "excluded interior" or "intimate exteriority," a kind of "vacuole".' The dictionary describes this word as a minute cavity in a cell, containing air or fluid, etc. In other words, it is inside the cell but it is 'the outside' within it. And like St Kevin's hand stretched out the window, it is space enough to create another world. A nest where birds can fly upwards. But before that happens, even as such a vacuole it remains at the heart of oneself, the centre of gravitation. And 'it is veiled by signifiers or "portents" in its setting that constitute a magic circle around it and represent it in its absence.'

The poet has to get to this place, first of all, and then speak from it. Getting there is described in 'The Swing':

To start up by yourself, you hitched the rope
Against your backside and backed on into it
Until it tautened, then tiptoed and drove off
As hard as possible. You hurled a gathered thing
From the small of your own back into the air.

That is the gymnastics of it. The inner 'swing' – what Rilke calls 'the turning'. Getting to the place. Once there, a transformation takes place. All the elements of the world we know are penetrated and transformed by the elements from the 'outside' coming through the vacuole. The cocoon of culture is transformed into a butterfly. 'And bigly, softly as breath of life / In a breath of air, a lime-green butterfly.'

All the different elements that make up his previous collections of poems – air, water, earth – have here been transmogrified to 'The Spirit Level':

The first words got polluted
Like river water in the morning
Flowing with the dirt
Of blurbs and the front pages.
My only drink is meaning from the deep brain,
What the birds and the grass and the stones drink.
Let everything flow
Up to the four elements,
Up to water and earth and fire and air.

To find the words that will express this reality 'you have good stamina / You stay on where it happens.' The poet has to 'wield and slice and poke and parry / The unhindering air; until he found the true extension of himself.' Writing through the 'unhindering air' is like a windscreen wiper swathing water off the glass. 'The watery grey / being lashed on in broad swatches, then drying out / Whiter on whiter.' Painting white on white. Or, 'a negative this time, in dazzle-dark', in a similar metaphor expressing the same apophatic approach.

'Where had we come from, what was this kingdom / We knew we'd been restored to?' This 'true extension of himself', which is beyond him, is a 'flight path' … 'that made him jubilant'. In fact, 'a dove rose in my breast' and rose to 'The Spirit Level'. But he also acknowledges that even though the where it came from was at the inmost intimacy of his own interiority, it led to somewhere else, to an inner exteriority, a 'somewhere' else. 'And somewhere the dove rose. And kept on rising.'

So, it is neither 'here' nor 'there'. In fact, as a kingdom, as a place, it can only exist through the words of the poet. The poet has to allow his heart to be blown open and then allow the breath of the 'Spirit' to breathe through his breath:

> You are neither here nor there,
> A hurry through which known and strange things pass
> As big soft buffetings come at the car sideways
> And catch the heart off guard and blow it open.

As Neil Corcoran points out, *Seeing Things* was dedicated to Derek Mahon, who in 1988 published his translations of the contemporary French poet, Philippe Jaccottet, whose abiding intuition is that '*Il y a une autre réalité mais elle est en celle-ci.*' (There is another reality but it is in this one.)

Helen Vendler has written what many might see as a definitive work on Heaney's *oeuvre* to date.[10] She is, in Denis Donoghue's words, 'the most influential reviewer of contemporary poetry in English', and her eloquence and command of the grammar and syntax of her subject make it difficult to suggest that she has missed a most important point about her subject. It is also difficult to show where exactly she has gone wrong. However, it seems to me that her deficiency is philosophical rather than literary: it has to do with the 'partial and somewhat domestic' (Donoghue again) definition of the lyric that underpins her critical analysis. Her book is dangerous because it is so dazzlingly comprehensive, articulate and convincing, that other, less muscular, manicured or self-assured commentators might baulk at the prospect of challenging so august an authority.

At the level of theory, my reservations have to do with her definition of the lyric: 'Its act is to present, adequately and truthfully, through the means of temporally prolonged symbolic form, the private mind and heart caught in the changing events of a geographical place and a historical epoch.' These requirements, as Denis Donoghue points out (talking of her book *Soul Says*):

> make it impossible to recognise words that don't issue from these given conditions, words which bring an incipiently imagined experience into being for the first time ... The effect of Vendler's taking the soul to mean the self when the self is alone is that the soul is deemed to be merely equal to its knowledge at any moment. There is nothing beyond what the soul knows. Knowledge is therefore deemed to be absolute; it extends itself to cover every occasion, and governs the entire field. The lyric voice utters that knowledge. There is no remainder. Nothing falls outside the range of that voice, or beneath it.
>
> This explains why Vendler appears to have little sense of the sublime or the demonic as states in excess of the soul's knowledge, states in which the soul is driven, dreading the loss of its powers, beyond itself or beside itself.[11]

Her gloss on two poems in particular can illustrate my reservations. The first is *viii* of 'Lightenings' in *Seeing Things*, where she fails to convey the humorous element in the poem. Heaney quoted it in his Nobel speech, called 'Crediting Poetry', thus referring back to the earlier poem in that same collection, 'Fosterling':

> Heaviness of being. And poetry
> Sluggish in the doldrums of what happens.
> Me waiting until I was nearly fifty
> To credit marvels.

This relationship between poetry and the marvelous, so present in Heaney, is absent in her commentary: 'The poem implies that just as it would be death for the man from heaven to remain in the thicker air of earth, so it would be equally fatal to human beings to attempt to breathe for any length of time the rarefied air of the transcendent. We may ascend to it for a short glimpse of the marvellous, but we must then return to the phenomenal world.' This is just after she quotes Heaney as saying that the poem's two realms represent 'two orders of knowledge which we might call the practical and the poetic'. In other words, poetry is the realm of the marvellous as perceived in and through the phenomenal: 'the frontier between them is there for the crossing.'

There is a whole difference in texture and tone in what Heaney himself says about this same poem:

I take it to be pure story. It has the entrancement of a narrative that's mysterious and absolute. It needs no explanation but even so, you could read it as a text about the necessity of being in two places at the one time, on the ground with the fatherly earthiness, but also keeping your mind open and being able to go up with the kite, on the magic carpet too, and live in the world of fantasy. To live in either world entirely and resolutely, and not to shift, is risky. For your wholeness you need to inhabit both worlds. I think the medieval notion of human beings occupying the angelic situation between the angels and the beasts is true. When I wrote *Seeing Things*, I think I had been quite close to the ground, and that then I lifted up my eyes to the hills, to the roof and to the Clonmacnoise boat.[12]

Not so Vendler. When she walks she treads upon the ground, resolutely and entirely. Her 'lyrical' order is of a quite different texture: 'These imagined grids and lines are the latitude and longitude lines ... by which mentality orders the world.' The poet as quantity surveyor or architect's assistant. 'Seeing Things' is an imposition of the categorical imperatives of 'mentality' upon the poet's surrounding history and geography.

No wonder she regards Heaney as a stoic. 'The other poems of *The Spirit Level* chiefly concern "keeping going", a stoic Afterwards.' I cannot believe that this is the same book that I have read so often. What she calls 'these usually stoic, but sometimes even joyful pieces ... are grounded in the doings of every day.' Yes, but they also take off and fly. There is an epiclesis in every anamnesis that 'spirits' it through the domain of the quotidien into that energising 'wonderland' of the marvellous.

'St Kevin standing motionless until the nest in his hand can hatch its eggs.' Yes, for God's sake, which means until what is in his hand takes off and flies! Not 'Kevin's pity obligating him to stoicism: "now he *must*" remain in his excruciating position for weeks.' Has she not misunderstood the whole meaning of this effort? Her analysis of *The Spirit Level* reminds me of F. W. H. Myers's account of his meeting with George Eliot in Cambridge, where she spoke to him of God, Immortality, and Duty. God, she said, was inconceivable. Immortality was unbelievable. But it was beyond question that Duty was 'peremptory and absolute'. 'Never, perhaps,' Myers says, 'have sterner accents affirmed the sovereignty of impersonal and unrecompensing Law. I listened and night fell; her majestic countenance turned towards me like a sybil in the gloom; it was as though she withdrew from my grasp the two scrolls of promise, and left me with the third scroll only, awful with inscrutable fate.'

Here's Vendler: 'Stoicism is by definition undramatic; it is the virtue of middle age, when one's progress is at best horizontal, and the future can hold only a decline. It is a matter of living with and within the choices one has made (like the married couple in 'A Walk'). And the formal beauty proper to stoicism – one of solidity, monumentality, simplification – has seldom been celebrated (and even more seldom enacted) in lyric.'

She gives us a *tour de force* analysis of the conjunction 'and' in Heaney on St Kevin.[13] 'The poem is strung on seven 'ands', she tells us, which means that 'there is no subordination of one item to another: they lie before us in the flat plane of medieval illustration.' She itemises the seven 'ands' and shakes them out comprehensively. But, and I find this symbolic of the protest I am trying to make, there are actually eight 'ands' in this poem. If you follow her analysis, you soon realise that the one she has left out is the one in the middle of verse three (all the others are meticulously and unmistakably accounted for), which reads: 'and, finding himself linked/Into the network of eternal life'. This 'and, comma,' is the 'conjunction' I find (whether deliberately or unconsciously) left out of all Vendler's considerations, the conjunction with the network of eternal life. Without that there is no sense to Kevin's life, actions, personality, prayer. My incredulity and disappointment reach their pinnacle when she translates the description of Kevin given by Heaney in the Nobel lecture, 'at the intersection of natural process and the glimpsed ideal', into her reductionist endurance test: 'It is as though the saint's stoic metabolism, without intervention by conscious will, keeps producing these serial heartbeats and breaths …' and, as far as I can understand her, this is what also makes the poetry 'distinctive and striking'. In other words, music for the middle-aged, poetry for the pot-bellied. Seamus Heaney as bard of the bald-headed, Dante to the disenchanted, Milton for the menopausal. Technicoloured photograph of an Irish fog! This is like describing Vermeer as a Dutch interior decorator, whereas all those cramped inscapes, those domestic details, those restricted settings are there also to describe the light: 'a Dutch interior gleam'.

As if on cue, Heaney's harvest of poems from the last decade of the twentieth century, his first published volume of the twenty-first, is called *Electric Light*. It opens with three poems that span the poetic task. There is the place of poetry, 'At Toomebridge', 'Where the flat water/came pouring over the weir', the ungraspable, unfathomable 'continuous/Present'. Then there is the poet as 'Perch', which is both a place, an attitude and a kind of creature. 'Perch on their water-perch hung …' Not without reason, these 'we called "grunts"'. Poetry is a kind of grunting as the perch hang on in there, 'runty and ready', 'guzzling the current' and 'bluntly holding the pass' … 'In the everything flows and steady go of the world'. Poets as perch are porous parmenidean, 'little flood-slubs' stuck into the water as counters to the otherwise inexorable flow of the all-consuming river. Their grunting efforts produce the only durable and enduring testimony to existence, symbolised by 'Lupins'. These are 'Seed packets to begin with'. These seeds are induced like pearls in the oyster, by the irritating and incessant flow of water over the half-opened shell of the 'runty' but 'ready'. The poems are the enduring standing stones:

> And cranial acoustic of the stone
> With its arch-ear to the ground, a listening post
> Open to the light, to the limen world
> Of soul on its lonely path, the rails on either side
> Shining in silence

Lupins as poems are also cathedrals composed in past historic as 'Lupin spires', but also 'small jittery promise[s]', 'erotics of the future'. Their span is from the depths of the earth to the height of heaven ('Lip-brush of the blue and earth's deep purchase') and their testimony is of time from dawn until midnight ('Rose-fingered dawn's and navy midnight's flower'). Poems/lupins are something we can understand, something in our language, something we can hold onto. Milosz calls them 'A dividend from ourselves', and Heaney adds, 'a tribute paid/By what we have been true to. A thing allowed'. They may not last forever, but at least they accompanied 'all our summer wending'. How long they will be there, will be read, will be acknowledged, is not for us to say. All we know is that: 'They stood. And stood for something. Just by standing'.

Poetry and the poet in this collection are connected as in a secret and sacred mystery. The child-poet (and the poet somehow always remains a child) finds himself in a place, a site, being – often reluctantly – introduced to a person. The place is 'A site of incubation, where 'incubation/Was technical and ritual, meaning sleep/When epiphany occurred and you met the god …' The person 'In the first house where I saw electric light' was like a witch: 'Candle-grease congealed, dark-streaked with wick-/soot …' Shades of Miss Havisham, a dark and scattered muse, whose bare feet were open to the earth: 'She sat with her fur-lined felt slippers unzipped.' But this was the first place where 'A touch of the little pip would work the magic.'

And the magic is the magic of poetry, which 'Year in, year out, in the same chair' – whether at Oxford, Harvard, or in Glanmore – 'whispered/In a voice that at its loudest did nothing else/But whisper'. And the poet confides: 'We were both desperate.' Because 'Her helplessness' was 'no help'. Inspiration from this muse was all 'Lisp and relapse. Eddy of sybilline English.' This is the rhythm and the churning of the poetic vocation, which involves 'The very "there-you-are-and-where-are-you?"/Of poetry itself'. And the work of writing it down, becoming 'all muscle and slur' in obedience to the impulse, is daunting and scary, because even though 'Electric light shone over us, I feared/The dirt-tracked flint and fissure of her nail,/So plectrum-hard'. And yet, this is the task and this is the light, without which there is no inspiration, no poetry of this kind. And it is 'Late in the Day' that the poet sees the similarity of his work to that of the monk in Clonard, of whom Sir William Wilde, in his *Beauties of the Boyne*, tells us:

How when his candle burnt out, his quill pen

Feathered itself with a miraculous light

So he could go on working.

What more illuminating picture of the haunted inkwell than 'his quill pen' feathering itself with 'miraculous light'.

Life is a 'loosening fodder-chute' and we are passing through. The poet is called to write an epitaph with something more durable than the

Condensation on the big windows

Where I drew with warm fingers once upon a time

To make a face that wept itself away

Down cold black glass.

Poetry's durability is a combination of sensitivity and memory and the mystery of electric light. Without the light, memory is a traitor and life is 'a green/Hurl of flood … so flown/And sealed I feared it would be lost/If I put it into words'. From the minute he comes 'Out of the Bag', the poet is 'incubating for real'. He or she is taking it all in, but without any redemptive understanding. The 'cure/By poetry that cannot be coerced' is the 'health and worth' supplied by 'talk':

> the main thing is
> An inner restitution, a purchase come by
> By pacing it in words that make you feel
> You've found your feet in what 'surefooted' means
> And in the ground of your own understanding

Heaney gives as an example of this his poem 'The Loose Box'. He describes himself as 'earthed' and 'heady' … 'As I am when I talk about the loose box.' He is rooted in the earth and yet open to whatever. A loose box is a covered stall where a horse is kept without having to be tied up.

This is the kind of freedom we need when growing up in the twenty-first century. 'Bann Valley Eclogue' has the poet asking Virgil for 'a song worth singing' for 'the child that's due. Maybe, heavens, sing/Better times for her and her generation'. Virgil is clear that 'Whatever stains you, you rubbed it into yourselves', but, if things are to get better, then as well as 'a flooding away of all the old miasma', he insists that 'you'll have to find a place for … Poetry'.

'Heaney takes the poet's right to compose following his own internal connections, inviting readers to drift with him from site to site', says Helen Vendler.[14] Such drifting she describes as 'the ruminative associations that surprise even the thinker'. Heaney himself uses similar vocabulary in an interview with Vincent Browne: 'It's a ruminant book in the sense of chewing the cud. It is stuff that's in the system, in the memory, that is being revisited.'[15] Something has to happen to make these layers of memory light up, to make them 'surprise even the thinker'. For such 'sites' to become 'electric', the poet has to go 'Where negative ions in the open air/Are poetry to me'. This word 'ion' is a Greek word, a neuter present participle of *einai*, meaning 'to go'.

The word, which has now entered our English vocabulary, describes 'an atom or group of atoms that has acquired a net electric charge by gaining electrons in or losing electrons from an initially electrically neutral configuration'. Something has to spark these memories, both as realities in themselves and as connected configurations in the poem. A stable on the Heaney farm, a Christmas crib in the parish church, a threshing scene from Thomas Hardy's *Tess of the D'Urbervilles*, and two scenes from the life of Michael Collins. All of them in the context of Heaney's admission that: 'By temperament, I'm caught between responding to the positive and being wary of the expression of the positive. The uplifting line is suspect to some extent. But there are moments when you have to let the abundance and let the shine come up.' It is a question of finding the site and waiting for the moment when 'a light that is down to earth' begins 'to fan out and open up' and then:

> We upped and downed and scissored arms and legs
> And spread ourselves on the wind's cross, felt our palms
> As tautly strung as Francis of Assissi's
> In Giotto's mural, where angelic neon
> Zaps the ping-palmed saint with the stigmata.

That is when the 'Wind blows through the open hayshed'. Sometimes it is a whisper, at other times it is 'turbulent/Sudden wind, a maelstrom'. But it blows things into perspective and allows what happened in early childhood, for instance, to reveal itself as a portent, and the poet is given also the light that allows him or her to read the signs of the times. A poem, too, has to be a loose box. There has to be room for manoeuvre. For:

> 'Since when,' he asked,
> 'Are the first line and last line of any poem
> Where the poem begins and ends?'

We have to start a new century by ridding ourselves of cliché and by opening ourselves to 'The whole mote-sweaty havoc and mania/Of threshing day'. The standard crib is no adequate representation of Christianity or incarnation; nor can 'any newsreel lying-in-state/Or footage of the laden gun-carriage/And grim

cortege' give us any adequate idea of who Michael Collins was
or what he stood for, or what it might mean to be an Irish person
on the threshold of another century, the two thousand and first
since '*they found the infant wrapped in swaddling clothes/ And laid in
a manger*'. There is a double obligation both to 'do this in remembrance of me' and at the same time to do justice to the original
experience of the thing:

> Back at the dark end, slats angled tautly down
> From a breast-high beam to the foot of the stable wall –
> Silked and seasoned timber of the hayrack.

> Marsupial brackets … And a deep-littered silence
> Off odourless, untainting, fibrous horsedung.

Such re-enactment of the real presence requires both anamnesis
and epiclesis, in technical terminology. Anamnesis is the Greek
word for remembrance, the bringing to mind of God's saving in-
terventions in history. Epiclesis is invocation for the light of the
Holy Spirit. Both together invite the assembly to appropriate the
freedom that has been effected by the rite. The strange facts that
Michael Collins began his life as a small boy by falling through a
trap-door in a hay-loft that had been covered in flowers, and
ended it in an ambush in *Béal na mblath* (The Mouth of Flowers)
are recorded by his biographer.[16] Heaney includes this anomaly
in his 'Loose Box' as a paradigm of how the poet has to re-enact
such childhood falls, 'Willingly, lastly, foreknowledgeably
deep', so that he may 'find his feet/In an underworld of understanding'.

When Heaney was awarded the Nobel Prize for Literature in
1995, the lecture he delivered as his acceptance speech in
Stockholm, 'Crediting Poetry', gives us his own considered testimony to what poetry can be. And it does not disappoint. Poetry
is an 'order'. The Nobel Prize confirms him sufficiently to provide a 'space-station' that allows him to take a 'space-walk'. And
the place we are being led to by the 'order' of poetry is 'the "temple inside our hearing" which the passage of the poem calls into
being.' His poetry and all real poetry is 'the unappeasable pursuit of this note' ('Sing yourself to where the singing comes

from'), which is identified and authenticated 'as a ring of truth within the medium itself'. 'As if the ripple at its widest desired to be verified by a reformation of itself, to be drawn in and drawn out through its point of origin.'[17]

This speech can be summed up in the words of Virgil, Eclogue IV, which are translated in *Electric Light* as 'Bann Valley Eclogue':

Here are my words you'll have to find a place for:
Carmen, ordo, nascitur, saeculum, gens.
Their gist in your tongue and province should be clear
Even at this stage. Poetry, order, the times,
The nation, wrong and renewal, then an infant birth
And a flooding away of all the old miasma.[18]

For the truth of Being to emerge in this next century, we have to get our priorities right. And the first of these, in our destitute times, is poetry. It is not the only or the most important thing, but without it there is danger of losing our way. Once it has 'spoken', then we can establish order. When we have, as 'Stable child, grown stabler', by hearing what poetry, genuine poetry, has to say about our condition, we can set about the business of arranging things accordingly.

What the 'necessary' poetry always does is 'touch the base of our sympathatic nature', in a way that is 'true to the impact of external reality', while remaining 'sensitive to the inner laws of the poet's being'. Such poetic form is 'both the ship and the anchor', both 'a buoyancy and a holding', which can help to usher in 'the birth of the future we desire'.[19]

CHAPTER EIGHT

Art and Our Future

This book is saying three things. The future is in our hands. It is a precious gift that we can squander, abuse, exploit or distort at will. Obviously, there are forces working, influences abounding, pressures surrounding, that diminish our autonomy and lessen our responsibility. However, it is still possible for those of us who live on this island of Ireland in the first years of the twenty-first century to shape our future within the limitations and con-strictions which global membership imposes.

There are many imperatives and considerations that should determine the steps forward we take, but prominent among these should be the voice of artists and the educating influence of art. This is not the only factor, but it should be a decisive one. Art can provide accurate and unflinching cardiography of the present with a prognosis of possibilities for the future, which politicians and leaders ignore at their peril.

One of the aspects of such future, which may be ignored by other inhabitants of the twenty-first century planet, but which cannot be gainsaid by those of us privileged to dwell on the last ditch of Europe (Beckett's designation) surveying the Atlantic ocean, is the religious or the spiritual. A socialism narrower than God and all humankind is a socialism too narrow for us. Our culture is incurably God-bespattered.

I was told of some ancient religion that performed its pro-foundest rites with two leopards present at the altar. The historical genesis of this peculiar ritual was apparently that, in former times, the celebrating priest was disturbed and devoured by a pair of such leopards. Since then, the importuning animals were incorporated into the official liturgy.

Ireland take note. Prophets are never recognised in their own countries. Until, that is, they make themselves irremovable landmarks. The once-banished artist returns as a statue in our most cherished square, a summer school in perpetuity, a novel being proposed as number one of the century. Our most noble antagonists must eventually be incorporated into mainstream culture. It is high time that churches and religious leaders recognised that such sons and daughters are not just their unacknowledged progeny, but their most creative critics and fastest friends, in Emerson's definition of friendship:

> Friendship requires that rare mean betwixt likeness and unlikeness. Let me be alone to the end of the world, rather than that my friend should overstep his real sympathy. I hate where I looked for furtherance or at least resistance, to find a mush of concession. Better be a nettle in the side of your friend than his echo. Let it be an alliance of two large formidable natures, mutually beheld, mutually feared, before they recognise the deep identity which beneath these disparities unites them. Let him be to thee forever a sort of beautiful enemy, untameable and devoutly revered.

We have to incorporate what Joyce has discovered and achieved into our religious and spiritual probings for the future. Not to do so is to risk delusionary misinstruction at the level of the orthodoxy of humanity, which is at least one half of the equation that church leadership is designed to effect. We also have to ensure that the kind of dismissive dogmatism, moral superiority and overbearing obtuseness that characterised the official attitude to such exploration in the past is removed, and precautions taken to preempt its return to future legislating mind-sets.

On the other hand, it is important to remind those who are artists of the prevailing possibility of the presence of the Spirit, which no amount of ill-treatment on the part of church authorities, implausibility in official manifesto or party line, should prevent from at least being entertained as an option. Specifically, in the case of writers, this book is suggesting that they can be surprised by this presence in the very act of creation by the phenomenon described by Joyce as the 'Holy Ghost in the Inkbottle'. There is no way of proving such intervention, but suggesting the suspicion can make the artist aware retrospectively of such a happening, and open to the possibility in current or future creative endeavour.

To philosophers and literary critics, this book would point to the extraordinary role that Heidegger attaches to art. Whether one accepts or rejects the argument, especially in the way it may have been distorted here, one is certainly obliged to keep an open mind in literary criticism to ontological dimensions and such a manifestation of Being.

Seamus Heaney as Nobel laureate has a very particular place in this investigation. Having reached the pinnacle of triumph as a poet, he should have no more worry about bad press, hostile critics, misunderstanding by the public. In some ways, he should be beyond all that. However, it is important for him, for the public, and for the critics to establish appropriate and symbiotic relationships so that the truth of art can emerge. In this sense, Heaney is a representative figure: the artist in residence. The danger for him is that of the comfort zone. What Robert Frost has asked in another way: How to be Dostoevsky in New Hampshire? What next after the Nobel prize? We and he can form a conspiracy of celebration, spending the next half century in laps of honour for this victory.

The other danger is the critic. Critics can stalk the poet and paralyse him or her into zero productivity for fear that the next utterance be grandiose, over the top, a signal of premature senility, a proof that prizes petrify and pollute. And yet, this study suggests, a certain kind of thinking can help the poet. The role of the critic in the circumstances here described is to support and affirm, to be like one of those who held the arms of Moses aloft on the mountaintop until the battle was won on the plain beneath. There should be no need for the poet to sway with the winds of change, to heed the calls of propagandists, the sneers of connoisseurs, the accusations of cowardice or self-satisfied couldn't-care-less-ness. Above all, there should be no guilt trip about poetry itself. The purpose of this book is to confirm the poet in a lonely and exigent task, which is all the more necessary in these times. There is an essential poetry, an absolute poetry, which certain wordsmiths have the calling and the capacity to create. It is possible to frighten them away, to distract them, drug them with alternative offers, time-consuming acclaim, duty-laden honours. The only important thing is that the work gets done and the poetry is harvested. Such poetry, in the words of Joseph Brodsky, is 'our anthropological, genetic goal, our linguistic, evolutionary beacon'.

It should be possible for a poet like Heaney to receive the support, the working conditions, the appropriate stimulation and atmosphere that would allow him to concentrate on the task in hand. As Van Gogh wrote about the portrait of himself that he dedicated to Gauguin: 'There is an art of the future, and it is going to be so lovely and so young that, even if we give up our youth for it, we must gain in serenity.'

Nor is this a further prescription to write a certain kind of poetry, another importunate tutoring tongue. It is confirmation, absolution. Absolving from everything that prevents; confirming the person and the work.

'This man can't bear our life here and will drown,'

The abbot said, 'unless we help him.' So

They did, the freed ship sailed, and the man climbed back

The comma between the freed ship and whatever they did who were standing around the altar, is the space that this book is attempting to excavate. Solitude and silence create the atmosphere that allows us to grow into circumambient space and relate to more than identifiable objects. It must become a space of trust, which is a phosphorescence exuding from belief that someone else is there. D. W. Winnicott, the child psychologist, describes play for children and what he calls the 'play-space', where a child is absorbed by some game on its own, as the basis for our capacity to be alone. Trust is built up by the paradoxical situation of 'the experience of being alone while someone else is present'. Something is allowed to happen then that would not happen unless you know there is someone there and without that other person interfering in any way. It is like learning to swim. If you believe there is someone there who will hold you up if you begin to drown, you have the confidence to learn how to swim out of your depth. This is intermediate space that allows us to become ourselves:

It is only when alone (that is to say, in the presence of someone) that the infant can discover his own personal life. The pathological alternative is a false life built on reactions to external stimuli. When alone in the sense that I am using the term, and only when alone, the infant is able to do the equivalent of what in an adult would be called relaxing. The infant is able to become unintegrated, to flounder, to be in a state in which there is no orientation, to be able to exist for a time without being either a reactor to an external impingement or an active person with a direction of interest or movement.[1]

Critics should be setting up such a space for artists, instead of being responsible for 'the pathological alternative' whereby artists simply respond to critics as hostile external stimuli. Artists and critics should be guardians of one another's solitude. There should be respect for the necessary anguish of the other. There should be no importunate sympathy, no attempt to capitalise on the other's apparent disarray in order to create dependency or win discipleship. Each one must fight against the temptation to plunder vulnerability for their own selfish purposes.

Why was Heaney's post-Nobel masterpiece a translation of *Beowulf*? Seamus Deane tells of Heaney's obsession with this poem from early on. Deane equates this story with 'the battle that lies at the heart of his work':

The deadly combat between the dragon and Beowulf is not only a story of a fight with a monstrous and evil force. It is also an emblem of the struggle between civilisation and its opposite. If freedom has the air as its natural habitat, violence clings to the ground. Yet, like the dragon, it can rise from its buried lair and infect the air: the 'ground-burner' is also the 'sky-roamer'. Since his undergraduate days, Heaney has been fascinated by this poem. His translation is one further act of retrieval, taking an Old English poem into the ambit of Northern Ireland, where the ancient combat between monstrous violence and the search for peace is even now being refought at a political level.

In Heaney's work, peace needs a space that is not emptiness: it needs to be a rich space, brimming with light.[2]

Perhaps. But, again, this is Deane shining his particular searchlight on the clearance, and more or less claiming privileged access to meaning because of friendship and family ties. This is part of the danger. Because there is much more to *Beowulf* than Northern Ireland. Heaney himself points to the European and hybrid nature of the original:

The motive was aesthetic and artistic, it was a linguistic pleasure and test. The further thing about it is that, as an English poem it's a problematic poem, because it's actually European.

Its subject is somebody from the south-west of Sweden coming down into Denmark and helping the Danes, then returning to the south-west of Sweden and clearing a dragon out of that place. It is written in England, perhaps in Northumbria, but then Northumbria itself was a hybrid enough place, also because of the Irish culture of the Scoti, those Irish monks who came down from Iona and settled there in Lindisfarne. I could go on about the hybrid nature of the thing, but the fundamental attraction was having a go at something that was impossible to do. There is no way that *Beowulf* can be definitively translated.[3]

Whatever the origin of the story, it is about a hero who has to go down under to deal with a persecuting monster. And while Beowulf is down there battling with the monster, the critics have to wait at the surface without pre-written scripts to cover the story on his return. Beowulf's friends wait all day at the very edge of the cold lake surface. The story says he is down there a very long time, to the point where he is given up for dead.

And friends can misunderstand their role and importance. Beyond the warmth and the love they may feel for each other as fellow human beings, there is, especially for fellow poets who are also friends, a deeper energy of first principle to first principle, where each is working towards a magnificent escape from such limitations. Like secret agents in some underground resistance movement, they should share the excitement of the new life that they are determined to usher in more fully.

The abyss separating each from each is essential distance. 'Deep is calling on deep in the roar of waters.'

Rainer Maria Rilke again symptomises the kind of solitude and community that should accompany such a process:

> He needed to be alone in order to molt, to fall apart in order to come together again as a writing poet … [He] believed that he had to go through a kind of mental disintegration as a preparatory stage for the emergence of his unique gifts of seeing and saying … At such a time he had to be alone, because, in the radically undifferentiated and unintegrated state which he needed to rediscover his genius, he felt extremely vulnerable to the impingements of other people upon his internal freedom, his unique sense of himself, and his emerging work. At such times the capacity to be alone, as Winnicott defines it, was essential to him, because it meant that he could feel sheltered and protected as he came apart, lost himself, and dissolved into the undifferentiated state which he celebrates and praises as *'das Offne'* ('the open') in the eighth Duino Elegy, in 'An Experience', and in a number of the Sonnets to Orpheus.
>
> When a child feels that he can be alone in himself because someone else is there who asks *'nothing but to be there functioning and protecting at the border of the invisible'* (Rilke's fantasy of the perfect companion …), then, as Winnicott says, the child 'is able to … exist for a time without being either a reactor to an external impingement or an active person with a direction of interest or movement'. Only the individual who has developed the capacity to be alone in this way, by internalising or creating such a 'protective environment,' is constantly able to rediscover the personal impulse.[4]

Another angle on the *Beowulf* poem is given by David Whyte, who combines the role of poet with that of prophet in an almost exemplary balance:[5] 'It is not the thing you fear that you must deal with, it is the mother of the thing you fear.' You may think you are dealing with, have dealt with, the monster in question. In fact you are just lying back with a glass in your hand, celebrating with your friends and your fellow countrymen, liberation from the 'evil' that had threatened you all since your childhood, when suddenly, taking you all unawares, the real monster makes itself felt. And this, it seems to me, is the ominous note of the *Beowulf* translation – the twenty-first century is preparing the mother of a monster that none of us has as yet anticipated or imagined. 'A good book,' says Whyte, quoting Kafka, 'should be an axe for the frozen sea within us.' Whyte goes on:

> Beowulf kills Grendel's mother, and the story does not attempt to soften this fact. Among different cultures, right down to the surviving hunter-gatherer peoples of today, one of the tribe would dress himself in the pelt or feathers of the animal to be hunted. The ensuing dance would be an imitation of the hunt to come, culminating in the pretended ritual killing of the masked human being ... The ritual was a reminder that we were stalking a part of ourselves ... we were in fact killing a part of ourselves. In a sense we *become* the animal that is killed, as it becomes a part of us when it is eaten. When the story announces that Beowolf has killed Grendel, we are being told that Beowulf has become Grendel, and that when he kills Grendel's mother, he has become Grendel's mother. He has wrestled with his interior and exterior monsters to the point where he admits them as himself.'

This is terrifying stuff. It reminds one of Ted Hughes. In his *Tales of Ovid*, powerful translations of *The Metamorphoses*, Hughes describes the fate of Actaeon who, out hunting with his hounds, happens to stumble upon the Goddess Diana bathing naked in a pool. For his foolhardiness she transforms him into a stag. His poem opens:

> Destiny, not guilt, was enough
> For Actaeon. It is no crime
> To lose your way in a dark wood.[6]

His is the possible fate of any poet, any Beowulf, who stumbles upon realities he or she was not meant to observe. The journey into the dark or into the deep, changed him into prey. The hunter became the hunted. 'But then as he circled, his own hounds found him.' He knew them all by name but:

> Where Actaeon had so often strained
> Every hound to catch and kill the quarry,
> Now he strained to shake the same hounds off –
>
> His own hounds. He tried to cry out:
> 'I am Actaeon – remember your master,'
> But his tongue lolled wordless, while the air
>
> Belaboured his ears with hounds' voices.
>
> Now the hills he had played on so happily
> Toyed with the echoes of his death-noises.
> His head and antlers reared from the heaving pile.
>
> And swayed – like the signalling arm
> Of somebody drowning in surf.
> But his friends, who had followed the pack
>
> To this unexpected kill,
> Urged them to finish their work. Meanwhile they shouted
> For Actaeon – over and over for Actaeon
> To hurry and witness this last kill of the day –
> And such a magnificent beast –
> As if he were absent. He heard his name
>
> And wished he were as far off as they thought him.
> He wished he was among them
> Not suffering this death but observing
>
> The terrible method
> Of his murderers, as they knotted
> Muscles and ferocity to dismember
>
> Their own master.

> Only when Actaeon's life
> Had been torn from his bones, to the last mouthful,
>
> Only then
> Did the remorseless anger of Diana,
> Goddess of the arrow, find peace.

It is, perhaps, a symptomatic image of ourselves as we goad ourselves on to devour those parts of ourselves that step out of line. It is also a bleak witness to the possible fate of a poet, especially a poet laureate.

Here is Heaney reviewing *Birthday Letters* by Ted Hughes in 1998: 'The immediate impression is one of wounded power healing and gathering and showing its back above the depths where it has been biding … It takes you down to levels of pressure where the undertruths of sadness and endurance leave you gasping.'[7] Heaney recognises the affinity between himself and Hughes, between both and Beowulf. These poems have, as he puts it, 'both an autobiographical and an archetypal resonance'. Both poets share the same dilemma, although Hughes's situation makes it more prurient, 'awakening the tabloid reader who lurks deep in even the most aesthetic critic':

> Hughes was impaled on the horns of a creative dilemma: to write directly about that which most desperately craved expression could seem like an exploitation of something sacrosanct, but not to write about it must have felt like an abdication of spiritual and imaginative responsibility.

The burden of this book is to prevent all of us from abdicating such spiritual and imaginative responsibility: we, through prurience or bullying postures; the artists through genuine fear of reprisals.

Not that there can be any prescriptions about what to do, other than 'what poetry told us to do', as Heaney quotes from *Birthday Letters*, but 'something sacrosanct', 'which most desperately craved expression', can remain unsaid because of fear of one kind or another. This fear can be cowardice in the child who knows he or she should speak, but it can also be generated by the surrounding adults, who, like the famous governess in Montgomery's memoirs, say: 'Go out and see what that child is doing and stop him.'

Ted Hughes remained silent for thirty years. Of these eighty-eight poems, called *Birthday Letters* – one is to Sylvia Plath's dead father, one to her living children – Heaney says in that same review: 'all the rest speak to a "you" who, as Sylvia Plath, is the other half of Hughes's consciousness in more ways than one'. These poems 'give credence to all kinds of telepathies and invite the reader to understand them as divine messages of a sort, like things "from some far region sent, / To give me human strength by apt admonishment". Consequently, whatever appears as a focus of attention in these *Birthday Letters* is transformed by the action of this uncanny magnetic field and immediately becomes charged with an aura and force and potential for revelation.' Heaney's description of *Birthday Letters* is a cautionary tale:

> The poems give the impression of utterance avalanching towards vision. They often seem to have been written swiftly, as if the writer's nose had taken up a scent and had run with it more or less blindly, astonished to be led back so unerringly into the moment-by-moment reality of what happened. But then suddenly the poem will take an extra jump, sure-footed and decisive, and land upon the thing that had been drawing it down the memory path towards itself all along.
>
> Mention of 'Daddy' there and in other poems is calculated to set off a chain reaction of responses … and is bound, in some quarters, to stir up old resentments against Ted Hughes. Known for three decades and more as the man who was having an affair when his wife committed suicide, doubly notorious after the 'other woman' also committed suicide and killed their little daughter at the same time, he has been under scrutiny by the media and the academy which has been mostly unsympathetic and on some occasions fiercely vindictive. As a result, there is a tendency within sections of the media and the academy (obvious in their response to the

appearance of this book) to regard Hughes as someone more or less in thrall to them, answerable to their accusations …

There is another use of the word 'Father' ('Abba' has been rendered as Daddy in some New Testament translations) that might cause as much resentment from the media and the academy, especially from a poet considered to be definitively in their thrall and answerable to their accusations. 'Ted Hughes,' Heaney continues, 'suggests that the origin of all true poems is in a place which he calls "the place of ultimate suffering and decision in us". And it is to that fatal place that *Birthday Letters* conducts us …' And this is the place in Heaney and in ourselves that I sense we all need to be conducted to, not out of prurience or voyeuristic excitement, but for poetic redress, in the way Heaney has described in his Oxford lectures, later published as *The Redress of Poetry*.

Heaney, again in this review, describes the kind of ontological poetry that this book is trying to advocate: 'On the one hand, there is the lens of personal recollection where the writing is a view-finder with telescopic and even microscopic powers of concentration … until they are finally brought to a point where illumination and definition coincide and everything seems to stand clear, backlit by a new transcendent understanding.' Heaney finds that Ted Hughes's *Birthday Letters*

remind us of something so obvious that it is astonishing it has been for so long ignored: namely, that the hounding Hughes has undergone from the outside has been a conventional enough affair compared with the hounding he must have suffered within himself. The deaths of a wife, a lover and a child would have had traumatic repercussions in any situation, but where the surviving party is a poet, it is more or less a genetic necessity that he himself tend to the personal wound he has been dealt, the dark embryo of sorrow and need, by giving it expression. Yet the work of poetry is also necessarily a work of the purest self-absorption and must therefore be inhibited by conditions such as those in which Hughes found himself.

When *Birthday Letters* won the 1998 Whitbread Book of the Year award, Frieda Hughes, the daughter of Ted Hughes and Sylvia Plath, read a letter at the award ceremony that her father had written shortly before he died. Hughes wished he had published the poems earlier, rather than keeping them hidden. He feared the public reaction to these poems addressed to Sylvia Plath, his wife, who had committed suicide in 1963. 'It was in a kind of desperation that I finally did publish them – I had always thought them unpublishably raw and unguarded, simply too vulnerable. But then I just could not endure being blocked any longer. How strange that we have to make these public declarations of our secrets. But we do. If only I had done the equivalent thirty years earlier, I might have had a more fruitful career – certainly a freer psychological life.'

One of the last works of Ted Hughes before he died on 28 October 1988 was a translation of a poem by Alexander Pushkin, called 'The Prophet'.[8] In the introduction to the collection in which it later appeared, the editor notes:

> Ted Hughes in the last months of his life collaborated over a period of days with Daniel Weissbort on 'The Prophet'. This is a poem, recognisably based on lines from Isaiah, in which Pushkin speaks of the poet as a man whose body has been physically torn open to have the fire of truth put inside by the hand of God. It was a poem that made Pushkin an iconic figure, both for those who opposed the Tsar and those who opposed the Soviet regime. Here, the poem reads as freshly as if written in our own time. It is something of a mystery of collaboration that Hughes's version of 'The Prophet', which adheres fairly closely to the vocabulary of Weissbort's literal version, nevertheless has the unmistakable vehemence of Hughes in its rhythms.[9]

Once again a mystery of collaboration, the haunted inkwell.

> Crazed by my soul's thirst
> Through a dark land I staggered.
> And a six-winged seraph
> Halted me at a crossroads.

With fingers of dream
He touched my eye-pupils.
My eyes, prophetic, recoiled
Like a startled eaglet's.
He touched my ears
And a thunderous clangour filled them,
The shudderings of heaven,
The huge wingbeat of angels,
The submarine migration of sea-reptiles
And the burgeoning of the earth's vine.
He forced my mouth wide,
Plucked out my own cunning
Garrulous evil tongue,
And with bloody fingers
Between my frozen lips
Inserted the fork of a wise serpent.
He split my chest with a blade,
Wrenched my heart from its hiding,
And into the open wound
Pressed a flaming coal.
I lay on stones like a corpse.
There God's voice came to me:
'Stand, Prophet, you are my will.
Be my witness. Go
Through all seas and lands. With the Word
Burn the hearts of the people.

But what of the wounded poet without any such sensational scandals or such archetypal monsters to contend with? As Heaney says, 'The sad fact is, there has been an element of spectator sport about the attention accorded to Hughes's work.' And at the same time it is easier to be Captain Ahab than Lord Jim; the fox hunted has enough to occupy him, to keep his mind off the inner wound, keeping the hounds at bay. Which does not excuse him from reaching the place and uttering the expressive cry, which, in terms of the time it took, as Heaney says, was '… not an evasion of the reality but an attempt to get at it without importing a prurience factor'. In *Electric Light*, Heaney too has a poem taken 'from the Russian of Alexander Pushkin':

> Then turbulent
> Sudden wind, a maelstrom:
> The helmsman and the sailors perished.
> Only I, still singing, washed
> Ashore by the long sea-swell, sing on,
> A mystery to my poet self,
> And safe and sound beneath a rock shelf
> Have spread my wet clothes in the sun.

There is something in Heaney's review of Ted Hughes's *Birthday Letters* that suggests that there is a truth here for us all, which now rests with him, and which 'poetry [could] finally and absolutely resolve ... into the unshakeable order of the totally imagined'. But perhaps, as in Heaney's poem 'On His Work in the English Tongue', which he dedicates to the memory of Ted Hughes, 'Soul has its scruples. Things not to be said. / Things for keeping, that can keep the small-hours gaze / Open and steady. Things for the aye of God / And for poetry.'

The area and the texture of 'the place' were hinted at in the Oxford lectures,[10] which, it heartened me to hear, were almost as much a surprise to him, who was just following and obeying the poetic impulse: 'I did not notice this correspondence between their thematic and imaginative concerns until the whole book had been assembled in manuscript. Once I saw the link, however, I was delighted. It confirmed my trust – the trust in which the subjects of these lectures were chosen – that a reliable critical course could be plotted by following a poetic sixth sense' (*RP*, xiii).

The labyrinth we find ourselves lost in at this time is also the one in which Ted Hughes was imprisoned. It causes the most pain and receives the least amount of enlightenment or understanding. Poetry can help us here: 'The imaginative transformation of human life is the means by which we can most fully grasp and comprehend it ... The poem is ... a fleeting glimpse of a potential order of things' (*RP*, xv). The people Heaney chooses

to illustrate the 'redress' (which also has connotations of naked-
ness and clothing) are surely significant – Christopher Marlowe
for instance and his death by stabbing at a tavern in Deptford:
'The story has always had a slightly sinister feel to it, something
to do with the mystery that hangs over those four companions
withdrawn quietly out of the early summer day, the stealth of
their privacy, the hovering possibility of underhand exchanges
or undercover deeds. And, of course, the fascination of the event
was every bit as potent for Marlowe's contemporaries, for it did
not escape their notice that the whole thing had been vaguely
foreshadowed in the dramatist's own writing' (*RP*, 17).

The kind of 'poetry' that we crave at this level is also described: 'Some works continue to combine the sensation of liberation with that of consolidation; having once cleared a space on
the literary and psychic ground, they go on to offer, at each re-
reading, the satisfaction of a foundation being touched and the
excitement of an energy being released' (*RP*, 20). Such poetry
provides 'an intimation of a far more generous and desirable
way of being alive in the world' (*RP*, 36). Enunciation of such,
for a poet, issues from 'the thing behind his voice and ear which
Nadezhda Mandelstam called 'the nugget of harmony'. 'To locate
this phonetic jewel, to hit upon and hold one's true note, is a
most exacting and intuitive discipline' (*RP*, 73-4).

My advocacy here is similar to the one Heaney makes in his
analysis of the work of Dylan Thomas, where 'it was not possible for Thomas to admit into his poetry the presence of that
which Rilke calls the angels. The jurisdiction of the bone-bound
island, to which he had pledged his loyalty, forbade the necessary widening of scope' (*RP*, 140-41). This could also be true for
the admission of the Spirit into the world of poetry. I see no contradiction between such an admission of presence and 'something that I have repeatedly tried to establish through several
different readings and remarks in the course of these lectures:
namely, that the goal of life on earth, and of poetry as a vital factor in the achievement of that goal, is what Yeats called in
"Under Ben Bulben" the "profane perfection of mankind".'

'... We go to poetry, we go to literature in general, to be for-
warded within ourselves. The best it can do is to give us an
experience that is like foreknowledge of certain things that we
already seem to be remembering. What is at work in this most
original and illuminating poetry is the mind's capacity to con-
ceive a new plane of regard for itself, a new scope for its own
activity' (*RP*, 159-160). Heaney says of Wordsworth that: '*The
Prelude* is about a consciousness coming together through the effort of articulating its conflict and crises' (*RP*, 189). 'When I took
up the theme of redress in the Michaelmas Term of 1989, I was
... clear ... that the theme is in fact an aspect or consequence of
my autobiography ... The artist, the poet must in some sense set
the world free to have a new go at its business. As I said also in
that first lecture, if our given experience is a labyrinth, then its
impassability is countered by the poet's imagining some equivalent of the labyrinth and bringing himself and the reader
through it.' (*RP*, 191)

The important thing is to do 'what poetry told us to do', 'to
write directly about that which most desperately craved expression'.

And how should this be done? Heaney has already been tu-
tored by the voice of James Joyce in the car park of Station
Island:
> 'Your obligation
is not discharged by any common rite.
What you do you must do on your own.

The main thing is to write
for the joy of it ...

Take off from here. And don't be so earnest,

so ready for the sackcloth and the ashes.
Let go, let fly, forget.
You've listened long enough. Now strike your note.'

It was as if I had stepped free into space
alone with nothing that I had not known
already ...

'You lose more of yourself than you redeem
doing the decent thing. Keep at a tangent.
When they make the circle wide, it's time to swim

out on your own and fill the element
with signatures on your own frequency,
echo-soundings, searches, probes, allurements,

elver-gleams in the dark of the whole sea.'
The shower broke in a cloudburst, the tarmac
fumed and sizzled. As he moved off quickly

the downpour loosed its screens round his straight walk.[11]

For our part, we have to listen; and for those who are critics or
members of the academy, a respectful distance is recommended.
A kind of thinking, a kind of criticism, is required which is humble
and, ready, without abdication of professional judgement, to
confirm the marvellous beyond what we have known to date.
Such attention implies, by silent presence rather than spoken
word: 'Keep on doing what you yourself know you should do,
that for which you have been preparing yourself, and for which
all your work to date has been an exorcism.' It is not a question
of the poet doing anything different; it is a question of finding
the strength, the momentum, the will, to keep on doing the same
thing. 'Seeing things' as they are and saying them, is the way in
which something more can register on our radar screens. It is
not a question of making a special effort, of straining one's mus-
cles, of adjusting one's lenses to focus on light, for instance. As
Merleau-Ponty tells us about Cezanne:

> In his *Peau de Chagrin* Balzac describes a 'white tablecloth,
> like a covering of snow newly fallen, from which rose sym-
> metrically the plates and napkins crowned with light-
> coloured rolls.' 'Throughout my youth,' Cezanne said, 'I
> wanted to paint that table-cloth like freshly fallen snow ... I
> know now that one must try to paint only: 'the plates and
> napkins rose symmetrically, and 'the light-coloured rolls.' If I
> paint: 'crowned,' I am finished, you see. And if I really bal-
> ance and shade my napkins and rolls as they really are, you

may be sure that the crowning, the snow and all the rest of it will be there.'[12]

'"Light came from the east" he sang, / 'Bright guarantee of God …' The future can only be brighter if at one and the same time 'The room I came from and the rest of us all came from / Stays pure reality', but with the artist 'at the bedside, incubating for real, / Peering … / Into a faraway smile whose precinct of vision / I would enter every time'.

The subject of Seamus Heaney's first book of poetry in the twenty-first century is 'origin'.[13] He has elaborated on this theme in a way that summarises also the theme of this book:

Your origin is almost the equivalent of your subject in poetry. Wherever your energy, wherever your consciousness springs from, wherever the firstness of your very being springs from, that is your subject. It's what wakens you and re-awakens you.

Poetry works with subjects, but I think its effect – for the writer writing it, and for the reader reading it – is of renewal, refreshment, a new purchase on yourself and on consciousness through language.[14]

Notes

INTRODUCTION

1. Wallace Stevens, 'Of Modern Poetry', in *The Palm at the End of the Mind: Selected Poems and a Play by Wallace Stevens*, edited by Holly Stevens (New York: Vintage Books, 1990), pp. 174–5.

2. *The Eye's Mind: Bridget Riley Collected Writings 1965–1999*, edited by Robert Kudielka (London: Thames and Hudson, 1999), p. 11.

3. Thomas Mann, *Death in Venice* (Penguin Modern Classics, 1977) p. 53.

4. Martin Heidegger, *Poetry, Language, and Thought* (New York: Harper & Row, 1971), p. 96.

5. Quoted in Christopher Clausen, 'The Great Queen Died', *The American Scholar* (Winter 2001), vol. 70, no. 1, pp. 41–2.

6. W. B. Yeats, *Essays and Introductions* (London: Macmillan, 1961), p. 111.

7. T. S. Eliot, *The Three Voices of Poetry* (Cambridge University Press, 1953), p. 4, quoted in Denis Donoghue, *Words Alone* (Yale University Press, 2000), p. 27.

8. Yeats, *Essays and Introductions*, pp. 317-18.

9. Samuel Beckett, *Proust* (New York: Grove Press, 1957), p. 55. This study was written in 1931 as an examination of 'that double-headed monster of damnation and salvation – Time'.

10. Seamus Heaney, 'Unheard Melodies', *The Irish Times*, Saturday, 11 April 1998.

11. Yeats, *Essays and Introductions*, p. 318.

CHAPTER ONE

1. Conor Cruise O'Brien, *The Long Affair: Thomas Jefferson and the French Revolution 1785-1800*, (University of Chicago Press, 1996).

2. W. B. Yeats, *Essays and Introductions* (London, 1961), p. 341.

3. Ibid., p. 325.

4. Ibid., p. 318.

5. Ibid., p. 317.

6. Martin Heidegger, *Poetry, Language and Thought* (New York, 1981), p. 78.

7. James Joyce, *Finnegans Wake* (London: Faber, 1975), p. 182. 'The house O'Shea or O'Shame, Quivapieno, known as the Haunted Inkbottle, no number Brimstone Walk, Asia in Ireland …'.

8. Letter to Stanislaus Joyce, 31 August 1906, in *Selected Joyce Letters*,

edited by Richard Ellmann, (New York: Viking Press, 1976), p. 100. In another letter, Joyce ascribes the phrase to Stanislaus himself: 'Were I to rewrite the book as G. R. suggests 'in another sense' (where the hell does he get the meaningless phrases he uses) I am sure I should find again what you call the Holy Ghost sitting in the inkbottle and the perverse devil of my literary conscience sitting on the hump of my pen.' This is written in the context of his having perhaps been 'unnecessarily harsh' to Ireland and to Dublin and his surprise 'that there should be anything exceptional in my writing'. Letter to Stanislaus Joyce, September 1906, ibid. p. 110.

9. Yeats, Essays and Introductions, pp. 330-341.

10. C. G. Jung, 'Answer to Job', Collected Works, Vol. 11, Psychology and Religion in East and West, (Bollingen Series XX, 1966), pp. 468-470.

11. J. M. Synge, *Four Plays and the Aran Islands* (London: OUP, 1962), p. 222.

12. Heidegger, *Poetry, Language and Thought*, p. 96.

CHAPTER TWO

1. *The Irish Times*, 4 September 1992, p. 10.

2. I have tried to answer these accusations elsewhere – see 'De l'interdiction a l'écoute', in *Heidegger et la Question de Dieu*, edited by Kearney and O'Leary (Paris: Grasset, 1980).

3. The information in this paragraph comes from Clavert Watkins, 'Indo-European Metrics and Archaic Irish Verse', *Celtica* 6 (1963), pp. 194–249.

4. Hart Crane, quoted in *Modern Poets on Modern Poetry*, edited by James Scully (Fontana, 1966), p. 163.

5. W. B. Yeats, *Essays and Introductions* (London, 1961), p. 128.

6. C. G. Jung, 'The Relations between the Ego and the Unconscious', *Collected Works*, Vol. 7, *Two Essays on Analytical Psychology* (Bollingen Series XX, 1966), p. 221.

7. This last paragraph has been hammered out in dialogue with Edna Longley over the years, not that she might recognise or endorse the present wording. A sample of this process of refinement can be found in our debate in three parts: her article, my article and her reply to my reply, which forms the basis of my present wording and which is in *The Crane Bag*, vol 9, no. 1, (1985).

8. James Fenton, 'The Orpheus of Ulster,' *The New York Review*, 11 July 1996, p. 37.

9. Al Alvarez's review of *Field Work* in *The New York Review*, 6 March 1980, p. 16, quoted in James Fenton, op. cit.

10. See, for example, Edna Longley, '"Inner Émigré" or "Artful Voyeur"?' in *The Art of Seamus Heaney*, edited by Tony Curtis (Poetry Wales Press, 1982), pp. 65-95; and 'Poetry and Politics in Northern Ireland', *The Crane Bag*, vol 9, no. 1, (1985), pp. 26–40.

11. James Simmons, 'The Trouble with Seamus', reprinted in *Seamus*

Heaney: A Collection of Critical Essays, edited by Elmer Andrews (New York: St Martin's Press, 1990), p. 39, quoted in James Fenton, op.cit.

12. *The Irish Times Supplement,* Wednesday, 27 December 2000, p. 1.

13. Helen Vendler, 'The Three Acts of Criticism', *London Review of Books,* 26 May 1994, p. 5.

14. Helen Vendler, *The Breaking of Style* (Harvard University Press, 1995), p. 40.

15. Helen Vendler, *Soul Says* (Harvard University Press, 1995), p. 211.

16. James Wood, 'Scruples', *London Review of Books,* 20 June 1996, p. 3.

17. Desmond Fennell, 'Whatever You Say, Say Nothing: Why Seamus Heaney is No. 1', *STAND,* vol. 32, no. 4 (Autumn 1991), pp. 38–55.

18. Ibid., p. 35-6.

19. Ibid., p. 38.

20. James Wood, 'Scruples', *London Review of Books,* 20 June 1996, p. 3.

21. Neil Corcoran, *The Poetry of Seamus Heaney: A Critical Study* (London: Faber & Faber, 1998), see footnote on p. x.

22. Fennell, 'Whatever You Say', p. 42–3.

23. Ibid., p. 33-4.

24. Ibid., p. 42.

25. Since then reprinted in Seamus Heaney, *The Redress of Poetry* (Oxford University Press, 1995).

26. Vendler, *Soul Says,* pp. 196-7.

27. Ibid., p. 197.

28. Ibid., p. 198.

29. Ibid., p. 187.

30. Vendler, *The Breaking of Style,* p. 43.

31. Vendler, *Soul Says,* p. 197.

32. Clifford Geertz, *Works and Lives, The Anthropologist as Author* (Oxford University Press, 1988), pp. 4–11.

33. Clifford Geertz, *The Interpretation of Cultures* (New York: Basic Books, 1973), p. 18.

CHAPTER THREE

1. I am giving here the outline and results of a more extended study, which I have published in more depth and detail in 'Heidegger's Reading of Poetry: Art as Spiritual Exploration', in *Anáil Dé, The Breath of God: Music, Ritual and Spirituality,* edited by Helen Phelan (Dublin: Veritas, 2001), pp. 121–139; and in 'De l'interdiction a l'écoute', in *Heidegger et la Question de Dieu,* edited by Richard Kearney and J.S. O'Leary (Paris, 1980), pp. 285-295.

2. See all the accounts, especially that of Hannah Arendt in Walter Biemel, *Martin Heidegger: An Illustrated Study* (London, 1977).

3. Ernst Juenger, in *Der Spiegel,* 18 August 1986, p. 167.

4. Martin Heidegger, *Poetry Language and Thought* (New York, 1971), p. 40.

5. All quotations from Rilke's Letters are taken from Stephen Garmey's

Introduction to R. M. Rilke, The Duino Elegies, translated by Stephen Garmey and Jay Wilson (London: Harper & Row, 1972). Hereafter in the text, *The Duino Elegies* will be referred to by the letter 'D' followed by the number of the Elegy.

6. Quoted in Garmey, *Introduction to Rilke's Elegies.*

7. Heidegger, *Poetry Language and Thought,* p. 98.

8. Ibid. p. 110.

9. Rainer Maria Rilke, *The Sonnets to Orpheus,* 3. I have taken the German version from Stephen Mitchell's bilingual edition (New York: Touchstone Books, Simon & Schuster, 1985), p. 22.

10. Heidegger, *Poetry, Language and Thought,* p. 127.

11. Ibid. p. 128.

12. Ibid. p. 129.

13. Ibid. p. 185.

14 Rainer Maria Rilke, letter dated Monday, 24 June 1907, in *Letters on Cezanne,* edited by Clara Rilke (London: Vintage, 1991), p. 4.

CHAPTER FOUR

1. Iris Murdoch was born in Dun Laoghaire on 15 July 1919, the only daughter of an opera singer and a British army cavalry officer. She was educated in and lived in England. From 1938-42 she studied 'Greats' (Ancient History, Greek, Latin and Philosophy) at Oxford. From 1944-6 she was an administrative officer for the United Nations Rehabilitation and Relief Association, working during the war in Belgium and Austria. Two of her lovers were victims of Hitler: Frank Thompson, whom it was assumed she would marry, was parachuted into Macedonia and was marching with the Partisans towards Sofia, Bulgaria, when he was captured by the Nazis. He was regularly beaten and finally executed. A volume of poems by Catullus and a Byzantine coin found in his pocket when arrested were later presented to Dame Iris by the Bulgarians.

The second was the poet and anthropologist Franz Bauermann Steiner, a scholarly Czech-Jewish refugee from Prague, whose parents were killed in a concentration camp. The suitcase containing his doctorate on the sociology of slavery was stolen from the luggage van on the London-Oxford train in 1942. The year he re-submitted, 1949, he had a coronary, and he died in 1952.

From 1947 to 1963 she was a tutor of philosophy and a fellow of St Anne's in Oxford. At thirty-five years of age she began to write novels. Her first novel, *Under the Net,* which was actually the fourth she wrote, was published in 1954 (she destroyed two of the four; the other was the second one she published, *The Flight from the Enchanter*). In 1956, at the age of thirty-seven, she married John Bayley, later Wharton Professor of English Literature and fellow of St Catherine's College, Oxford. She wrote twenty-six novels and three major works of philosophy, one book of poetry and three plays. Her last novel, *Jackson's Dilemma,* was published in 1995. She developed Alzheimer's disease in 1997. She died on 8 February 1999 at the age of seventy-nine. Her husband John wrote two accounts of her last illness and their life together while he nursed her at the end. One of these, *Iris*, became a bestseller.

2. D. H. Lawrence, 'Why the Novel Matters', *Phoenix I* (1936). Written c. 1925. Reprinted in *Lawrence on Education*, edited by Joy and Raymond Williams (Penguin Education, 1973).

3. Iris Murdoch, *Sartre: Romantic Rationalist* (London: Bowes & Bowes, 1965), p. 75. She met Sartre and read his *L'Etre et le Néant* in Brussels. 'People were liberated by that book after the war', she says, 'It made people happy, it was like the Gospel. Having been chained up for years, you were suddenly free and could be yourself.' She published her first book, *Sartre: Romantic Rationalist*, in 1953.

4. E. M. Forster, *Aspects of the Novel* (Pelican, 1962), p. 34.

5. Caroline Spurgeon, *Shakespeare's Imagery* (Cambridge, 1965), p. xi.

6. Iris Murdoch, *The Message to the Planet* (London: Chatto & Windus, 1989), p. 214.

7. Iris Murdoch, *The Bell* (London: Panther, 1976), pp. 189-91.

8. Iris Murdoch, *The Sovereignty of Good* (London: RKP, 1970), pp. 65–7.

9. Gabriel Garcia Marquez, *Love in the Time of Cholera*, (Alfred A. Knopf, New York, 1988).

10. Iris Murdoch, *Metaphysics as a Guide to Morals* (London: Chatto & Windus, 1992).

11. Ibid., p. 472.

12. Iris Murdoch, *The Unicorn* (London: Chatto & Windus, 1963), p. 181.

13. Henry James, *The Golden Bowl*, Book Second, Part Fourth, XXV (Oxford University Press, 1999), p. 299.

14. Iris Murdoch, Jackson's Dilemma (London: Chatto & Windus, 1995)

15. A. S. Byatt, *Degrees of Freedom: The Early Novels of Iris Murdoch* (Vintage, 1994), p. 224.

16. Interview with Iris Murdoch by Edward Whitley, published in his book *The Graduates* (London: Hamish Hamilton, 1986), pp. 63-74.

17. Last line of Gerard Manley Hopkins's poem 'That Nature is a Heraclitean Fire and of the Comfort of the Resurrection'.

CHAPTER FIVE

1. Léopold Sédar Senghor, *Les Fondaments de l'Africanité* (Paris, 1967).

2. Abiola Irele, 'Negritude – Philosophy of African Being', *Nigeria Magazine*, Festac Edition, 122, 123 (1977), pp. 1-13.

3. Interview in *Newswatch*, 29 July 1991.

4. O. R. Dathorne, *African Literature in the Twentieth Century* (London: Heinemann, 1976), pp. 218-19.

5. Aimé Césaire, 'Cahier d'un retour au pays natal', originally published in Paris in *Volantes*, no 20 (August 1939), translated into English as *Return to my Native Land* (Penguin, 1969).

6. Dathorne, *African Literature*, p. 2.

7. Wole Soyinka was born in 1934 in Abeokuta, Nigeria. He has written over twenty plays as well as some novels and a considerable body of poetry. He was awarded the Nobel Prize for Literature in 1986.

8. Wole Soyinka, *Myth, Literature and the African World* (Cambridge, 1978), p. 126.

9. Ibid., pp. 127-9.

10. L. S. Senghor, 'Negritude et Marxisme', in *Pierre Teilhard de Chardin et la politique Africaine* (Paris: Editions du Seuil, 1962), English trans. in *Africa in Prose* (Penguin African Library, 1969), pp. 337-43.

11. L. S. Senghor, 'New York', in *Modern Poetry from Africa*, edited by Gerald Moore and Ulli Beier (Penguin, 1976), pp. 56-8.

12. Dathorne, *African Literature*, p. 235.

13. Senghor, 'Negritude et Marxisme', p. 342.

14. Abiola Irele, 'Negritude – Philosophy of Being', p. 6.

15. W. E. Abraham, quoted in Dathorne, *African Literature*, pp. 229-30.

16. Léopold Senghor, 'Nuit de Sine', in *Poèmes* (Paris: Editions du Seuil, 1964), English translation in *Modern Poetry from Africa*, op. cit., p. 231.

17. Soyinka, *Myth, Literature and the African World*.

18. R. Garaudy, *Danser sa vie* (Paris: Editions de Seuil, 1973).

19. Ulli Beier, *Year of Sacred Festivals in one Yoruba Town*, Lagos, 1959.

20. Wole Soyinka, *The Road*, in *Collected Plays*, vol. 1 (Oxford University Press, 1973), pp. 186-7.

21. Wole Soyinka, *Idanre and Other Poems* (London: Methuen,1967), pp. 28-9.

22. Wole Soyinka, *Ake: The Years of Childhood* (Ibadan: Spectrum Books, 1991).

23. Olumuyiwa Awe, 'Before My Very Eyes', in *Before Our Very Eyes* (Ibadan: Spectrum Books, 1987), pp. 57-89. Olumuyiwa Awe is Professor of Physics at the University of Ibadan. He has been a friend of Wole Soyinka since they began secondary school together at Government College, Ibadan in 1945. This quotation comes from pp. 84-85.

24. Wole Soyinka, *The Man Died* (Ibadan: Spectrum Books, 1988), p. 158.

25. Soyinka, *Myth Literature and the African World*, p. 13.

CHAPTER SIX

1. Denis Donoghue, 'Joyce and the Finite Order', *Sewanee Review* 68 (Spring 1960), p. 256.

2. Richard Ellmann, *James Joyce, The First Revision of the 1959 Classic* (Oxford University Press, 1983), p. 27 (hereafter referred to in the text as Ellmann, with the relevant page number).

3. Louis Golding, *James Joyce* (London, 1933), p. 55 (hereafter referred to in the text as Golding, with the relevant page number).

4. *Chamber Music* first published in 1907, *Pomes Penyeach* first published in 1927. Both are contained in *The Essential James Joyce*, edited by Harry Levin (Triad/Panther Paperback, 1977).

5. *Ulysses*, 1958 edition, p. 236 (hereafter referred to in the text as *Ulysses*, with the relevant page number).

6. Clive Hart, *Structure and Motif in Finnegans Wake* (London: Faber, 1962), pp. 25-6.

7. See for example Stan Gebler Davies, who takes this point of view.

8. Louis Gillet, 'Stele for James Joyce', *James Joyce Yearbook* (Paris, 1949), pp. 42-3.

9. William T. Noon, SJ, *Joyce and Aquinas* (Yale University Press, 1957), p. 105f.

10. Thomas Aquinas, *Summa Theologiae*, I, q.39.a.8.

11. Samuel Beckett, 'Dante ... Bruno ... Vico ... Joyce' in *Our Examination Round His Factification for Incamination of Work in Progress* (Faber & Faber, 1929). This essay is reproduced in *A Bash in the Tunnel*, edited by John Ryan, see p. 28 for the above quotation.

12. Letter from Stanislaus dated 7 August 1924, reproduced in *Selected Joyce Letters*, edited by Richard Ellmann (New York, 1975), p. 589.

13. Letter from H. G. Wells dated 15 November, 1926, in *Selected Joyce Letters*, op. cit., p. 597.

14. Letter from Ezra Pound dated 15 November 15 1926, in *Selected Joyce Letters*, op. cit., p. 597.

15. *Selected Joyce Letters*, edited by Richard Ellmann, (New York: The Viking Press, 1975), p. 129.

16. Lionel Trilling, *The Liberal Imagination* (London: Secker & Warburg, 1951), p. 40.

17. In this section I am indebted to Colin MacCabe, *James Joyce & the Revolution of the Word* (London: MacMillan, 1978).

18. Ibid., p. 54.

19. Ibid., pp. 4-5.

20. Ibid., pp. 28-9.

21. 'Le titre nous indique que c'est aussi, en un certain sens, l'histoire de la jeunesse de l'artiste en général, c'est-à-dire de tout homme doué du temperament artiste', Valery Larbaud, 'James Joyce', *La Nouvelle Revue Française*, nouv. ser., 9e annee, 16, no 103, (April 1922).

22. Sheldon R. Brivic, *Joyce between Freud and Jung* (New York: NUP, 1980), p. 136.

23. Ibid., p. 137.

24. Ibid., p. 137.

25. Ibid., p. 165.

26. Sheldon Brivic, 'Joyce and the Metaphysics of Creation', *The Crane Bag*, vol. 6, no. 1, (1982).

27. Ibid.

28. C. G. Jung, 'Synchronicity: An A-Causal Connecting Principle', in *The Collected Works*, vol. 8, (Bollingen Series XX, New York, 1960), pp. 419-531.

29. Ibid., p. 531.

30. These influences would be Dante, Vico and Bruno (see the article by

Samuel Beckett already quoted here in note 11) and Thomas Aquinas (see William Noon as quoted here in note 9). In the first case, that of Dante, there was a process of identification. Temperamentally, Joyce was a medieval artist (see Vivian Mercier, 'James Joyce as Medieval Artist', *The Crane Bag*, vol. 2, nos. 1 and 2, pp. 11-17). In the case of Bruno and Vico, the influence was more structural and paradigmatic. By structural I mean that he built *Finnegans Wake*, for instance, on Vico's division of history into recurring cycles of theocratic, aristocratic and democratic ages, each set off by a thunderclap. The fact that the book begins and ends on the same sentence is an imitation of Vico's *ricorso* or return to the beginning. He was also influenced by Vico's use of etymology and mythology to uncover the significance of events, as if these were only superficial manifestations of underlying energies.

His interest in Giordano Bruno of Nola goes back to his undergraduate days. His first published work, 'The Day of the Rabblement', opens with Joyce taking the role of Bruno, who was burned at the stake as a heretic by the Church of Rome. As a Renaissance philosopher who fuses classical and Christian thought, Bruno seeks the 'real' world of Plato and Paradise of which our imperfect world contains intimations. In *Ars Memoriae*, he suggests that certain sounds are reminiscent of this lost reality. The *anima mundi* infuses our world, and to invoke this special power, Bruno composed a list of 150 sounds that recall parts of some one word or Logos, which evokes the Godhead. Bruno had spent three years in London as the friend of Sir Philip Sidney, the 'defender of poetry'. Bruno claimed that his mission was to arouse men from their 'theological stagnation'. Wishing to escape condemnation, he, a lapsed Dominican, set forth his own personal philosophy under the guise of interpreting the writings of Thomas Aquinas.

Of all these influences, Joyce wrote to Miss Weaver: 'I would not pay overmuch attention to these theories, beyond using them for all they are worth, but they have gradually forced themselves on me through circumstances of my own life.' Thus, he identified himself with the heretic who was burnt by the Catholic Church, and, some would claim, Joyce built the story of his own martrydom in *A Portrait of the Artist as a Young Man* as a parallel to the Bruno life-story; he identified himself with Vico's pathological fear of thunderstorms. In the same way he was convinced that there was a secret affinity between himself and James Stephens, the author, because he found out that they were born on the same day. This meant that if he were not able to finish *Finnegans Wake*, Stephens would be able to take over where he left off. He even set about making preparations for such an eventuality.

Such instances show his very idiosyncratic use of influences and sources. It is almost impossible, under such circumstances, to trace the exact nature or extent of any, or all, the influences upon his 'thought'.

31. Lionel Trilling, 'James Joyce in His Letters', *Commentary* (February 1968), pp. 57-8.

32. C. J. Jung, 'Ulysses: A Monologue', *The Collected Works* (Bollingen XX, New York, 1966), vol. 15, pp. 122-3.

33. Ibid, p. 137, note 3.

34. Jung, 'Synchronicity', pp. 513, 119.

35. Ibid., p. 513.

36. Herman Broch, 'Joyce and the Present Age', *Yearbook,* (1949), pp. 106-107.

37. *Finnegans Wake* (Faber, 1975, paperback edition), p. 269 (hereafter referred to in the text as *FW*, with the relevant page number).

38. David Sylvester, *Interviews with Francis Bacon* (London, 1975), p. 58.

39. Ibid, p. 53.

40. Ibid, p. 105.

41. '… what do you think Vulgariano did but study with stolen fruit how cutely to copy all their various styles of signature so as one day to utter an epical forged cheque on the public for his own private profit …' (*FW*, 181).

42. Ellmann, *Selected Joyce Letters*, p. 321.

43. Ibid.

CHAPTER SEVEN

1. John Wilson Foster, *The Achievement of Seamus Heaney* (Dublin: Lilliput Press, 1995), p. 40.

2. Seamus Heaney, *The Redress of Poetry* (London: Faber, 1995), pp. 191-3.

3. W. B. Yeats, 'Samhain: 1905', in *Explorations*, quoted by Heaney in *Preoccupations* (London: Faber, 1980), as an epigraph.

4. *The Crane Bag*, vol. I, no. 1 (1977), pp. 61-7.

5. Ibid., p. 63.

6. Mark Patrick Hederman, 'Seamus Heaney: The Reluctant Poet', *The Crane Bag*, vol. 3, no 2 (1979), pp. 61-70.

7. Seamus Heaney, 'The Golden Bough', in *Seeing Things*, p. 3.

8. Helen Vendler, *Soul Says* (Harvard University Press, 1995), p. 211.

9. What I say about Lacan is borrowed from William J. Richardson's article, 'Long Day's Journey into Sublimation', which I have been fortunate to read in its unpublished form.

10. Helen Vendler, *Seamus Heaney* (London: Faber, 1999).

11. Denis Donoghue, 'The Supreme Fiction' *The New York Review*, November 28, 1996, p. 60.

12. *Reading the Future,* Irish Writers in Conversation with Mike Murphy, (Dublin: Lilliput Press, 2000), p. 90.

13. Ibid., pp. 160-61.

14. Helen Vendler, 'Heaney, the Survivor', *The Irish Times*, 24 March 2001.

15. The Vincent Browne Interview, *The Irish Times*, 31 March 2001.

16. Tim Pat Coogan, *Michael Collins: A Biography* (London: Hutchinson, 1990).

17. Seamus Heaney, *Crediting Poetry, The Nobel Lecture* (Dublin: Gallery Press, 1995), p. 28.

18. Seamus Heaney, *Electric Light* (London: Faber, 2001), p. 11.

19. Heaney, *Crediting Poetry*, p. 28.

CHAPTER EIGHT

1. D.W. Winnicott: *Playing and Reality*, and *Through Paediatrics to Psycho-Analysis* (London: Hogarth, 1977), p. xxxvii.

2. Seamus Deane, 'The Famous Seamus', *The New Yorker*, 20 March 2000, p. 66.

3. *Reading the Future*, Irish Artists in Conversation with Mike Murphy, (Dublin: Lilliput Press, 2000), pp. 94-95.

4. David Kleinbard, *The Beginning of Terror: A Psychological Study of Rainer Maria Rilke's Life and Work* (New York University Press, 1993) p. 240.

5. David Whyte, *The Heart Aroused*, (New York: Currency Doubleday, 1994) pp. 33-71.

6. Ted Hughes, *Tales from Ovid* (London: Faber & Faber, 1997), pp. 105-112. I was introduced to this poem and to a similar reading of it applied to the work of psychoanalysis by John Hughes.

7. Seamus Heaney, 'A Wounded Power Rises from the Depths', *The Irish Times*, 31 January 1998.

8. In *After Pushkin: Versions of the Poems of Alexander Sergeyevich Pushkin by Contemporary Poets*, edited and introduced by Elaine Feinstein (London: The Folio Society, 1999), p. 26. Hughes's translation was done from an annotated literal translation by Daniel Weissbort.

9. Ibid. p. 12.

10. Seamus Heaney, *The Redress of Poetry: Oxford Lectures* (London: Faber 1995), hereinafter referred to as *RP* with the relevant page number.

11. Seamus Heaney, *Opened Ground, Poems 1966-1996* (London: Faber & Faber, 1998), pp. 267-8.

12. Maurice Merleau-Ponty quoting Cezanne, in *Phenomenology of Perception* (London: Routledge & Kegan Paul, 1962), pp. 197-8.

13. Vincent Browne Interview in *The Irish Times*, 31 March 2001.

14. *Reading the Future, Irish Writers in Conversation with Mike Murphy* (Dublin: Lilliput Press, 2000), p. 82.

Samuel Beckett already quoted here in note 11) and Thomas Aquinas (see William Noon as quoted here in note 9). In the first case, that of Dante, there was a process of identification. Temperamentally, Joyce was a medieval artist (see Vivian Mercier, 'James Joyce as Medieval Artist', *The Crane Bag*, vol. 2, nos. 1 and 2, pp. 11-17). In the case of Bruno and Vico, the influence was more structural and paradigmatic. By structural I mean that he built *Finnegans Wake*, for instance, on Vico's division of history into recurring cycles of theocratic, aristocratic and democratic ages, each set off by a thunderclap. The fact that the book begins and ends on the same sentence is an imitation of Vico's *ricorso* or return to the beginning. He was also influenced by Vico's use of etymology and mythology to uncover the significance of events, as if these were only superficial manifestations of underlying energies.

His interest in Giordano Bruno of Nola goes back to his undergraduate days. His first published work, 'The Day of the Rabblement', opens with Joyce taking the role of Bruno, who was burned at the stake as a heretic by the Church of Rome. As a Renaissance philosopher who fuses classical and Christian thought, Bruno seeks the 'real' world of Plato and Paradise of which our imperfect world contains intimations. In *Ars Memoriae*, he suggests that certain sounds are reminiscent of this lost reality. The *anima mundi* infuses our world, and to invoke this special power, Bruno composed a list of 150 sounds that recall parts of some one word or Logos, which evokes the Godhead. Bruno had spent three years in London as the friend of Sir Philip Sidney, the 'defender of poetry'. Bruno claimed that his mission was to arouse men from their 'theological stagnation'. Wishing to escape condemnation, he, a lapsed Dominican, set forth his own personal philosophy under the guise of interpreting the writings of Thomas Aquinas.

Of all these influences, Joyce wrote to Miss Weaver: 'I would not pay overmuch attention to these theories, beyond using them for all they are worth, but they have gradually forced themselves on me through circumstances of my own life.' Thus, he identified himself with the heretic who was burnt by the Catholic Church, and, some would claim, Joyce built the story of his own martrydom in *A Portrait of the Artist as a Young Man* as a parallel to the Bruno life-story; he identified himself with Vico's pathological fear of thunderstorms. In the same way he was convinced that there was a secret affinity between himself and James Stephens, the author, because he found out that they were born on the same day. This meant that if he were not able to finish *Finnegans Wake*, Stephens would be able to take over where he left off. He even set about making preparations for such an eventuality.

Such instances show his very idiosyncratic use of influences and sources. It is almost impossible, under such circumstances, to trace the exact nature or extent of any, or all, the influences upon his 'thought'.

31. Lionel Trilling,'James Joyce in His Letters', *Commentary* (February 1968), pp. 57-8.

32. C. J. Jung, 'Ulysses: A Monologue', *The Collected Works* (Bollingen XX, New York, 1966), vol. 15, pp. 122-3.

33. Ibid, p. 137, note 3.

34. Jung, 'Synchronicity', pp. 513, 119.

35. Ibid., p. 513.

36. Herman Broch, 'Joyce and the Present Age', *Yearbook*, (1949), pp. 106-107.

37. *Finnegans Wake* (Faber, 1975, paperback edition), p. 269 (hereafter referred to in the text as *FW*, with the relevant page number).

38. David Sylvester, *Interviews with Francis Bacon* (London, 1975), p. 58.

39. Ibid, p. 53.

40. Ibid, p. 105.

41. '... what do you think Vulgariano did but study with stolen fruit how cutely to copy all their various styles of signature so as one day to utter an epical forged cheque on the public for his own private profit ...' (*FW*, 181).

42. Ellmann, *Selected Joyce Letters*, p. 321.

43. Ibid.

CHAPTER SEVEN

1. John Wilson Foster, *The Achievement of Seamus Heaney* (Dublin: Lilliput Press, 1995), p. 40.

2. Seamus Heaney, *The Redress of Poetry* (London: Faber, 1995), pp. 191-3.

3. W. B. Yeats, 'Samhain: 1905', in *Explorations*, quoted by Heaney in *Preoccupations* (London: Faber, 1980), as an epigraph.

4. *The Crane Bag*, vol. I, no. 1 (1977), pp. 61-7.

5. Ibid., p. 63.

6. Mark Patrick Hederman, 'Seamus Heaney: The Reluctant Poet', *The Crane Bag*, vol. 3, no 2 (1979), pp. 61-70.

7. Seamus Heaney, 'The Golden Bough', in *Seeing Things*, p. 3.

8. Helen Vendler, *Soul Says* (Harvard University Press, 1995), p. 211.

9. What I say about Lacan is borrowed from William J. Richardson's article, 'Long Day's Journey into Sublimation', which I have been fortunate to read in its unpublished form.

10. Helen Vendler, *Seamus Heaney* (London: Faber, 1999).

11. Denis Donoghue, 'The Supreme Fiction' *The New York Review*, November 28, 1996, p. 60.

12. *Reading the Future*, Irish Writers in Conversation with Mike Murphy, (Dublin: Lilliput Press, 2000), p. 90.

13. Ibid., pp. 160-61.

14. Helen Vendler, 'Heaney, the Survivor', *The Irish Times*, 24 March 2001.

15. The Vincent Browne Interview, *The Irish Times*, 31 March 2001.

16. Tim Pat Coogan, *Michael Collins: A Biography* (London: Hutchinson, 1990).

17. Seamus Heaney, *Crediting Poetry, The Nobel Lecture* (Dublin: Gallery Press, 1995), p. 28.

18. Seamus Heaney, *Electric Light* (London: Faber, 2001), p. 11.

19. Heaney, *Crediting Poetry*, p. 28.

CHAPTER EIGHT

1. D.W. Winnicott: *Playing and Reality*, and *Through Paediatrics to Psycho-Analysis* (London: Hogarth, 1977), p. xxxvii.

2. Seamus Deane, 'The Famous Seamus', *The New Yorker*, 20 March 2000, p. 66.

3. *Reading the Future*, Irish Artists in Conversation with Mike Murphy, (Dublin: Lilliput Press, 2000), pp. 94-95.

4. David Kleinbard, *The Beginning of Terror: A Psychological Study of Rainer Maria Rilke's Life and Work* (New York University Press, 1993) p. 240.

5. David Whyte, *The Heart Aroused*, (New York: Currency Doubleday, 1994) pp. 33-71.

6. Ted Hughes, *Tales from Ovid* (London: Faber & Faber, 1997), pp. 105-112. I was introduced to this poem and to a similar reading of it applied to the work of psychoanalysis by John Hughes.

7. Seamus Heaney, 'A Wounded Power Rises from the Depths', *The Irish Times*, 31 January 1998.

8. In *After Pushkin: Versions of the Poems of Alexander Sergeyevich Pushkin by Contemporary Poets*, edited and introduced by Elaine Feinstein (London: The Folio Society, 1999), p. 26. Hughes's translation was done from an annotated literal translation by Daniel Weissbort.

9. Ibid. p. 12.

10. Seamus Heaney, *The Redress of Poetry: Oxford Lectures* (London: Faber 1995), hereinafter referred to as *RP* with the relevant page number.

11. Seamus Heaney, *Opened Ground, Poems 1966-1996* (London: Faber & Faber, 1998), pp. 267-8.

12. Maurice Merleau-Ponty quoting Cezanne, in *Phenomenology of Perception* (London: Routledge & Kegan Paul, 1962), pp. 197-8.

13. Vincent Browne Interview in *The Irish Times*, 31 March 2001.

14. *Reading the Future, Irish Writers in Conversation with Mike Murphy* (Dublin: Lilliput Press, 2000), p. 82.

Colum Kenny